During a season in which the 21st-century church is grappling with constant cultural change and advancements in virtual teaching, discipleship is being reimagined. Sadly, in some sectors, even redefined. Against this backdrop Burggraff's book challenges us to revisit the Scriptural basis for why we mentor and train new believers and learn from the instructional approach of our early church fathers. This text will enrich new believers and veteran mentors alike.

Kenneth S. Coley, Ed.D.

Senior Professor of Christian Education
Southeastern Baptist Theological Seminary

Dr. Andy Burggraff explores the problems with discipleship in today's churches and presents twelve principles from the New Testament regarding discipleship. He then carefully examines the history of the early church's process of discipling new believers. We need these insightful lessons so we can apply them to our own context. An excellent study!

Les Lofquist, D.Min.

Professor of Pastoral Theology
Shepherds Theological Seminary

Former Executive Director
IFCA International

The commission to make disciples continues unchanged. Burggraff's work points modern disciple makers to the most important lessons from our predecessors in the post-apostolic period. We can learn much from them about fostering in believers a deep commitment to Jesus Christ, even in the face of persecution by a morally corrupt and heretical culture, government, and society.

Tim M. Sigler, Ph.D.

Provost & Dean
Shepherds Theological Seminary

Discipleship
in the
Early Church

Discipleship
in the
Early Church

A Study of the Catechumenate
and Its Implications for Discipleship Today

Andrew T. Burggraff, Ed.D., M.Div.

SHEPHERDS PRESS

Cary, North Carolina

Editorial assistance: Trevor Robinson

Layout & cover: Andrew N. "Marcus" Corder

Published by Shepherds Press
6051 Tryon Road
Cary, NC 27518

First printing 2022

Printed in the United States of America

Trade paperback ISBN: 978-1-959454-01-4
Hardback ISBN: 978-1-959454-02-1

To my wife, Delecia,
and our children, Andrew, Anna, Aaron, Brody, and Tanner.
I love you!

Contents

Preface

This current historical research study examines the catechumenate and its implications for discipleship in 21st-century churches. The primary goal of this research is to provide Christian leaders an understanding of the current issues facing discipleship, provide an exegesis of several New Testament passages and the principles that derive from these passages regarding discipleship, provide an analysis of post-apostolic culture and religious setting that influenced the start of the catechumenate, and analyze the catechumenal process with implications for modern discipleship curriculum and programs.

Chapter one identifies the need to examine trends occurring in modern methods of discipleship. Contemporary research has revealed several concerns that the church must acknowledge as it seeks to disciple believers.

1. There appears to be a decline of biblical literacy among believers today.
2. There appears to be an exodus of believers from evangelical churches today.
3. There appears to be an acceptance of inactivity among current evangelical Christians.
4. There appears to be a de-emphasis of discipleship training within the church.

When taken collectively, these four areas present a dismal picture of the current state of discipleship taking place (or not taking place) within American churches. These concerns ought to arouse an alarm over the loss of understanding and practice of biblically based and historically practiced discipleship.

Chapter two examines select NT passages and draws principles from these texts regarding discipleship. As the post-apostolic church prepared to train individuals for membership to their community, it based its foundation for theological teaching and personal commitment upon the instruction of the NT Scriptures. The principles that were gleaned from the NT provided the basis for the catechumenate. An examination of NT instruction regarding discipleship is essential to understanding post-apostolic discipleship as well as discipleship in 21st-century church settings. This section examines select NT passages to provide an understanding of key principles in the development of NT disciples.

Chapter three examines the catalysts that led the church to begin an intentional catechumenal process. As the church moves into the post-apostolic period, there develops widespread testimony of a focused, coherent plan to instruct new believers, the catechumenate. What influences impacted the church which ultimately provided an impetus to begin the catechumenal process? In this chapter, three catalysts are examined that influenced the development of the catechumenate: pre-Christian religious influences, sociological influences, and doctrinal influences.

Chapter four examines the characteristics of the catechumenal process. Before examining this process, an overview of the corporate education in the OT and NT is provided. Once the role of corporate education is established, the chapter examines the history of the catechumenate, the procedures of the catechumenal process, mentorship during catechesis, and the value of the catechumenate for churches in the 21st century.

Chapter five provides a summary of the research. In addition, a large portion of chapter five is dedicated to examining the implications of the research for discipleship programs today. Recommendations are provided for church leaders who are involved in discipleship ministries in their churches. The purpose of chapter five is to provide the application of the research to 21st-century discipleship contexts. The chapter concludes with recommendations for further research.

Keywords: Discipleship, Disciple, Disciple-Making, The Great Commission, Catechumenate, Catechesis, Catechumens, Godparents, Mentorship, Christian Education, Corporate Education, μαθητης.

Discipleship
in the
Early Church

CHAPTER 1

Introduction

Discipleship: Our Mandate, Our Mission

As Jesus prepared to leave His disciples, He provided them with a final command.[1] "Go therefore and make disciples of all the nations, baptizing them in the name of the Father and the Son and the Holy Spirit, teaching them to observe all that I commanded you; and lo, I am with you always, even to the end of the age"[2] (Matt 28:19–20). Jesus commands his disciples to disciple others. To understand what Jesus was calling his followers to accomplish, one must ask the question, what is a *disciple?* The simple definition of the Greek word μαθητης (disciple) means one who learns or is a pupil of another.[3]

In biblical times, a disciple was one who followed a recognized teacher. In the gospels, Jesus had many disciples. There are the twelve disciples of Jesus in Matthew 10:1–4 and Luke 6:12–16. Jesus commissioned and sent out 70–72 disciples in Luke 10:1. In addition, a large group of disciples are identified in Luke 6:17: "Jesus came down with them and stood on a level place; and *there was* a large crowd of His disciples, and a great

---

1 Portions of the introduction were published previously by the author. Andrew Buggraff, "Devleoping Discipleship Curriculum: Applying the Systems Approach Model for Designing Instruction by Dick, Carey, and Carey to the Construction of Church Discipleship Courses," *Christian Education Journal* 12 (2015): 397–414.

2 All Scripture quotations are from the NASB unless otherwise stated.

3 BAGD s.v. μαθητης, 486. An expanded definition for μαθητης and its derivations will be provided in chapter 2 of the dissertation.

throng of people from all Judea and Jerusalem and the coastal region of Tyre and Sidon."

In Matthew 28:19–20, Jesus urged his disciples to go and make other followers of His teachings. Jesus commanded His disciples to be in the pattern of "discipling" disciples. They were to baptize those individuals who accepted Jesus Christ as their Savior and to continually teach/instruct them in the truths of God's Word. Therefore, discipling involves identification (baptizing) and instruction (teaching).

The disciple of Christ is urged, throughout the NT Scriptures, to grow in his spiritual life. Once the believer has accepted the gift of salvation, he becomes a new creation. Paul states, "Therefore if anyone is in Christ, he is a new creature; the old things passed away; behold, new things have come" (2 Cor 5:17). Part of the obligation as a new creation is to become more like Jesus. A disciple is a believer in Christ who is becoming "transformed into the likeness of Jesus Christ."[4] To become a mature follower of Christ, the believer must strive to develop the mind of Christ. In 1 Corinthians 2:16, Paul states the following: "For who has known the mind of the Lord, that he will instruct him? But we have the mind of Christ." The believer needs to live, act, respond, and think like his Savior. This demands that there is constant transformation of thinking and of one's mindset, so that he/she can become more like Jesus in every aspect of life. A disciple, then, is a born-again believer who desires to learn what the Bible teaches, seeks to obey God's instruction, is committed to following Christ's example, and teaches the truths of Scripture to others.

The term *discipleship* may be difficult at times to define. Today, it is being used as a catchall term for anything from mentorship to small-group discussion, to meetings at a coffee house, to the title for a conference at a sports arena. However, it is best to understand discipleship as "a deliberate process of moving Christians forward spiritually."[5] Discipleship has also been explained both as "becoming a complete and competent follower of Jesus Christ" and "the intentional training of people who voluntarily submit to the lordship of Christ and who want to become

---

4 George Barna, *Growing True Disciples: New Strategies for Producing Genuine Followers of Christ* (Colorado Springs, CO: WaterBrook Press, 2001), 18.

5 Brad J. Waggoner, *The Shape of Faith to Come: Spiritual Formation and the Future of Discipleship* (Nashville, TN: B & H Pub. Group, 2008), 14.

imitators of Him in every thought, word, and deed."[6] The process of discipleship has been committed to the church, the Bride of Christ (Eph 4:4–16). The church is to be involved in the process of transforming the believer from a babe in Christ to a mature follower of Christ (1 Pet 2:2). Discipleship, then, is the process of learning the teachings of Scripture, internalizing them to shape one's belief system, and then acting upon them in one's daily life.

Present Concerns in Church Discipleship

Contemporary research has revealed several concerns that the church must acknowledge as it seeks to disciple believers. 1) There appears to be a decline of biblical literacy among believers today. 2) There appears to be an exodus of believers from evangelical churches today. 3) There appears to be an acceptance of inactivity among current evangelical Christians. 4) There appears to be a de-emphasis of discipleship training within the church.

There Appears to be a Decline of Biblical Literacy Among Believers Today

Prior to the invention of the printing press by Johannes Gutenberg in A.D. 1440, the Bible was copied line by line by scribes and copyists. Due to the tedious process of copying Scripture accurately, an entire town or city usually would have only one copy of the Scriptures, often chained inside the church so that it could not be stolen. Very few believers possessed even a portion of Scripture, much less a complete copy of the canon. Due to the inaccessibility of Bibles and the lack of individual possession of the Word of God, biblical illiteracy was common. Since the invention of the printing press, the production of Bibles has rapidly increased. The following statistics are staggering as one realizes the volume of Bibles produced and sold:

- 25 million copies of the Bible are sold in the United States annually.
- Nine out of 10 homes in the United States have a Bible.

---

6 Barna, *Growing True Disciples*, 18.

• More than 400 million copies of all or part of the Bible are distributed through Bible societies each year.[7]

With the sheer volume of Bibles being produced and distributed, one would assume that biblical literacy would be at an all-time high. The question is, "How much has biblical literacy improved?" George Guthrie, a professor at Union University, acknowledges confounding research regarding Bible reading among believers:

> In a recent survey by LifeWay Research, the No. 1 predictor of spiritual maturity among church goers was whether or not they read the Bible on a daily basis. Yet, only 16 out of 100 of those who regularly attend our churches read the Bible every day; another 32 percent read the Bible at least once per week. This means that more than 50 percent of people who come through our doors on a regular basis only read their Bibles occasionally, perhaps one or two times per month, if at all. Even more sobering, only 37 percent of those who attend church regularly say that reading and studying the Bible has made a significant difference in the way they live their lives. Only 37 percent.[8]

It would appear from this research that Biblical literacy has improved some, but not nearly to the level that one would expect. George Barna has made the following statement based upon his research findings regarding biblical literacy:

> Bible reading has become the religious equivalent of sound-bite journalism. When people read from the Bible, they typically open it, read a brief passage without much regard for the context, and consider the primary thought or feeling that the passage provided. If they are comfortable with it, they accept it; otherwise, they deem it interesting but irrelevant to their life, and move on. There is shockingly little growth evident in people's understanding of the fundamental themes of the Scriptures and amazingly little interest in deepening their knowledge and application of biblical principles.[9]

---

7 Russ Rankin, "Lack of Bible Literacy is Spotlighted," *Baptist Press—Baptist Press News with a Christian Perspective,* accessed March 22, 2012, http://www.bpnews. net / bpnews.asp?id=35125.

8 George H. Guthrie, *Will We Rise to Biblical Literacy?* accessed March 12, 2012, http://www.bpnews.net/bpnews.asp?id=34558.

9 George Barna, "Barna Studies the Research, Offers a Year-in-Review Perspec-

A startling fact from Barna's research is that those individuals who read the Bible spend little time allowing the truths of Scripture to impact their lives.

A recent study by the Barna Group highlighted the decrease of Bible reading during the national pandemic. While the pandemic eliminated various time distractions with a lockdown, the number of people that read Scripture decreased drastically. David Roach cited the following in *Christianity Today* from the Barna research:

> Between early 2019 and 2020, the percentage of US adults who say they use the Bible daily dropped from 14 percent to 9 percent, according to the State of the Bible 2020 report released today by the Barna Group and the American Bible Society (ABS). A decrease of 5 percentage points in a single year was unprecedented in the annual survey's 10-year history; between 2011 and 2019, daily Bible readers had basically held steady at an average of 13.7 percent of the population.[10]

With a decrease in Bible reading, it would appear obvious that there is a decrease in biblical literacy because individuals do not know the contents of Scripture. They are not reading God's Word.

Research has shown that the church is continuing to witness a recurrent lack of literacy among believers. Stephen Prothero states the following regarding America as "A Nation of Biblical Illiterates":

> Evangelical pollsters have lamented for some time the disparity between Americans' veneration of the Bible and their understanding of it, painting a picture of a nation that believes God has spoken in Scripture but can't be bothered to listen to what God has to say.... According to recent polls, most American adults cannot name one of the four Gospels, and many high school seniors think Sodom and Gomorrah were husband and wife.[11]

---

tive," *The Barna Group—Barna Update,* accessed March 22, 2012, http://www.barna.org/barna-update/article/12-faithspirituality/325-barna-studies-the-research-offers-a-year-in-review-perspective.

10 David Roach, *Bible Reading Drops During Social Distancing,* accessed May 4, 2022, https://www.christianitytoday.com/news/2020/july/state-of-bible-reading-coronavirus-barna-abs.html

11 Stephen R. Prothero, *Religious Literacy: What Every American Needs to Know—and Doesn't* (New York, NY: HarperOne, 2008), 7.

In 2010, one of the six "megathemes" for American churches as listed by *The Barna Group* was that "the church is becoming less theologically literate." The results of various surveys led George Barna to state, "The data suggests that biblical literacy is likely to decline significantly."[12] Stephen Marlin summarizes several surveys to reveal how bad the trend of biblical illiteracy has become:

Consider these results:

- Fewer than half of all adults can name the four Gospels
- Many professing Christians cannot identify more than two or three of the disciples
- 60 percent of Americans can't name even five of the Ten Commandments
- 82 percent of Americans believe the phrase, "God helps those who help themselves" is a Bible verse
- 12 percent of adults believe that Joan of Arc was Noah's wife
- A survey of graduating high school seniors revealed that over 50 percent thought that Sodom and Gomorrah were husband and wife
- A considerable number of respondents to one poll indicated that the Sermon on the Mount was preached by Billy Graham. (This old saint has been around a while, but not that long!).[13]

Albert Mohler, after examining various surveys related to biblical illiteracy, stated the following about the source of the biblical literacy problem in America:

Christians who lack biblical knowledge are the products of churches that marginalize biblical knowledge. Bible teaching now often accounts for only a diminishing fraction of the local congregation's time and attention. The move to small group ministry has certainly increased opportunities for fellowship, but many of these groups never get beyond superficial Bible study. Youth ministries are asked

---

12 The Barna Group, *Six Megathemes Emerge from Barna Group Research in 2010,* accessed March 12, 2012, https://www.barna.org/barna-update/culture/462-six-megathemes-emerge-from-2010.

13 Stephen Marlin, *Barna Research Group: Megatheme: Biblical Illiteracy!* accessed May 14, 2012, http://hopeforbrazil.com/wordpress/barna-research-group-megatheme-biblical-illiteracy/.

to fix problems, provide entertainment, and keep kids busy. How many local-church youth programs actually produce substantial Bible knowledge in young people? Even the pulpit has been sidelined in many congregations. Preaching has taken a back seat to other concerns in corporate worship. The centrality of biblical preaching to the formation of disciples is lost, and Christian ignorance leads to Christian indolence and worse. This really is our problem, and it is up to this generation of Christians to reverse course.[14]

Mohler provided a challenging reminder that biblical knowledge is a critical component in the discipleship and spiritual growth of an individual. If churches marginalize Bible knowledge, they will be filled with believers who have superficial knowledge of God's Word.

Due to the lack of Biblical literacy, basic truths from Scripture are overlooked and subsequently unlearned. Sadly, many believers do not even realize how little Scripture they know. George Barna made the following statement regarding believer's lack of recognition as to the Bible's impact in their lives:

> The problem facing the Christian Church is not that people lack a complete set of beliefs; the problem is that they have a full slate of beliefs in mind, which they think are consistent with biblical teachings, and they are neither open to being proven wrong nor to learning new insights. Our research suggests that this challenge initially emerges in the late adolescent or early teenage years. By the time most Americans reach the age of 13 or 14, they think they pretty much know everything of value the Bible has to teach and they are no longer interested in learning more scriptural content. It requires increasingly concise, creative, reinforced, and personally relevant efforts to penetrate people's minds with new or more accurate insights into genuinely biblical principles.[15]

Similarly, Kenneth Gourlay, in a 2010 survey assessing the biblical knowledge of adult Southern Baptist Sunday school attendants, revealed the following about his findings:

---

14 Albert Mohler, *The Scandal of Biblical Illiteracy: It's Our Problem*, accessed March 28, 2014, http://www.albertmohler.com/2005/10/14/the-scandal-of-biblical-illiteracy-its-our-problem/.

15 Barna, *Barna Studies the Research*, 2009.

An analysis of the data indicates that the adult SBC Sunday school participants who took the basic Bible knowledge survey (BKS) for this research scored an average of 65.6 percent (m = 32.79). Teaching or learning factual Bible knowledge is not the major purpose of teachers in SBC Sunday schools, but it is a worthy purpose. If seventy were passing, then this study reveals that the average adult Sunday school participant would fail a basic test on knowledge of his text book, the Bible.[16]

Echoing the above findings, similar research led Craig Keener to make the following statement regarding the state of the church in relationship to the importance of Scripture:

> At least in the United States, the church has lost much of its emphasis on teaching Scripture. Most things are driven by marketing; while marketing can be a useful tool, it is not a criterion of truth or morality. Some messages are more popular than others because they are more marketable to consumers. Many churches across the theological spectrum succumb to the culture's values, whether its sexual mores or its materialism; many churches fight for their tradition, or focus on charismatic speakers' experiences. Yet most of the western church today neglects the very Scriptures that we claim to be our arbiter of truth and a living expression of God's voice.[17]

Keener presents a significant concern for the church. Churches today deemphasize the Scriptures and as a result many believers are biblically illiterate.

The Christian church is witnessing a lack of biblical literacy in the lives of believers today. The statistics are staggering as to the lack of biblical knowledge that most believers possess regarding basic biblical truths. How can one be a true follower (disciple) of the Savior if he does not know Christ's message and instruction?

---

16 Kenneth Gourlay, "An Assessment of Bible Knowledge Among Adult Southern Baptist Sunday School Participants" (Ed.D. diss., Southeastern Baptist Theological Seminary, 2010), 126.

17 Craig S. Keener, *The Gospel of Matthew: A Socio-Rhetorical Commentary* (Grand Rapids, MI: William B. Eerdmans Pub., 2009), 14.

There Appears to be an Exodus of Believers from Evangelical Churches Today

Another area of concern in discipleship is the exodus of evangelical believers from evangelical churches. John Dickerson in his book, *The Great Evangelical Recession*, describes this exodus. According to Dickerson's surveys, the evangelical church is losing members at the rate of "2.6 million per decade."[18] He continues to highlight the growing concern that this figure indicates: "If the evangelical church is only about 22 million Americans, as a growing crowd of respected sociologists estimate ... then we lost more than 10 percent of our people in the last ten years. That's worth losing sleep over."[19]

David Kinnaman, a lead researcher for The Barna Group, in his book, *You Lost Me: Why Young Christians Are Leaving Church ... and Rethinking Faith*, conveys several disturbing statistics about the young generation of Christians in America.

> The ages eighteen to twenty-nine are the black hole of church attendance; this age segment is "missing in action" from most congregations.... Overall, there is a 43 percent drop-off between the teen and early adult years in terms of church engagement. These numbers represent about eight million twentysomethings who were active churchgoers as teenagers but who will no longer be particularly engaged in a church by their thirtieth birthday.[20]

Kinnaman continues to describe the exodus of young adults from the church by presenting the research conducted by The Barna Group:

> In one of Barna Group's most recent studies, conducted in early 2011, we asked a nationwide random sample of young adults with a Christian background to describe their journey of faith.... The research confirmed what we had already been piecing together from other data: 59 percent of young people with a Christian background report that they had or have "dropped out of attending church, after going regularly." A majority (57 percent) say they are

---

18 John S. Dickerson, *The Great Evangelical Recession: 6 Factors That Will Crash the American Church...and How to Prepare* (Grand Rapids, MI: Baker Books, 2013), 22.

19 Ibid., 22–23.

20 David Kinnaman, *You Lost Me: Why Young Christians are Leaving Church...and Rethinking Faith* (Grand Rapids, MI: Baker Books, 2011), 22.

less active in church today compared to when they were age fifteen. Nearly two-fifths (38 percent) say they have gone through a period when they significantly doubted their faith. Another one-third (32 percent) describe a period when they felt like rejecting their parents' faith.[21]

It is not only the young evangelicals who are leaving the church. In a 2009 study by The Barna Group adults with children in the home are leaving the church as well.

Demographics suggest that the mainline churches may be on the precipice of a period of decline unless remedial steps are taken. For instance, in the past decade there has been a 22% drop in the percentage of adults attending mainline congregations who have children under the age of 18 living in their home.[22]

These trends indicate that a growing number of evangelicals, especially younger evangelicals, are leaving the church. This exodus reveals an area of concern as to how the church is discipling believers.

There Appears to be an Acceptance of Inactivity Among Current Evangelical Christians

In addition to the decline of biblical literacy and the exodus of evangelical believers from the church, another area of concern surfaces within discipleship. There appears to be an acceptance of inactivity among Christians as well. Again, from the 2009 study conducted by *The Barna Group*, the following statistics reveal the level of involvement among Christians in evangelical churches:

Volunteerism in these churches is down by an alarming 21% since 1998. Adult Sunday school involvement has also declined, by 17% since 1998. The tenuous ties that millions of mainline adults have with their church are exemplified by their willingness to consider other spiritual options. Just half (49%) describe themselves as "absolutely committed to Christianity." Slightly more (51%) are willing to try a new church. Two-thirds (67%) are open to pursuing faith in environments or structures that are different from those

---

21 Ibid., 23.

22 Barna, *Barna Studies the Research*, 2009.

of a typical church. Almost three-quarters (72%) say they are more likely to develop [their] own religious beliefs than to adopt those taught by their church. And nine out of ten (86%) sense that God is motivating people to stay connected to Him through different means and experiences than in the past. Evidence of waffling commitment is found elsewhere, as well. A minority of mainline attenders are presently involved in some type of personal discipleship activity. Less than half contend that the Bible is accurate in the life principles it teaches. Only half of all mainline adults say that they are on a personal quest for spiritual truth. And when asked to identify their highest priority in life, less than one out of every ten mainline adults (9%) says some aspect of faith constitutes their top priority.[23]

There is an acceptance for inactivity among evangelical believers. Since a core element in the very definition of the term *disciple* is the idea of someone who serves Christ, these statistics should concern church discipleship leaders.

There Appears to be a De-Emphasis of Discipleship Training Within the Church

In addition to the above concerns, a final concern is the de-emphasis of discipleship within churches. Noted leaders have made claims as to the lack of discipleship occurring within the church. This lack of emphasis on discipleship is not a new phenomenon. James Montgomery Boice, a noted Bible expositor, voiced many years ago a concern about the deficiency of discipleship within the church:

> There is a fatal defect in the life of Christ's church ... a lack of true discipleship. Discipleship means forsaking everything to follow Christ. But for many of today's supposed Christians—perhaps the majority—it is the case that while there is much talk about Christ and even much furious activity, there is actually very little following of Christ Himself.[24]

More recently, George Barna made the following statement after an extensive interview process with Christian adults: "Not one of the adults

---

23 Ibid., 2009.

24 James M. Boice, *Christ's Call to Discipleship* (Chicago, IL: Moody Press, 1986), 13.

we interviewed said that their goal in life was to be a committed follower of Jesus Christ or to make disciples."[25] The result of his study led Barna to conclude the following about discipleship: "To pastors and church staff, *discipleship* is a tired word. To most laypeople, it is a meaningless word. But let's not get hung up on terminology for the moment. Let's get hung up on our failure to produce indefatigable imitators of Christ."[26] Barna challenged our churches not to forsake the importance of discipleship, but rather make discipling others a key component of our church ministries.

Within the last five years, a team of researchers from LifeWay Research sought to evaluate the discipleship outcomes of churches. After extensive research, they made the following claim, "Since Christ-centered discipleship results in transformation, we can confidently assert that most churches are deficient in discipleship. This is a scathing claim as our entire mission as believers and churches is to 'make disciples.'"[27] This claim was made after two different surveys were conducted by LifeWay Research in 2008 and 2010. The first study (2008) surveyed seven thousand churches. The second study (2010) was a multi-faceted, mixed-method study which began with an interview of twenty-eight experts in the field of discipleship. This initial interview process was followed by a survey of one thousand Protestant pastors in the United States. Finally, a survey was conducted of four thousand Protestants in North America. After the respective surveys were completed for the 2010 study, the research team would state, "Sadly, we can make this bold diagnosis based on the far-reaching and sobering research: There is a discipleship deficiency in most churches resulting in a lack of transformation.... The sad reality is that the daily lives, aspirations, and desires of many people in our churches mirror those who do not claim to know Christ."[28]

When taken collectively, these four areas present a dismal picture of the current state of discipleship taking place (or not taking place) within American churches. These concerns ought to arouse an alarm over the loss of understanding and practice of biblically based and historically

---

25 Barna, *Growing True Disciples*, 6.

26 Ibid., 6–7.

27 Eric Geiger, Michael Kelley and Philip Nation, *Transformational Discipleship* (Nashville, TN: B&H, 2012), 10.

28 Ibid., 16.

practiced discipleship. As a step toward addressing these concerns, this study will examine the New Testament teaching regarding discipleship (selected New Testament texts). In addition, this study will examine the catechumenate, the post-apostolic discipleship program of the church. This post-apostolic period from A.D. 150 to 420 witnessed the rapid growth of Christianity through a deep commitment by believers to Jesus Christ. This growth occurred during a period of persecution by a morally corrupt and heretical culture, government, and society.

The early church formulated a method of education (discipleship) for believers to train new Christians in the knowledge and defense of their faith. Much of this training was required to take place prior to believer's baptism and membership into the church. Through this process, commitment to Christ was evaluated, discipleship was implemented, education in theology and apologetics was taught, and moral character was mentored and enhanced.

The first official Christian education program for the church was the catechumenate. The catechumenate, from κατηχεω meaning "to teach" or "instruct,"[29] was designed for the education of adult converts prior to joining the church through baptism. A question is posed as to whether these individuals who entered the catechumenate were believers or unbelievers. At the beginning of the Apostolic Tradition (an accumulation of material from different sources from a variety of geographical regions dating to the mid-second century A.D.) the following statement appears which provides insight into the question of whether the individuals entering the catechumenal process were believers: "Concerning newcomers, those who will give their assent to the faith."[30] The initial interviewing teacher was further instructed: "Let them be asked the reason why they have given their assent to the faith."[31] One can infer from these statements that the new people coming to the church and entering the catechumenal process have a rudimentary level of faith. They have heard the gospel message and have exercised faith in that message. These individuals, after a profession of faith, now desire to join the community of

---

29 BAGD, κατηχεω, 423.

30 Paul F. Bradshaw et al., *The Apostolic Tradition: A Commentary* (Minneapolis, MN: Fortress Press, 2002), 82.

31 Ibid., 82.

believers by giving themselves to a period of rigorous study and preparation for baptism.[32]

Three intended purposes are noteworthy as the church created this Christian educational program. The first purpose was to help develop a disciplined lifestyle among new believers. A second purpose was to acquaint the catechumen with the Christian tradition. The final purpose was to create a profound devotion to the Christian faith and way of life.[33] Individuals passed through stages of increasingly intimate fellowship and participation within the Christian community. As they progressed through these stages, the catechumens would be introduced to deeper levels of instruction until they were admitted to baptism and then participation in the Lord's Supper.

The catechumenate developed as a corporate educational tool to be used to train new believers to understand what they believe, why they believe it, how to defend it, and how to live it in a hostile world. This process was not a quick procedure (not the customary 4–8 weeks, as is often seen in churches today), but rather was accomplished through various interviews, lectures, and mentorship over a period of two to three years. The pastors/bishops of the Patristic period saw the value and need for this corporate education for the growth of individuals within their congregations. Are there lessons that we can learn from the early church? Are there practices from the catechumenate that should be incorporated in discipleship programs today? Is essential biblical and theological content omitted today in our discipleship programs that were present in the early church?

Purpose of the Study

The purpose of this historical study is to explore the catechumenate and its implications for discipleship in 21st-century churches. To accomplish this purpose, this study will investigate the New Testament teaching on discipleship (Jesus and Paul); the pre-Christian, sociological factors, and doctrinal influences that led to the development of the catechumenate;

---

32 Clinton E. Arnold, "Early Church Catechesis and New Christians' Classes in Contemporary Evangelicalism," *JETS* 47 (2004), 39–54.

33 Lewis J. Sherrill, *The Rise of Christian Education* (New York, NY: The Macmillan Company, 1950), 186.

the history of the catechumenate; and the characteristics of the catechumenate. This research will contribute to current discipleship materials by providing an analysis of a successful discipleship program in church history and providing implications from this program for 21st-century churches.

CHAPTER 2

Principles of New Testament Discipleship

As the post-apostolic church prepared to train individuals for membership to their community, it based its foundation for theological teaching and personal commitment upon the instruction of the NT Scriptures. The principles that were gleaned from the NT provided the basis for the catechumenate. Twelve discipleship principles will be identified from Matthew 28:19–20, Luke 6:40, Luke 14:26–27, John 13:34–35, John 15:7–8, Romans 12:1–2, Ephesians 4:11–16, and 2 Timothy 2:2.

1. Disciples are commanded to make disciples of all peoples.
2. The means by which disciples are made is by baptizing (initiation) and teaching (instruction).
3. Disciples of Christ strive to be like their Master not just cognitively but also in conduct.
4. Disciples are singular in their allegiance to Christ.
5. Disciples must be willing to sacrifice all for Christ.
6. Disciples display genuine love to fellow believers.
7. Disciples are characterized by an intimate relationship with Jesus Christ, a passion for the Bible, a consistent prayer life, and a heart for ministry and service.
8. Disciples dedicate their lives as a consistent, blameless sacrifice to God.
9. Disciples consistently allow themselves to be transformed through meditation on the Word of God.
10. Disciples are actively involved in ministry.

11. Disciples are grounded in the truth and are not persuaded to follow false teaching.

12. Disciples replicate themselves into the spiritual lives of others.

An examination of NT instruction regarding discipleship is essential to understanding post-apostolic discipleship as well as discipleship in 21st-century church settings. This section examines select NT passages to provide an understanding of key principles in the development of NT disciples.

Matthew 28:19–20: The Command to Make Disciples

πορευθέντες οὖν μαθητεύσατε πάντα τὰ ἔθνη, βαπτίζοντες αὐτοὺς εἰς τὸ ὄνομα τοῦ πατρὸς καὶ τοῦ υἱοῦ καὶ τοῦ ἁγίου πνεύματος, διδάσκοντες αὐτοὺς τηρεῖν πάντα ὅσα ἐνετειλάμην ὑμῖν καὶ ἰδοὺ ἐγὼ μεθ' ὑμῶν εἰμι πάσας τὰς ἡμέρας ἕως τῆς συντελείας τοῦ αἰῶνος.[1]

As Jesus prepared to leave His disciples, He provided them with a final command. "Go therefore and make disciples of all the nations, baptizing them in the name of the Father and the Son and the Holy Spirit, teaching them to observe all that I commanded you; and lo, I am with you always, even to the end of the age." William Barclay, Scottish theologian and commentator, summarizes Jesus' command by simply stating, "He sent them out to make all the world His disciples."[2] The primary goal then of Christ's commission was to challenge his disciples to make disciples throughout the world.

Jesus had spent several years training His disciples (making disciples), and now He requires them to make disciples of others. The command that Jesus provides His disciples is to reproduce themselves into the lives of others. They were to take the treasure that Jesus had given to them (His life, teaching, and example) and share that treasure with all nations. John Nolland, Australian biblical scholar and NT commentator, describes the command that Jesus provides His disciples: "The imagery was of

---

1 Kurt Aland et al., *Novum Testamentum Graece*, 28th Edition. (Stuttgart: Deutsche Bibelgesellschaft, 2012), Mt 28:19–20.

2 William Barclay, *The Gospel of Matthew, Vol. 2* (Philadelphia, PA: Westminster Press, 1958), 417.

the disciples being discipled to be scribes of the kingdom and where the scribe was seen, as are the Eleven now in 28:19, as a discipling disciple: the treasure he has gained is a treasure he passes out to others."[3] This "treasure" that was received from Christ is to not be horded by Jesus' disciples, but rather the "treasure" is to be dispensed throughout the world.

The disciples were to be discipling others. Christ's disciples were to reproduce themselves into the lives of others. Three aspects of this passage need to be examined as one seeks to understand the command that Jesus is giving to His disciples.

The Meaning of the Term Disciple

The Greek term translated "make disciples" in Matthew 28:19 (μαθητευσατε) is from the root μαθητης meaning "pupil, learner, disciple."[4] The term "disciple" is not a new concept introduced in NT writings. The term "disciple" was used in the OT period as well as in Greek philosophical schools of the classical and koine Greek time periods.[5] In the OT, the term "*talmidh* appears to be the Hebrew equivalent of μαθητης."[6] *Talmidh* derives from the Hebrew verb *lamadh* meaning "to learn" or "to be taught."[7] *Talmidh* is used once in the OT in 1 Chronicles 25:8 and conveys the idea of "an apprentice learning a trade."[8] The adjective *limmudh*, "taught," also derives from the verb *lamadh*, is used six times in the OT (Isa 8:16; 50:4 [2x]; 54:13; Jer 2:24; 13:23), and has been translated as "disciples" (NASB, NIV, KJV, RSV). The OT records the concept of a disciple as a "learner," "follower," "apprentice," and "beginning scholar."[9]

---

3 John Nolland, *NIGTC: The Gospel of Matthew: A Commentary on the Greek Text* (Grand Rapids, MI: W.B. Eerdmans Pub. Co., 2005), 1265.

4 BAGD s.v. μαθητης, 486.

5 Richard N. Longenecker, *Patterns of Discipleship in the New Testament* (Grand Rapids, MI: William B. Eerdmans Pub., 1996), 2.

6 Michael J. Wilkins, *Discipleship in the Ancient World and Matthew's Gospel,* (2nd ed.) (Grand Rapids, MI: Baker Books, 1995), 45.

7 Francis Brown, S. R. Driver, and Charles A. Briggs, *The New Brown, Driver, Briggs, Gesenius Hebrew and English Lexicon: With an Appendix Containing the Biblical Aramaic* (Peabody, MA: Hendrickson, 1979), 541.

8 Wilkins, *Discipleship*, 46.

9 Ibid., 45–51.

In Greek culture, the term μαθητης dates back to the time of Herodutus.[10] The term and its derivations were used in the writings of Homer, Xenophanes, Plato, Socrates, Aristotle, Josephus, Philo, and others, and carried a range of meanings such as "apprentice," "follower," "learner," "pupil," "disciple," etc.[11] Gerhard Kittel in his classic work, *Theological Dictionary of the New Testament (TDNT)*, describes the meaning of the term μαθητης in the relationship of Socrates, the philosopher, as a μαθητης of the poet Homer:

> The centre [sic] of gravity of μαθητην ειναι is thus removed from the formal side of the relation between μαθητης and διδασκαλος to the inner fellowship between the two and its practical effects, and this to such a degree that the latter is basic to the whole relationship. This is not without considerable significance in relation to the development of the Christian use of μαθητης.[12]

Not only was a disciple a "learner" but was also an "apprentice" of a teacher. The relationship of μαθητης (disciple) to διδασκολος (teacher) is more than just "student" to "lecturer" and implies an intimate relationship such as "apprentice" to "mentor."

In the NT the term μαθητης is used to describe the "disciples" of Christ. The term will also include those who in the future enter a saving relationship with Jesus Christ and become a follower of the Savior. David Turner, NT scholar, professor, and commentator, describes the NT

---

10 James Orr, *The International Standard Bible Encyclopedia* (Peabody, MA: Hendrickson Publishers, 1984), 851. Michael Wilkins expounds that in Classical Greek, the word was used to describe three main groups:

1) In a general sense with reference to someone who is learning from another (i.e., apprentice).

2) In a technical sense referencing an individual who studies under a particular teacher (i.e., student).

3) In a restricted sense referring specifically to a Sophist pupil.

Michael J.Wilkins, "Disciples," in *Dictionary of Jesus and the Gospels: A Compendium of Contemporary Biblical Scholarship*, ed. Joel B. Green, Scot McKnight, and I. Howard Marshall (Downers Grove, IL: InterVarsity, 1992), 176–182.

11 Gerhard Kittel, *Theological Dictionary of the New Testament: Vol. 4*, edited and translated by G.W. Bromiley, (Grand Rapids, MI: Wm. B. Eerdmans Pub. Co., 1967), 391–461.

12 Ibid., 417.

disciple, as well as future disciples, as being characterized by the following: "A disciple is literally one who follows an itinerant master, as have Jesus' disciples. But Jesus will soon depart from this world, and discipleship will take on a more metaphorical meaning. Following Jesus will entail understanding and obeying his teaching."[13]

Donald Carson, theologian and NT scholar, describing the processes of discipleship and thus providing characteristics of a disciple of Jesus, states:

> To disciple a person to Christ is to bring him into the relation of pupil to teacher, "taking his yoke" of authoritative instruction (Matt 11:29), accepting what he says is true because he says it, and submitting to his requirements as right because he makes them. Disciples are those who hear, understand, and obey Jesus' teaching (Matt 12:46–50).[14]

Expounding upon this definition of a disciple, Donald Hagner, George Eldon Ladd Professor Emeritus of New Testament and Senior Professor of New Testament at Fuller Theological Seminary, provides an explanation of the Matthean concept of discipleship described in Matthew 28:19–20 (The Great Commission):

> The word "disciple" means above all "learner" or "pupil." The emphasis in the commission thus falls not on the initial proclamation of the gospel but more on the arduous task of nurturing into the experience of discipleship, an emphasis that is strengthened and explained by the instruction "teaching them to keep all that I have commanded" in v 20a. To be made a disciple in Matthew means above all to follow after righteousness as articulated in the teaching of Jesus.[15]

The concept of NT discipleship did not strictly apply to only the twelve apostles but further involves those individuals who will accept Christ in the future and follow His teachings. Therefore, the concept of a disciple of Christ has clear application to 21st-century Christians. Ulrich

---

13 David L. Turner, *Matthew* (Grand Rapids, MI: Baker Academic, 2008), 689–690.

14 Donald A. Carson, *EBC: Matthew (Vol. 8)* (Grand Rapids, MI: Zondervan Pub. House, 1984), 595–596.

15 Donald A. Hagner, *WBC: Matthew 14–28. (Vol. 33b)* (Nashville, TN: Thomas Nelson, 1995), 887.

Luz, Swiss theologian and professor at the University of Bern, explains that The Great Commission in Matthew 28:19–20 involves discipleship beyond the twelve apostles and impacts believers today.

> "Disciples" are not only the twelve disciples of the earthly Jesus; Jesus' discipleship occurs at every place where his power becomes active among people (v. 18b; cf. 9:8; 10:1) and his commandments are kept (v. 20a). Therefore the mission command of the Risen One is also transparent for the present. It is directed not only to the eleven apostles at the beginning of church history; the apostles are figures with whom all disciples of Jesus in all times can identify. The mission of the risen Jesus is for them also.[16]

Therefore, the Matthean concept of a disciple as described in Matthew 28:19 is a born-again believer who desires to learn what the Bible teaches, seeks to obey God's instruction, is committed to following Christ's example, and teaches the truths of Scripture to others.

The Nature of the Command

It has often been mistaken that the command in Matthew 28:19 is "go." Many churches, mission groups, and denominations misunderstand the command within Matthew 28 and spend their efforts winning new converts instead of anchoring them in the Christian faith.[17] The command that Jesus gives to His disciples is to "make disciples" of other individuals. Jesus' commission, which is imperative to all His followers, involved one primary command: "make disciples." This command is accompanied by three participles in the Greek: going, baptizing, and teaching.[18] Craig Blomberg, New Testament scholar and Distinguished Professor of the New Testament at Denver Seminary, provides important insight into the relationship of the command "make disciples" regarding the participles.

> The verb "make disciples" also commands a kind of evangelism that does not stop after someone makes a profession of faith. The truly subordinate participles in v. 19 explain what making disciples

---

16 Ulrich Luz, *Hermeneia: Matthew 21–28* (Philadelphia, PA: Fortress Press, 2005), 625–626.

17 Grant R. Osborne, *Matthew* (Grand Rapids, MI: Zondervan, 2010), 1080.

18 John F. Walvoord and Roy B. Zuck, *The Bible Knowledge Commentary: New Testament ed.* (Wheaton, IL: Victor Books, 1983), 94.

involves: "baptizing" them and "teaching" them obedience to all of Jesus' commandments. The first of these will be a once-for-all, decisive initiation into Christian community. The second proves a perennially incomplete, life-long task.[19]

Daniel Wallace, Greek scholar and Professor of New Testament Studies at Dallas Theological Seminary, describes the first participle, πορευθεντες ("going"), as an "attendant circumstance participle." The definition of the "attendant circumstance participles" is as follows:

> The attendant circumstance participle is used to communicate an action that, in some sense, is coordinate with the finite verb. In this respect it is not dependent, for it is translated like a verb. Yet it is still dependent *semantically*, because it cannot exist without the main verb. It is translated as a finite verb connected to the main verb by *and*.[20]

With this definition in focus, Wallace explains the connection of the participle πορευθεντες, "going", with the main verb μαθητευσατε, "make disciples." Wallace claims that the participle "going" is an "attendant circumstance participle" due to the following reasons:

1. πορευθεντες fits the structural pattern for the attendant circumstance participle: aorist participle preceding an aorist main verb (in this case, imperative).

2. There is no good grammatical ground for giving the participle a mere temporal idea. To turn πορευθεντες into an adverbial participle is to turn the Great Commission into the Great Suggestion! In Matthew every other instance of the aorist participle of πορευομαι followed by an aorist main verb (either indicative or imperative) is clearly attendant circumstance.

3. The commission must be read in its historical context, not from the perspective of a late twentieth-century reader.

---

19 Craig L. Blomberg, *NAC: Matthew* (Nashville, TN: B&H Publishing Group, 1992), 431.

20 Daniel B. Wallace, *Greek Grammar Beyond the Basics: An Exegetical Syntax of the New Testament with Scripture, Subject, and Greek Word Indexes* (Grand Rapids, MI: Zondervan, 1996), 640.

These apostles of the soon-to-be inaugurated church did not move from Jerusalem until after the martyrdom of Stephen. The reason for this reticence was due, in part at least, to their Jewish background. As Jews, they were ethnocentric in their evangelism (bringing prospective proselytes to Jerusalem); now as Christians, they were to be *ektocentric*, bringing the gospel to those who were non-Jews.[21]

According to the above reasons, Wallace believes that the way to interpret the participle "going" is as an "attendant circumstance participle."

Wallace's third reason for interpreting πορευθεντες as an "attendant circumstance particle" provides important insight regarding the way in which the disciples are to be discipling others. To "make disciples *of all nations*" does require many people to leave their homelands. However, Jesus' focus remains for all believers to duplicate themselves wherever they may be.[22] The activity demanded in the Great Commission is not to "go," but rather to "make disciples." It is critical to note that the command is not to evangelize but to perform the broader and deeper task of "discipling" the nations.[23] Jesus previously commissioned the disciples to proclaim the kingdom to Israel alone (Matt 10:5–6; 15:24–27), but now He commands them to disciple all the nations.[24] The commission is not simply to proclaim the good news, but it has the end result in mind, to "make disciples." It is not enough that the nations hear the message; they must also respond with the same wholehearted commitment which was required of those who became disciples of Jesus during his ministry.[25]

The Means by which Disciples are Developed: Baptizing and Teaching

Jesus stated at the close of Matthew 28:19 that the disciples were to make disciples by baptizing (βαπτιζοντες) and teaching (διδασκοντες). The two participles should not be interpreted as "attendant circumstance" like πορευθεντες because they do not fit the normal pattern for an "attendant

---

21 Ibid., 645.

22 Blomberg, *Matthew*, 431.

23 Osborne, *Matthew*, 1080.

24 Turner, *Matthew*, 689.

25 R. T. France, *NIGTC: The Gospel of Matthew* (Grand Rapids, MI: William B. Eerdmans Pub., 2007), 1115.

circumstance participle" (they are present tense and follow the main verb). Rather, they should be interpreted as participles of "means" (i.e., the means by which the disciples were to make disciples was to baptize and then to teach).[26] Baptizing (βαπτιζοντες) and teaching (διδασκοντες) "beautifully describe both the sacramental and experiential sides of discipleship which are essential aspects of ecclesiology."[27]

Baptizing

The first "means" by which new believers are discipled is through baptism. The eleven disciples were to make disciples by proclaiming the truth concerning Jesus. Their hearers were to be evangelized and enlisted as Jesus' followers (i.e., become new disciples). Those who believed were to be baptized in water in the name of the Father and of the Son and of the Holy Spirit. This act would associate a believer with the person of Jesus Christ and with the Triune God.[28]

Jesus, in the Great Commission, makes baptism an essential component of discipleship. The new believer is baptized under the rulership of Christ. Baptism was an act of initiation, and Matthew 28:19 states that disciples initiate others (after salvation) into the church. Baptism was part of Christian practice universally and from the beginning, and it is unlikely that the early Jewish Christians would baptize fellow Jews without some sort of approval from Jesus (cf. John 4:1–2); therefore, a command of Jesus to baptize was important to the eleven disciples.[29]

Baptism would become the key first step that initiates new disciples into the church (that will be established later in Acts 2). This baptism is a single act, distinct from repeated Jewish ritual washings. It is done with the Trinitarian formula invoking the Father, Son, and Holy Spirit, and so it also contrasts from John's baptism (Mark 1:4; Jn 3:3).[30] Baptism will be a once-for-all, decisive initiation into Christian community.[31]

---

26 Wallace, *Greek Grammar Beyond the Basics*, 645.

27 Osborne, *Matthew*, 1081.

28 Walvoord and Zuck, *The Bible Knowledge Commentary*, 93–94.

29 Craig S. Keener, *The Gospel of Matthew: A Socio-Rhetorical Commentary* (Grand Rapids, MI: William B. Eerdmans Pub., 2009), 720.

30 Turner, *Matthew*, 690.

31 Blomberg, *Matthew*, 431.

Teaching

Those who are baptized are to be taught not only to know all of Jesus' commands but also to obey all of them (Matt 28:20). Therefore, in discipleship the intellectual component is secondary, the means to the end, which is spiritual formation.[32] Throughout the book of Matthew, Jesus has functioned as the teacher, but now the disciples are to teach on His behalf (because Jesus is physically leaving the earth). But though the disciples are now to do the teaching, the teacher-disciple relationship is with Jesus. The disciples are not the ones that the new disciples are to emulate, but rather new Christians are to be imitators/disciples of Jesus. What the disciples are to teach is what they have been taught by Jesus; and as they teach, Jesus will, but now in a new way, be present as mentor/model for the new disciple (Matt 28:20b).[33]

In Matthew 28:20, the content of the teaching is given to the disciples—"all that I have commanded you." This expression has in mind the teaching of Jesus in the Gospels as was directed to the disciples. First and foremost, the disciples are to be obedient to what Jesus has commanded them, and then as a by-product of this obedience they are to pass on his teachings to others. The idea of replication is fundamental to Matthew's thought here.[34]

There are two different Greek words which convey the idea of "teaching" in verses 19–20 (μαθητευσατε—"make disciples" v. 19 and διδασκοντες—"teaching" v. 20). The "teaching" in these two verses seems to include two things: (1) Bringing those who are out of Christianity into it, "teach all nations." The word "teach" (μαθητευσατε) carries the sense of, "make disciples, proselytize them, bringing them over to my religion." (2) An indoctrinating of those who are brought into the new religion into a practical observance of its holy truths. "Teaching them to observe all that I commanded you" (v. 20). Once the initiatory work is done (proselytizing), this is the work to be pursued (indoctrination). The proselyte having been brought to the faith is to be practically taught how to live by faith.[35] "Teaching" obedience to all of Jesus' commands (the two parts

---

32 Turner, *Matthew*, 690.

33 Nolland, *The Gospel of Matthew*, 1270.

34 Ibid., 1271.

35 David Thomas, *The Gospel of St. Matthew: An Expository and Homiletic Commentary* (Grand Rapids, MI: Baker Book House, 1956), 559.

of the teaching process in mind) forms the heart of disciple making. If non-Christians are not hearing the gospel and not being challenged to make a decision for Christ, then the church has disobeyed one part of Jesus' commission. If new converts are not faithfully and lovingly nurtured in the whole counsel of God's disclosure, then the church has disobeyed the other part.[36]

Once new believers are initiated, mature disciples must build the new believers into stronger disciples by teaching them Jesus' message. The summaries of Jesus' teachings earlier in Matthew's Gospel (chs. 5–7; 10; 13; 18; 23–25) work well as a discipling manual for young believers.[37] This instruction (discipleship) proves a perennially incomplete, life-long task.[38]

Interestingly, as will be described in Chapter 3, the order in which these two participles occur—baptizing (βαπτίζοντες) and teaching (διδάσκοντες)—differs from what becomes common practice in subsequent Christian history in that baptism is administered only after a period of "teaching" to those who have already learned. Baptism will become in the catechumenal process a graduation ceremony rather than an initiation to the Christian community. If the order of Matthew's participles is meant to be observed and practiced, the catechumenate presented a different model whereby baptism is the point of enrollment into a process of learning which is never complete. The Christian community then becomes a school of learners at various stages of development rather than divided into the baptized (who have "arrived") and those who are "not yet ready."[39]

Matthew 28:19–20 provides for the believer a commission to obey the command of Jesus to "make disciples" of all peoples. The requirement of "going" is assumed by Jesus as a byproduct of a saving relationship with Christ. The means by which believers are to "make disciples" is by "baptizing" and "teaching" them. "Baptism" is the introduction into the Christian community while "teaching" involves a lifelong task of becoming more like Jesus Christ. From this passage the first two discipleship principles are gleaned:

---

36 Blomberg, *Matthew*, 432.

37 Keener, *The Gospel of Matthew*, 720.

38 Blomberg, *Matthew*, 431.

39 France, *The Gospel of Matthew*, 1115–1116.

Discipleship Principles:

Disciples are commanded to make disciples of all peoples.

*The means by which disciples are made is by baptizing (initiation)
and teaching (instruction).*

Luke 6:40: The Goal of Discipleship

οὐκ ἔστιν μαθητὴς ὑπὲρ τὸν διδάσκαλον κατηρτισμένος δὲ πᾶς ἔσται
ὡς ὁ διδάσκαλος αὐτοῦ.[40]

In Luke 6:40, Jesus provides his disciples with a maxim regarding the relationship between a teacher and his pupils. "A pupil is not above his teacher; but everyone, after he has been fully trained, will be like his teacher."
This passage not only provides an important principle in relation to NT
discipleship, but also provides a beautiful picture of the relationship that
disciples have to the Master Teacher (Jesus Christ).

The maxim contains several elements that are critical to the understanding of this unit.

1. The maxim contains two participants—a disciple and a
   teacher.
2. The maxim consists of two parts—two declarative
   statements.
3. The second half of the maxim focuses on the effect that
   one participant has on the other participant—the disciple
   will become like his/her teacher.
4. The second half of the maxim is designed to be more
   inclusive than the first half. The use of "everyone" extends
   the principle beyond one individual disciple and includes all
   future disciples.[41]

This maxim reveals the relationship that Jesus (the teacher) currently
has with his disciples and which he will possess with future disciples.

---

40 Kurt Aland et al., Lk 6:40.

41 Thomas W. Hudgins, "Luke 6:40 and the Theme of Likeness Education in the
New Testament" (EdD Diss., Southeastern Baptist Theological Seminary, 2013), 48–49.

The Nature of the Teacher-Pupil Instruction

In the Greco Roman world, the teacher-pupil relationship was a personal one. Before the widespread availability of books, a pupil depended on his teacher's instruction.[42] Because books were not readily available and oral instruction was normative, a student (disciple) virtually lived alongside his teacher.[43] Teachers were regarded as authorities, and the student's role was not simply to get information from the teacher—or, as is often the case in modern classrooms, to challenge the instruction of the teacher—but rather to follow a teacher by adopting his teaching as normative for life.[44] A critical point to understand is that Jesus describes the end result of the disciple's instruction when he states, "after he has been fully trained, he will be like his teacher." The disciple would eventually mimic the teacher's instruction and the instructor himself.

The verb "fully trained" (κατηρτισμενος) means "restored" (1 Pet 5:10, NIV) or "perfectly united" (1 Cor 1:10, NIV). The term is also used in Mark 1:19 to describe James the son of Zebedee and John his brother "mending the nets." "Christian discipleship implies mending one's ways."[45] The instruction in the teacher-pupil relationship involves reordering one's personal and spiritual life. Ceslas Spicq, internationally recognized biblical scholar, writes, "the Christian life involves steady progress in preparation for glory, or the restoration and reordering of whatever is deficient either in one's personal life or in one's relations with one's neighbor."[46] This depth of instruction is not achieved in a one-time sermon series or in a six-week discipleship course. Rather, this instruction requires continuous spiritual formation (Phil 3:12–16).[47]

---

42 I. H. Marshall, *The Gospel of Luke: A Commentary on the Greek Text* (Grand Rapids, MI: Eerdmans, 1978), 269.

43 Darrell L. Bock, *Luke* (Grand Rapids, MI: Baker Books, 1996), 612. Bock describes the following of the teacher by the student by stating, "In addition, these teachers were followed, because they were regarded as authorities."

44 Ibid., 612.

45 David E. Garland, *Luke* (Grand Rapids, MI: Zondervan, 2011), 284.

46 Ceslas Spicq, *Theological Lexicon of the New Testament, Vol. 2* (Peabody, MA: Hendrickson, 1994), 274.

47 Garland, *Luke*, 284. In Philippians 3:12–16, Paul is calling believers to make it their life's goal to strive toward attaining the prize. This passion and pursuit are a lifelong process. This prize is not achieved by a casual commitment to Christ. Rather, Paul

The Content of the Teacher-Pupil Instruction

In the ancient world, the content of the instruction was critically important within the teacher-pupil relationship. It is often assumed in modern teaching that content should drive the instruction. However, modern research on teaching suggests that though content is important the teacher and his/her methods of instruction are a critical component in the education of individual students.[48]

In the NT time period, the teacher-pupil relationship is assumed to be one in which the teacher does not merely impart a body of information (content) but rather praxis (to mimic the actions of the teacher).[49] Thomas Hudgins states, "mere cognition was never the exclusive goal

---

urges the Philippians to press on toward the goal. "Paul elaborates the point of v. 12 with an athletic metaphor, picturing himself as a runner whose every muscle and nerve is singularly focused on the goal, in hopes of winning the prize." Gordon D. Fee, *NIC-NT: Paul's Letter to the Philippians* (Grand Rapids, MI: W.B. Eerdmans Pub. Co., 1995), 346.

48 Modern educational researchers and experts suggest that other factors beyond simply content are involved in the education of an individual. 1) <u>Teachers</u>. Robert Marzano, a world-renowned educational specialist, argues that the teacher and his/her methods of instruction are a critical component to the education of an individual. "The conclusion that individual teachers can have a profound influence on student learning even in schools that are relatively ineffective, was noticed in the 1970s when we began to examine effective teaching practices." Robert J. Marzano, Debra Pickering, and Jane E. Pollock. *Classroom Instruction That Works: Research-Based Strategies for Increasing Student Achievement* (Alexandria, VA: Association for Supervision and Curriculum Development, 2001), 3. In a comprehensive research study involving more than 100,000 students from hundreds of schools, the research reveals that the teacher is the significant difference in student achievement rather than content. "The results of this study will document that the most important factor affecting student learning is the teacher. … Effective teachers appear to be effective with students of all achievement levels, regardless of the level of heterogeneity in their classrooms." S. Paul Wright, Sandra P. Horn, and William L. Sanders, "Teacher and Classroom Context Effects on Student Achievement: Implications for Teacher Evaluation," *Journal of Personal Evaluation in Education 11* (1997), 63. 2) <u>Differentiated instruction</u>. Carol A. Tomlinson and Marcia B. Imbeau, *Leading and Managing a Differentiated Classroom* (Alexandria, VA: ASCD, 2010). 3) <u>Multiple Intelligences</u>. Howard Gardner, *Multiple Intelligences: New Horizons in Theory and Practice*. Rev. and updated ed. (New York, NY: BasicBooks, 2006). 4) <u>Learning Conditions</u>. Rita Dunn and Kenneth Dunn, *Teaching Secondary Students Through Their Individual Learning Styles* (Boston, MA: Allyn and Bacon, 1993).

49 John Nolland, *WBC: Luke* (Dallas, TX: Word Books, 1989), 307.

of learning and education in the Old and New Testaments."[50] Rather, education involved taking the cognitive and relating this information to relational aspects of one's life.[51] A key component of the content in the μαθητης-διδασκολος relationship was not only a transfer of knowledge from teacher to pupil but also the transmission of experience and the character of the teacher himself. The pupil was not only to learn from the teacher (cognitive), but he was also to imitate the teacher (conduct).[52]

The Goal of the Teacher-Pupil Instruction

The text in Luke 6:40 highlights the goal of discipleship from a Jewish mindset. Francois Bovon, the late Frothingham Professor of the History of Religion Emeritus at Harvard Divinity School, states, "the goal of instruction for a disciple in Judaism consisted in becoming like his or her teacher in order eventually to become a teacher himself or herself."[53] Luke however does not expect the disciples to be teachers exactly like Jesus Christ (this is impossible because Jesus is omniscient and holy). However, Luke is challenging the disciples to strive to be like the Master in one's ethical behavior (as a byproduct of gaining spiritual knowledge). Discipleship involves more than intellectual learning; it involves learning that impacts head, heart, will, and body.[54] Once an individual enters a salvation relationship with Jesus Christ, he then has the power or ability to mimic the Master (through the power of the Holy Spirit).[55]

The point of this passage is not for disciples (the twelve) to make disciples who resemble themselves (the twelve). Rather, the disciple should ultimately resemble the Master. Future disciples are not to become carbon copies of the copies. Rather, through the study of the Scriptures (in conjunction with the teaching of the disciples), they are to resemble the

---

50 Hudgins, *Luke 6:40*, 55.

51 James Limburg comments on Psalm 25 and highlights the theological-relational and cognitive-practical aspects of OT education. One must understand who God is (his attributes and character) and allow this knowledge to change the way that he/she lives (conduct). James Limburg, *Psalms* (Louisville, KY: Westminster John Knox, 2000), 81.

52 Hudgins, *Luke 6:40*, 57.

53 Francois Bovon, *Luke a Commentary on the Gospel of Luke 1:1–9:50* (Minneapolis, MN: Fortress Press, 2002), 249.

54 Ibid., 249.

55 Ibid., 249.

Master, Jesus Christ. Thomas Hudgins explains this relationship: "Jesus becomes the center of an individual's relationship to God, not just salvifically but also instructionally."[56] A disciple must be ready to learn, not strictly from human wisdom but rather from wisdom from above.[57]

Discipleship Principle:

Disciples of Christ strive to be like their Master not just cognitively but also in conduct.

Luke 14:26–27: The Cost of Discipleship

εἴ τις ἔρχεται πρός με καὶ οὐ μισεῖ τὸν πατέρα ἑαυτοῦ καὶ τὴν μητέρα καὶ τὴν γυναῖκα καὶ τὰ τέκνα καὶ τοὺς ἀδελφοὺς καὶ τὰς ἀδελφὰς ἔτι τε καὶ τὴν ψυχὴν ἑαυτοῦ, οὐ δύναται εἶναί μου μαθητής. ὅστις οὐ βαστάζει τὸν σταυρὸν ἑαυτοῦ καὶ ἔρχεται ὀπίσω μου, οὐ δύναται εἶναί μου μαθητής. [58]

"If anyone comes to Me and does not hate his own father and mother and wife and children and brothers and sisters, yes, and even his own life, he cannot be My disciple. Whoever does not carry his own cross and come after Me cannot be My disciple."

The pericope which contains these two verses regarding discipleship is Luke 14:25–35. The purpose of this pericope was for Jesus to explain to his followers the cost of being His disciple. The section begins with an introduction (v. 25), transitions to two parallel sayings on discipleship (vv. 26–27), continues by providing two parabolic sayings with application regarding discipleship (vv. 28–33), and concludes with a challenge against half-hearted discipleship (vv. 34–35).[59]

The opening sayings (vv. 26–27) and the application (v. 33) express the total commitment required from disciples of Jesus Christ. This pericope

---

56 Hudgins, *Luke 6:40*, 52.

57 Bovon, *Luke a Commentary on the Gospel of Luke 9:51–19:27*, 387.

58 Kurt Aland et al., Lk 14: 26–27.

59 I. Howard Marshall, *The Gospel of Luke: A Commentary on the Greek Text* (Grand Rapids, MI: Eerdmans, 1978), 591.

describes what it will take to be a disciple of Jesus.[60] The reason Jesus provides the two parables (vv. 28–32) is to provide an illustration of the importance of correct evaluation before venturing into a task (building a tower, v. 28) or large undertaking (war, v. 31). In both examples, it is critical for an individual to "count the cost" before venturing into the task. These illustrations (parables) challenge the individual to consider the cost of discipleship. The disciple of Christ must be willing to pay the cost or else the task will go uncompleted, and he will be considered useless (vv. 34–35).[61]

Jesus challenges those who are following him that there is a cost to being his disciple (vv. 26–27, 33). In verses twenty-six and twenty-seven, Jesus makes two challenging statements related to the cost of discipleship.[62] It is critically important to understand what these two statements mean so that one can understand the true cost of being a disciple of Christ.

The Meaning of the Verb μισει

What does Jesus mean when he calls his disciples to "hate" father, mother, wife, children, brothers, sisters, and his own life? The verb μισεω, "hate," probably reflects a Semitic origin. The Semitic languages often used contrasts to express things in a comparative degree of preferences.[63] Therefore, "to hate" used in this Semitic sense would mean "to love less." I. Howard Marshall, Professor Emeritus of New Testament Exegesis at the University of Aberdeen, Scotland, affirms such an understanding of the Semitic sense of the term "to hate": "this is no doubt how the phrase was understood by Matthew's tradition."[64] It would seem odd for Jesus to instruct his disciples to love their enemies (Luke 6:35) but to hate their families. But when one understands the verb "to hate" in this Semitic sense, one understands that Jesus is calling his disciples to show preference for one over another. David Garland, Dean and Professor of New Testament at Talbot School of Theology, explains that the passage should not be viewed as "I love A and hate B," but should be read "I prefer A

---

60 Bovon, *Luke a Commentary on the Gospel of Luke 9:51–19:27,* 389.

61 Marshall, *The Gospel of Luke,* 591.

62 "If anyone comes to Me and does not hate his own father and mother and wife and children and brothers and sisters, yes, and even his own life, he cannot be My disciple. Whoever does not carry his own cross and come after Me cannot be My disciple."

63 Bovon, *Luke,* 386.

64 Marshall, *The Gospel of Luke,* 592.

to B" (A being Jesus and B being the list of individuals).[65] The thought then behind the meaning of μισεω is not psychological hate, but rather renunciation. "I choose one over another."[66]

The image that is conveyed by this verb is strong. It does not involve a call to be insensitive or to leave all feeling towards our families behind. But, following Jesus is to be the disciple's "first love" (Rev 2:4). Being a disciple of Christ should have priority over any family member and even over one's own life. Jesus, and being his disciple, should be the passion of our lives.[67] The idea of "hating" is tantamount to "leaving."[68] The crowds who were following Christ, to become a true disciple of Jesus, needed to be willing to part with those individuals closest to their hearts. Francois Bovon explains the choice that is involved in "hating": "in this connection hate is not, in the first instance, an emotion; it is an act."[69]

With a proper understanding of the verb μισει in mind, the requirement for discipleship becomes clear. Discipleship to Christ is fundamentally a call to allegiance; as it pertains to importance in a believer's life, Jesus must be first even above family.[70] One must understand the context of the passage's first-century setting. When a Jewish person made a choice to follow Jesus, he would inevitably alienate his or her family. Darrell Bock explains the cost of discipleship and the level of allegiance required to follow Jesus in a first-century context.

> If someone desired acceptance by family more than a relationship with God, one might never come to Jesus, given the rejection that would inevitably follow. In other words, there could be no casual devotion to Jesus in the first century. A decision for Christ marked a person and automatically came with a cost.[71]

---

65 Garland, *Luke*, 600. Garland lists the following references as examples of this Semantic interpretation as to preference to one over another: Gen 29:30–33 (speaking of Jacob, "he loved Rachel more than Leah"); Deut 21:15–17; Mal 1:2–3; Luke 16:13; and Rom 9:13.

66 Marshall, *The Gospel of Luke*, 592.

67 Bock, *Luke*, 1284–1285.

68 Bovon, *Luke*, 387.

69 Ibid., 387.

70 Bock, *Luke*, 1284.

71 Ibid., 1285.

The language of the passage is clear: if one does not make Jesus the priority of one's life, he/she cannot be his disciple.

If one does not fully forsake his family, he/she will not be fully committed to Christ. Disciples are to distance themselves from the high cultural value placed on family.[72] If a disciple is not diligent, family ties will become a greater pull for one's allegiance then that of Jesus Christ.[73] One's family is not to be the primary priority of one's life; only Jesus is to have that role. David Garland states, "love for him is to take precedence over all other loves."[74] A disciple must make a choice. He/she cannot have divided loyalties, pulling in opposite directions. He/she must be singular in his or her devotion to Jesus Christ.[75]

The Call to Endure Persecution for Christ

In addition to the call for a singular allegiance to Christ, Jesus provides a second requirement to be his disciple. He calls disciples to be willing to endure persecution. In Luke 14:37, Jesus states: "Whoever does not carry his own cross and come after Me cannot be My disciple."

Again, it is of great importance that one understands the first-century context in which this call is found. The call to bear one's cross denotes a willingness to bear the pain of persecution because of following Jesus. It is a call to have a constant willingness to suffer shame and reproach.[76] It is often impossible for 21st-century individuals to understand the shame associated with crucifixion in the ancient world.[77] Crucifixion, understood to be of Persian origin, was a well-known Roman practice during the time of Christ. Crucifixions were such a feared means of execution that various revolts had been suppressed by means of such killings.[78]

History reveals that crucifixion was used by the Assyrians, Phoenicians, and Persians during the first millennium B.C. It was introduced to the West from eastern cultures, and, though it was not used regularly in

---

72 Joel B. Green, *The Gospel of Luke* (Grand Rapids, MI: W.B. Eerdmans Pub. Co., 1997), 565.

73 Bock, *Luke*, 1285.

74 Garland, *Luke*, 601.

75 Bovon, *Luke*, 386.

76 Bock, *Luke*, 1286–1287.

77 Garland, *Luke*, 601.

78 Bovon, *Luke*, 389.

Greece, it became a frequently used punishment in Sicily and southern Italy.[79] During the Hellenistic Period, crucifixion became a popular form of execution, used frequently by the Seleucids and Ptolemies after the death of Alexander.[80]

During the Hasmonean Dynasty, crucifixion was employed by the Jews to stop rebellions. Josephus records the horrific account of Alexander Jannaeus crucifying 800 Pharisees because of a revolt against him.

> He brought them to Jerusalem, and did one of the most barbarous actions in the world to them; for as he was feasting with his concubines, in the sight of all the city, he ordered about eight hundred of them to be crucified; and while they were living, he ordered the throats of their children and wives to be cut before their eyes.[81]

Vassilios Tzaferis, noted archaeologist and historian, states:

> At the end of the first century B.C., the Romans adopted crucifixion as an official punishment for non-Romans for certain legally limited transgressions. Initially, it was employed not as a method of execution, but only as a punishment.[82]

---

79 Vassilios Tzaferis, "Crucifixion—The Archaeological Evidence," *BAR* Jan/Feb (1985), 48.

80 Ibid., 48.

81 Josephus, *Antiquities*, XIII:14.2.380, 361.

82 Tzaferis, *BAR*, 48. Tzaferis expounded on the view that initially crucifixion was designed for punishment for slaves.

> Moreover, only slaves convicted of certain crimes were punished by crucifixion. During this early period, a wooden beam, known as a *furca* or *patibulum* was placed on the slave's neck and bound to his arms. The slave was then required to march through the neighborhood proclaiming his offense. This march was intended as an expiation and humiliation. Later, the slave was also stripped and scourged, increasing both the punishment and the humiliation. Still later, instead of walking with his arms tied to the wooden beam, the slave was tied to a vertical stake. Because the main purpose of this practice was to punish, humiliate and frighten disobedient slaves, the practice did not necessarily result in death. Only in later times, probably in the first century B.C., did crucifixion evolve into a method of execution for conviction of certain crimes.

Crucifixion did not always result in death but rather was used as a punishment tool for slaves.

Crucifixion, as history reveals, was a common practice used to stop revolts or punish severe criminal offenses. It would later be used by the Romans as a method of execution for certain crimes.[83]

During a crucifixion, the wood was attached in such a way as to display a cross. The vertical bar was secured into the ground, and it appears that the condemned persons had to carry the horizontal part, the *patibulum*, to the place where they would be executed. The executioner would then attach the horizontal bar to the vertical bar and would hang the condemned person on the cross (usually with nails).[84] The horror of this punishment was well known.[85]

Jesus calls his disciples to be willing to bear their cross. To "bear one's cross" is not necessarily a call to death. Rather, the call is to the denial of oneself with a willingness to endure hardship which may result in death. To Jesus' Jewish audience, this demand "to bear one's cross" would be understood as an utterly offensive affair. The cross was viewed as "obscene" in the original sense of the word.[86] The illustration is that the disciples

---

83 Ibid., 48. Tzaferis expounded on the historical development of crucifixion under the Romans.

> Initially, crucifixion was known as the punishment of the slaves. Later, it was used to punish foreign captives, rebels, and fugitives, especially during times of war and rebellion. Captured enemies and rebels were crucified in masses. Accounts of the suppression of the revolt of Spartacus in 71 B.C. tell how the Roman army lined the road from Capua to Rome with 6,000 crucified rebels on 6,000 crosses. After the Romans quelled the relatively minor rebellion in Judea in 7 A.D. triggered by the death of King Herod, Quintilius Varus, the Roman Legate of Syria, crucified 2,000 Jews in Jerusalem. During Titus's siege of Jerusalem in 70 A.D., Roman troops crucified as many as 500 Jews a day for several months. In times of war and rebellion when hundreds and even thousands of people were crucified within a short period, little if any attention was paid to the way the crucifixion was carried out. Crosses were haphazardly constructed, and executioners were impressed from the ranks of Roman legionaries.

Crucifixion under the Romans expanded into a widely used punishment to quell rebellions.

84 Bovon, *Luke*, 389.

85 Tzaferis, *BAR*, 49–50. For a further examination of the process of crucifixion, see Appendix 1. Tzaferis provided a detailed explanation of the horrors of the crucifixion process.

86 Martin Hengel, *Crucifixion in the Ancient World, and the Folly of the Message of the Cross* (Philadelphia, PA: Fortress Press, 1977), 22. Hengel's work is an extensive revelation of the horrors of crucifixion. Hengel provides an examination of the historical

must be willing to suffer opposition for Jesus Christ. This opposition may result in death for Christ (martyrdom). A true disciple must be willing to sacrifice all to follow Jesus Christ.

Discipleship Principles:

Disciples are singular in their allegiance to Christ.

Disciples must be willing to sacrifice all for Christ.

John 13:34–35: A Distinguishing Mark of a Disciple

Ἐντολὴν καινὴν δίδωμι ὑμῖν, ἵνα ἀγαπᾶτε ἀλλήλους, καθὼς ἠγάπησα ὑμᾶς ἵνα καὶ ὑμεῖς ἀγαπᾶτε ἀλλήλους. ἐν τούτῳ γνώσονται πάντες ὅτι ἐμοὶ μαθηταί ἐστε, ἐὰν ἀγάπην ἔχητε ἐν ἀλλήλοις [87]

"A new commandment I give to you, that you love one another, even as I have loved you, that you also love one another. By this all men will know that you are My disciples, if you have love for one another."

In the Upper Room Discourse, Jesus provides a distinguishing mark of his disciples. "All mankind will know that you are my disciples if you display love for one another." John Phillips, noted commentator and former assistant director of the Moody Bible Institute's Correspondence School, states the following regarding this identifying mark of Jesus' disciples.

> The badge of true discipleship is not in the doctrinal statements to which we subscribe, not in the types of hymns and music we prefer, not in the rituals we observe or the ordinances we cherish, not in our soulwinning zeal, our faithfulness to the churches of our choice—but in our love for all those who love the Lord. When people see that, they will recognize Christ in his disciples and recognize that love as truly his own.[88]

---

evidence regarding crucifixion including the history of crucifixion, the various methods utilized in crucifixion, as well as the horror of the crucifixion process. After studying his book, the reader truly understands that ancient crucifixion is indeed "obscene."

87 Kurt Aland et al., Jn 13:34–35.

88 John Phillips, *Exploring the Gospel of John: An Expository Commentary* (Grand Rapids, MI: Kregel Publications, 2001), 260.

Jesus' disciples would distinguish themselves from others in the world by their love for one another.[89] This love is so uncharacteristic of the world's system that Jesus' disciples would stand out when they demonstrated this love for one another.

The Basis for the New Commandment

The form of this "new" command matches the example that Jesus previously provided for the disciples when he washed their feet. When Jesus finished washing his disciple's feet (John 13:3–12), he required that they go and do likewise (vv. 14–15).[90] The standard of comparison for the love the disciples are to display to the world is Jesus' love just exemplified in the foot washing of his disciples. These disciples, during the foot washing, had yet to understand the standard of love they are to follow. Days later they would understand the full meaning of Jesus' love for them—when he would die for their sins.[91]

---

89 Don Carson writes the following about this simplicity yet difficulty with obeying this new command. "The new command is simple enough for a toddler to memorize and appreciate, profound enough that the most mature believers are repeatedly embarrassed at how poorly they comprehend it and put it into practice: *Love one another. As I have loved you, so you must love one another.*" Donald A. Carson, *The Gospel According to John* (Leicester, England: Inter-Varsity Press, 1991), 484.

90 Ramsey J. Michaels, *NICNT: The Gospel of John* (Grand Rapids, MI: William B. Eerdmans Pub, 2010), 759–760. Michaels goes on to write regarding the comparison between the example of foot washing and the present command to "love one another."

> While Jesus did not speak of the latter as a "command;" only as an obligation, something the disciples "ought" to do (v. 14), and are "blessed" for doing (v. 17), the similarity of structure is evident. Both pronouncements combine a "vertical," one-way relationship (that is, from a Lord or King to subordinates) with a "horizontal," two-way relationship (that is, a mutual relationship among peers). Jesus takes the initiative to love (and show his love for) his disciples. Nothing is said of their loving him first, or even in return, and they are not allowed to reciprocate by washing his feet. Instead, they extend his love to "each other," whether specifically by washing each other's feet (vv. 14–15), or more generally in the daily conduct of their lives (vv. 34–35). Such a structure, with its "vertical" and "horizontal" axis, can be seen not only here but in several other New Testament passages, whether the subject matter is mutual love (see 15:12; 1 Jn 3:16; 4:11; Eph 5:2), forgiveness (Eph 4:32; Col 3:13), or acceptance (Rom 15:7).

According to Michaels the act of "loving one another" was an outward demonstration of the love that the believer has for God.

91 Carson, *The Gospel According to John,* 484. Carson goes on to write that until we

The command to "love" is not a new commandment but finds its basis in the OT where God instructs the Israelites to "love your neighbor as yourself" (Lev 19:18).[92] In fact, the Mosaic Law mandated two different love commandments: "You shall love the LORD your God with all your heart and with all your soul and with all your might" (Deut 6:5); and "You shall not take vengeance, nor bear any grudge against the sons of your people, but you shall love your neighbor as yourself; I am the LORD" (Lev 19:18). Jesus himself taught that all the law and the prophets were summed up in these two commands (Mark 12:28–31).[93] Johannine tradition also recognizes that the commandment was not "new" (in that it had never been given before). Second John 1:5 states, "Now I ask you, lady, not as though I *were* writing to you a new commandment, but the one which we have had from the beginning, that we love one another." In addition, love within a community of individuals was not only on display but also highly regarded in the Qumran community.[94]

Therefore, if love was not only previously commanded and displayed within Jewish communities, why does Jesus state that he is giving the disciples a "new commandment"? The "new" portion of this command appears to be the affection that the disciples should have for one another

---

understand our own sin, we will never fully understand the level of love that Christ displayed to us and we are likewise to display to others.

> The more we recognize the depth of our own sin, the more we recognize the love of the Saviour; the more we appreciate the love of the Saviour, the higher his standard appears; the higher his standard appears, the more we recognize in our selfishness, our innate self-centeredness, the depth of our own sin. With a standard like this, no thoughtful believer can ever say, this side of the parousia, "I am perfectly keeping the basic stipulation of the new covenant."

Without a proper view of self, believers cannot comprehend the depth of Jesus' love for them.

92 Craig S. Keener, *The Gospel of John: A Commentary* (Peabody, MA: Hendrickson Publishers, 2003), 924. "Jewish tradition continued the emphasis on love of neighbor. Still, loving one's neighbor as oneself was such a radical demand that biblical tradition might depict its actual occurrence only in the most intimate relationships (1 Sam 18:1,3; 20:17)."

93 Carson, *The Gospel According to John*, 484.

94 Flavius Josephus, *The Works of Josephus: Complete and Unabridged*. New updated ed. (Peabody, MA: Hendrickson Publishers, 1987), 605. "These last [Essenes] are Jews by birth and seem to have a greater affection for one another than the other sects have" 2.8.2 § 119.

based upon Christ's great love for them.[95] A new community (the church) will be created based on Jesus' work, and there is a new relationship within that community. The love of Christ's disciples for Jesus' sake was a new thing in the world. Jesus himself has set the example for his disciples to follow. They are now to follow in his steps and display to one another a love the world has never seen previously.[96]

Andreas Köstenberger, noted commentator, theologian, and Greek Scholar, states the following regarding this "new" commandment.

> What was new was Jesus' command for his disciples to love one another as he has loved them—laying down their lives. This rule of self-sacrificial, self-giving, selfless love, a unique quality of love inspired by Jesus' own love for the disciples, will serve as the foundational ethic for the new messianic community.[97]

What is new in Jesus' admonition to His disciples is the standard for this love: "as I have loved you" (John 13:34). By laying down His life for others on the cross of Calvary, Jesus loved the disciples more than His own life (John 11:5; 13:1). This is now the standard by which the disciples are to show love toward one another.[98] The commandment, "to love one another," has no meaning apart from the demonstration of Christ's love for us. Such a command becomes philosophically a lofty ideal without being rooted. One cannot make people love others unconditionally without the foundation of God's love for the world displayed in the sacrifice of Jesus Christ.[99]

The Demonstration of the New Commandment

Once the meaning and basis for the "new" commandment are understood, it is important to note the demonstration of this command to a

---

95 Alfred Plummer, *The Gospel According to St. John* (Cambridge, England: Cambridge University Press, 1906), 271.

96 Leon Morris, *The Gospel According to John* (Rev. ed.), (Grand Rapids, MI: William B. Eerdmans Publishing Co., 1995), 562.

97 Andreas J. Köstenberger, *John* (Grand Rapids, MI: Baker Academic, 2004), 423–424.

98 Keener, *The Gospel of John,* 924.

99 Gerald L. Borchert, *NAC: John 12–21* (Nashville, TN: Broadman & Holman, 2002), 98.

lost and dying world. The content of the commandment is provided for the disciples: "love one another." Jesus is not speaking here of love to all people (the world in general, though that truth is provided elsewhere in Scripture—Rom 9:1–4), but of love within the new community of believers (the Church—established in Acts 2).[100]

This way of loving one another is to take on a radically different approach to that which was demonstrated previously by the nation of Israel. Because this new community (church) has the basis of Jesus' example of love at the center of its motivation, the church is to display a love which the world had yet to witness. The demonstration of love was to epitomize God's intention in the OT when he instructed Israel to love him (Deut 6:4–5) and love their neighbor (Lev 19:18). Jesus' Sermon on the Mount (Matt 5–7) presents a sense in which this radical display will result in a different love and obedience to Christ.[101]

The newness of the command goes beyond simply a new standard ("as I have loved you"—though that has been demonstrated as a critical basis for this new command), but with the new directive it both dictates and represents.[102] "This commandment is presented as the marching order for the newly gathering messianic community, brought into existence by the redemption long purposed by God himself."[103] It is therefore not simply the obligation of the church to obey this new command but also, through the disciples' demonstration of love to one another, to display to the world the new relationship that has been established between believers. This demonstration of love serves as a proclamation of God's love before a watching world.[104]

Discipleship Principle:

Disciples display genuine love to fellow believers.

---

100 Morris, *The Gospel According to John,* 562.

101 Borchert, *John 12–21,* 98.

102 Carson, *The Gospel According to John,* 484.

103 Ibid., 484–485. Carson continues, "It is not just that the standard is Christ and his love; more, it is a command designed to reflect the relationship of love that exists between the Father and the Son (cf. 8:29; 10:18; 12:49–50; 14:31; 15:10), designed to bring about amongst the members of the nascent messianic community the kind of unity that characterizes Jesus and his Father (Jn. 17)."

104 Ibid., 485.

John 15:7–8: The Characteristics of a Disciple

ἐὰν μείνητε ἐν ἐμοὶ καὶ τὰ ῥήματά μου ἐν ὑμῖν μείνῃ, ὃ ἐὰν θέλητε αἰτήσασθε, καὶ γενήσεται ὑμῖν. ἐν τούτῳ ἐδοξάσθη ὁ πατήρ μου, ἵνα καρπὸν πολὺν φέρητε καὶ γένησθε ἐμοὶ μαθηταί.[105]

"If you abide in Me, and My words abide in you, ask whatever you wish, and it will be done for you. My Father is glorified by this, that you bear much fruit, and *so* prove to be My disciples."

In the Upper Room Discourse, Jesus provides for his disciples characteristics that should be evidenced in their lives. In addition to the command to love one another (John 13:34–35—as previously discussed), Jesus provides four additional characteristics that should be displayed in the lives of his disciples.

Characteristic 1: Disciples have an Intimate Relationship with Jesus Christ

The first characteristic of a disciple of Christ is found within the initial phrase "If you abide in Me." The Greek term for "abide", μείνητε, from the root μενω, means "to remain," "to stay," "to wait," "to abide."[106] Gerhard Kittel, in the *Theological Dictionary of the New Testament* states, "the concept of remaining or abiding takes different forms according to the different relations or antonyms in view."[107] Therefore, the context is the determining factor as to the translation of the term μενω.

In Johannine theology, "abiding" describes the close communion of a believer with Christ.[108] The vine metaphor (John 15:1–6—the preceding

---

105 Kurt Aland et al., Jn 15:7–8.

106 Henry G. Liddell and Robert Scott, *A Greek-English Lexicon.* 8th ed. (New York, NY: American Book Company, 1882), 941.

107 Kittel, *Theological Dictionary of the New Testament: Vol.4,* 574.

108 Joel B. Green, Green, Jeannine K. Brown and Nicholas Perrin, *Dictionary of Jesus and the Gospels.* Second ed. (Downers Grove, IL: InterVarsity Press, 2013), 1. The term *meno* is used multiple times in the NT corpus.

> Over half of the 118 NT occurrences of the word *meno* ("to abide" or "to remain") are found in the Johannine corpus (40x in John's Gospel and 27x in the Johannine Epistles, compared with three references in Matthew, two in Mark and seven in Luke). Believer's need to "abide" in Christ, in turn, is presented as part of John's Trinitarian mission theology, according to which Jesus' follow-

context and the continuation of the vine theme into verse 7) illustrates the intimate relationship that Jesus desires with his disciples.[109] Jesus demands that the foundational commitment in a disciple's life is to abide in Him. This means that an intimate relationship with Christ is essential for a disciple. A disciple must be so intimately connected with the Savior that he/she is characterized by the words and actions of Jesus.[110]

Characteristic 2: Disciples have a Passion for the Word of God

Not only does Jesus state that disciples should "abide in Me," but he also expects that "My words abide in you." Just as the disciples were to have an intimate relationship with Christ, God's Word should have an intimate relationship with the disciples. This concept is described by commentators as a "mutual indwelling."[111]

The mutual indwelling described in this passage involves more than just obedience. The idea also entails a continued immersion of Jesus' teaching in one's understanding and life practice.[112] This mutual indwelling is equivalent to doing all that Jesus commands. Don Carson states, "Jesus' words must so lodge in the disciple's mind and heart that conformity to Christ, obedience to Christ, is the most natural (supernatural?) thing in the world."[113] To truly abide in Christ is to allow his words to truly abide within the disciple's life.[114] God's Word continually cleanses the life of a disciple (Ps 119) and therefore must be allowed to "remain" in our daily walk.[115]

---

ers are taken up into the love, unity, and mission of Father, Son, and Spirit and charged to continue Jesus' mission until he returns.

As believers "abide" in Christ, they reflect the intimate relationship between the Trinity.

109 Ibid., 2.

110 Borchert, *John 12–21,* 145.

111 Kostenberger, *John,* 454 and Carson, *The Gospel According to John,* 517.

112 Kostenberger, *John,* 454.

113 Carson, *The Gospel According to John,* 517.

114 Raymond E. Brown, *The Gospel According to John (xii–xxi). 2nd ed.* (Garden City, NY: Doubleday, 1966), 662.

115 Craig S. Keener, *The Gospel of John: A Commentary* (Peabody, MA: Hendrickson Publishers, 2003), 1000. Keener explains this idea of *meno* involving more than just "dwell" but also "remain."

Characteristic 3: Disciples have a Consistent Prayer Life

Once disciples display an intimate relationship with Christ and allow God's Word to permeate their lives, they will not only display a dependence on God through prayer, but they will also pray according to God's will. Disciples understand the importance that prayer plays in the life of a believer.[116] This consistent prayer life is displayed in the life of an individual who knows God and seeks to "abide in him." Jesus assumes ("ask whatever you wish, and it will be done for you") that those who know Him well will ask Him to help in life's situations (cf. Mark 4:35–41).

Leon Morris expounds on the connection of the term "abide" with the answering of the prayers of Jesus' disciples: "When believers abide in Christ and Christ's words abide in them, they live as close to Christ as well may be. Then their prayers will be prayers that are in accord with God's will, and they will be fully answered."[117] A true disciple of Christ proves

---

The demand for perseverance plays a central role in this pericope. In this context, μενω signifies not only "dwell" (as in 14:10, 17) but "remain" (both are legitimate components of the term's semantic range functioning in this context). John 8:31 warns initial believers that they must "abide" in his "word" so that they may be his "disciples" in truth. The passage alludes back to all the major concepts of 8:31, expanding them in connection with the image of the vine: they must "abide" (15:4–7); his "word" has cleansed them (15:3) and his "words" should abide in them (15:7); those who abide bear fruit and hence prove to be his "disciples" (15:8).

The term implies that this "remaining" should be evident in our daily actions as disciples of Christ.

116 E. M. Bounds, *The Weapon of Prayer* (New Kensington, PA: Whitaker House, 1996), 8. Bounds describes the importance of prayer in the life of a believer:

In dealing with mankind, nothing is more important to God than prayer. Prayer is likewise of great importance to people. Failure to pray is failure in all of life. It is failure of duty, service, and spiritual progress.... We must pray to God if love for God is to exist. Faith and hope and patience and all strong, beautiful, vital forces of piety are withered and dead in a prayerless life. An individual believer's life, his personal salvation, and his personal Christian graces have their being, bloom, and fruit in prayer. All this and much more can be said about how prayer is necessary to the life and piety of the individual. But prayer has a larger sphere, a loftier inspiration, a higher duty. Prayer concerns God.

According to Bounds prayer is an essential dynamic of the Christian's life and is important to God.

117 Morris, *The Gospel According to John*, 562.

effective in prayer because what he or she asks for conforms to the will of God.[118]

Characteristic 4: Disciples have a Heart for Ministry and Service

In addition to abiding in Christ, allowing God's Word to remain in them, and having a passion for prayer, disciples desire to serve their Master. "My Father is glorified by this, that you bear much fruit." The disciples will glorify the Father by their continual fruit-bearing. However, disciples cannot bear fruit of themselves, but rather the fruitfulness is confirmation of the Father's work in them. The bearing of fruit reveals that they are disciples.[119]

John's audience would understand the imagery of "fruit bearing." In the 1st-century, northern Mediterranean region, the harvest arrived in autumn.[120] During the harvest, the farmers would gather the grapes and then they would be trodden to yield their juice.[121] In Palestine, the grapes ripen in late summer around August and September.

John obviously is writing figuratively when he states that believers should bear much fruit. John is describing the "fruit" of Christian ministry.[122] By involving themselves in Christian service, the disciples will glorify God the Father and prove that they are true disciples.

---

118 Carson, *The Gospel According to John*, 517–518.

119 Morris, *The Gospel According to John,* 597.

120 Longus, *Daphnis, and Chloe*, 1:28, 2:1, Translated by William B. Tyrrell, Accessed April 20, 2014, https://www.msu.edu/~tyrrell/daphchlo.htm.

121 Ovid, *Metamorphoses*, 2:29, Translated by A. S. Kline, accessed April 20, 2014, http://ovid.lib.virginia.edu/trans/Metamorph2.htm#476707488.

122 Keener, *The Gospel of John*, 997. Keener expounds on the interpretation of the "fruit" described in John 15:7–8.

> In John's larger usage, one might suppose the fruit of Christian witness (4:36; 12:24), but the immediate context, which bears more weight than John's usage elsewhere when the usage is so rare (two texts), suggests moral fruit. This is the most common sense of the metaphor in other traditions about Jesus and John the Baptist with which this Gospel's first audience may have been familiar (Matt 3:8, 10; 7:16–20; 12:33; Luke 3:8–9; 6:43–44; 13:6–9; probably Mark 11:14; 12:2); other early Christian writers also develop it (Gal 5:22; Phil 1:11; Eph 5:9; Col 1:10; Heb 12:11; Jas 3:18; Jude 12).

According to Keener, the idea of "fruit" is moral fruit that is displayed in the life of a believer.

Discipleship Principle:

Disciples are characterized by an intimate relationship with Jesus Christ, a passion for the Bible, a consistent prayer life, and a heart for ministry and service.

Romans 12:1–2: The Mindset of a Disciple

Παρακαλῶ οὖν ὑμᾶς, ἀδελφοί, διὰ τῶν οἰκτιρμῶν τοῦ θεοῦ παραστῆσαι τὰ σώματα ὑμῶν θυσίαν ζῶσαν ἁγίαν εὐάρεστον τῷ θεῷ, τὴν λογικὴν λατρείαν ὑμῶν καὶ μὴ συσχηματίζεσθε τῷ αἰῶνι τούτῳ, ἀλλὰ μεταμορφοῦσθε τῇ ἀνακαινώσει τοῦ νοὸς εἰς τὸ δοκιμάζειν ὑμᾶς τί τὸ θέλημα τοῦ θεοῦ, τὸ ἀγαθὸν καὶ εὐάρεστον καὶ τέλειον.[123]

"Therefore, I urge you, brethren, by the mercies of God, to present your bodies a living and holy sacrifice, acceptable to God, *which is* your spiritual service of worship. And do not be conformed to this world, but be transformed by the renewing of your mind, so that you may prove what the will of God is, that which is good and acceptable and perfect."

Though the term *disciple* is not found within Romans 12:1–2, Paul's exhortation to the believers in Rome speaks to the mindset that all disciples should exhibit in their spiritual lives. "Therefore" (the first word in English translations but the second word in Greek—οὖν) demonstrates that Paul wants to show that the exhortations of Romans 12:1–15:13 are built firmly on the theology of chapters 1–11. The exhortations and application sections that conclude Romans are firmly built upon the soteriology and sanctification described in Romans 1–11.[124]

The first word of Romans 12:1 carries the plea upon which verses 1 and 2 will be built. The verb παρακαλῶ, "I urge," has a wide range of meanings including "to call to one's side," "to exhort," "to implore," "to encourage."[125] C. E. B. Cranfield, New Testament scholar and professor emeritus of theology at the University of Durham in England, states that

---

123 Kurt Aland et al., Rom 12:1–2.

124 Douglas J. Moo, *The Epistle to the Romans* (Grand Rapids, MI: W.B. Eerdmans Pub. Co., 1996), 748.

125 Robert H. Mounce, *NAC: Romans,* Vol. 28 (Nashville, TN: Broadman & Holman Pub., 1995), 231.

παρακαλω is a technical term for Christian exhortation. It is "the earnest appeal, based on the gospel, to those who are already believers to live consistently with the gospel they have received."[126] Robert Mounce reveals the importance of the exhortation considering the content that will follow in verses 1–2. "Holiness of life rarely progresses apart from deliberative acts of the will. While sanctification is gradual in the sense that it continues throughout life, each advance depends upon a decision of the will."[127] What has Paul exhorted believers to do?

Believers are Called to be a Living Sacrifice

In the Septuagint, παριστημι (to present) was often used as a technical term for a priest's placing an offering on the altar.[128] In the ancient world the term was also used to describe the presentation of sacrifices.[129] The idea of the term was to indicate a "surrendering" for sacrifice or "yielding up" for the altar.[130] However, sacrifices of dead animals on an altar (as practiced in the OT) are no longer acceptable to God. Jesus Christ being the perfect Lamb of God (John 1:29) was sacrificed once for all in our place.[131] Christians are not to offer animals to God but rather to offer themselves to God as "living sacrifices."[132]

Paul's use of sacrificial imagery here is a pattern that is used throughout the NT. As stated above, Christians no longer offer literal sacrifices to Christ, because he has fulfilled, through his death, the requirements for salvation ending the OT sacrificial system. However, with the common understanding of sacrifice in ancient religious systems, using sacrificial

---

126 Charles E. B. Cranfield, *ICC: A Critical and Exegetical Commentary on the Epistle to the Romans: Volume 2* (Edinburgh, Scotland: T. & T. Clark, 2000), 597.

127 Mounce, *Romans,* 231.

128 Marvin R. Vincent, *Word Studies in the New Testament: Volume III* (Peabody, MA: Hendrickson, 1991), 153.

129 Josephus, *The Works of Josephus,* 109. *Ant 4:113.*

130 John MacArthur, *Romans 9–16* (Chicago, IL: Moody Press, 1994), 142. "As members of God's present 'holy priesthood' (1 Pet. 2:5), Christians are here exhorted to perform what is essentially a priestly act of worship. Because the verb is in the imperative, the exhortation carries the weight of a command."

131 John 1:29—"The next day he saw Jesus coming to him and said, 'Behold, the Lamb of God who takes away the sin of the world!'"

132 MacArthur, *Romans 9–16,* 145.

imagery was an important tool to convey the spiritual convictions of the early church.[133]

That the sacrifice is "living" reflects the voluntary nature of the act. F. F. Bruce comments that "the sacrifices of the new order do not consist in taking the lives of others, like the ancient animal sacrifices, but in giving one's own (Heb 13:15–16; 1 Pet 2:5)."[134] Paul qualifies the sacrifice that we offer by stating that it is a "living" sacrifice. This adjective refers "to the nature of the sacrifice itself: one that does not die as it is offered but goes on living and therefore continues in its efficacy until the person who is offered dies."[135] John MacArthur explains the "living" sacrifice we are to offer "is the willingness to surrender to Him all our hopes, plans, and everything that is precious to us, all that is humanly important to us, all that we find fulfilling."[136] Believers are called upon to make an ongoing sacrifice of not only their lives but also their desires.

When Paul calls believers to offer their "bodies" as living sacrifices, the term σωματα (bodies) is to be interpreted as the entirety of the individual.[137] Wright describes it as "the complete person seen from one point of view: the point of view in which the human being lives as a physical object within space and time."[138] The sacrifice that Paul exhorts believers

---

133 Douglas J. Moo, *NICNT: The Epistle to the Romans* (Grand Rapids, MI: W.B. Eerdmans Pub. Co., 1996), 750. Moo expounds on this understanding of sacrifice:

> At the same time, the NT use of cultic language has an important salvation-historical and polemical function, claiming for Christianity the fulfillment of those institutions so central to the OT and to Judaism. Christians offer no bloody sacrifice on an altar; but they offer "spiritual sacrifices" (1 Pet. 2:5), such as the "sacrifice of" praise to God, which is the fruit of lips that acknowledge his name" (Heb. 13:15). In Rom. 15:16, Paul describes his own missionary work in cultic terms (see also Phil. 2:17; and note Phil. 3:3 and 4:18).

NT believers do not offer the OT bloody sacrifices to God, but rather they are involved in spiritual sacrifices or acts of service to God.

134 F. F. Bruce, *Tyndale New Testament Commentary: Romans* (Grand Rapids, MI: William B. Eerdmans Publishing Co. 1993), 213.

135 Moo, *The Epistle to the Romans,* 751.

136 MacArthur, *Romans 9–16*, 146.

137 Colin G. Kruse, *Paul's Letter to the Romans* (Grand Rapids, MI: William B. Eerdmans Pub. Co., 2012), 461.

138 N. T. Wright, *The New Interpreter's Bible, Vol. X: Letter to the Romans* (Nashville, TN: Abingdon Press, 2002), 704.

to offer is their "bodies" themselves. Unlike the OT sacrificial system in which the gift was of central importance (Gen 4:3–7),[139] God, in the NT sacrificial imagery, demands the giver himself.[140] This reemphasizes once again the aspect of "living" sacrifice. Colin Kruse states, "Paul employs the idea of a 'living sacrifice' deliberately because the sacrifice he has in mind is not martyrdom, but rather lives that are pleasing to God."[141] Paul is making a special point to emphasize that this sacrifice is not once and done. Rather, the sacrifice calls for continual dedication to the service of God even in the face of opposition from the world.[142]

This type of ongoing, living, dedicated sacrifice of our bodies is "holy and pleasing to God." Believers must realize that the possibility of bringing pleasure to God should provide a powerful motivation for the complete surrender of our will and self to him.[143] "Holy" is a regular description of sacrifices in the OT (cf. Num 18). The idea behind the term implies that the offering is "set apart" from the profane and is dedicated to God. Likewise, as "living" sacrifices believers are to be "set apart" from this world.[144]

---

139 Genesis 4:3–7 describes the sacrifices that Adam and Eve and subsequently their offspring (Cain and Abel) were to offer to God.

> So it came about in the course of time that Cain brought an offering to the LORD of the fruit of the ground. Abel, on his part also brought of the firstlings of his flock and of their fat portions. And the LORD had regard for Abel and for his offering; but for Cain and for his offering He had no regard. So Cain became very angry and his countenance fell. Then the LORD said to Cain, "Why are you angry? And why has your countenance fallen? If you do well, will not *your countenance* be lifted up? And if you do not do well, sin is crouching at the door; and its desire is for you, but you must master it."

God demanded an animal sacrifice from Cain and Abel. When Cain brought his own sacrifice to the altar, God did not accept the offering. Sacrifices were an essential part of the OT Jewish religious system.

140 Moo, *The Epistle to the Romans,* 750–751. "'Body' can, of course, refer to the physical body as such, and the metaphorical associations with sacrifice make it an appropriate choice here. But Paul probably intends to refer to the entire person, with special emphasis on that person's interaction with the world."

141 Kruse, *Paul's Letter to the Romans,* 462.

142 Moo, *The Epistle to the Romans,* 751.

143 Mounce, *Romans,* 231.

144 Moo, *The Epistle to the Romans,* 751.

Paul said that the offering of one's body as a "living sacrifice" is a "spiritual act of worship." It is the reasonable act of service (worship) by Christians. God is not asking disciples to do something that is impossible or unthinkable. Rather, dedicating one's life to serving God should be a reasonable sacrifice by those who have been redeemed by the death of Christ.[145]

Believers are Commanded to Not Conform to the World's System

After Paul's exhortation to "present your bodies as living sacrifices," He urges Christians to involve themselves in two ongoing activities. These activities reveal how the believer is to become an acceptable "living sacrifice." The first activity is negative in nature; the second activity is positive. Believers are no longer to "conform themselves" to the world's system.[146] The term for "conform," συσχηματίζεσθε means to "squeeze you into its own mold."[147]

---

145 Mounce, *Romans,* 231. Mounce continues by describing the spiritual sacrifice that believers are to make to God.

> This expression has been variously translated as "spiritual service, reasonable worship, rational service," and so on. Perhaps the best paraphrase is that of Knox, "This is the worship due from you as rational creatures." In view of God's acts of mercy it is entirely fitting that we commit ourselves without reservation to him. To teach that accepting the free gift of God's grace does not necessarily involve a moral obligation on our part is a heresy of gigantic proportions. The popular cliche "He is Lord of all or not Lord at all" is absolutely right.

This worship that we as believers give to God is a necessary outpouring when disciples understand that God is King of all.

146 Ibid., 232. Mounce describes the world system and its negative influence on the life of believers.

> As citizens of heaven (Phil 3:20) we are to "set [our] minds on things above, not on earthly things" (Col 3:2). Paul reminded the Galatians that the present age is evil (Gal 1:4). It cannot, and must not, serve as a model for Christian living. Its values and goals are antithetical to growth in holiness. The church should stand out from the world as a demonstration of God's intention for the human race. To be culturally identified with the world is to place the church at risk. Believers are to be salt and light (Matt 5:13–14), purifying and enlightening contemporary culture.

According to Mounce, instead of being "conformed" to the wicked worldly system, disciples are to live in a distinctly different way than the world proposes.

147 John Phillips, *Exploring Romans* (Grand Rapids, MI: Kregel Publications, 1969), 186.

Paul's command that we "not be conformed to this world" calls Christians to resist the pressure to "be squeezed into the mold" of this world. Believers are not to fall into the "pattern" of behavior that typifies the world's system.[148] Disciples are to think differently than the world's mindset. Disciples should have a different perspective on life, and their actions should demonstrate this alternate viewpoint.

Believers are Commanded to be Transformed by The Renewing of Their Mind

Instead of being fitted into the world's mold, believers are commanded to be "transformed by the renewing of your mind." The tense of the verb is present and therefore describes a continuing process of constant transformation.[149] This transformation is not a once and done activity but rather is a consistent work of being altered in one's thinking. The verb occurs in two other settings in the New Testament. In Mark 9:2 (Matt 17:2) Jesus "transfigured" before his three disciples. In 2 Corinthians 3:18, Paul taught that believers who behold the glory of the Lord are being "transformed" into his likeness. The transformation Paul is describing in Romans 12:2 is not a change effected from outside the individual but rather a radical reorientation that begins deep within the human heart.[150]

"The renewing of your mind" is how this transformation takes place. "Mind" is a word that Paul uses specifically to indicate a person's "practical reason" or "moral consciousness."[151] Christians are to adjust their way of thinking. This process does not occur overnight but is a lifelong process of altering one's thinking to resemble the way that God desires that he/she think about life and service.[152]

There is continuing pressure by the "world" on disciples to adopt the customs and mind-set of the world in which we live. Though Christians may reject that pressure, this action alone will never create the kind of change God has in mind for his followers. Real and lasting change comes

---

148 Moo, *The Epistle to the Romans,* 755.

149 Ibid., 756.

150 Mounce, *Romans,* 232.

151 Moo, *The Epistle to the Romans,* 756.

152 Ibid., 756–757.

from within.[153] Disciples must let themselves be transformed by the "renewing of the mind." A renewed mind is concerned with those issues of life that are of lasting importance.[154]

Discipleship Principles:

Disciples dedicate their lives as a consistent, blameless sacrifice to God.

Disciples consistently allow themselves to be transformed through meditation on the Word of God.

Ephesians 4:11–16: The Maturity of a Disciple

Καὶ αὐτὸς ἔδωκεν τοὺς μὲν ἀποστόλους, τοὺς δὲ προφήτας, τοὺς δὲ εὐαγγελιστάς, τοὺς δὲ ποιμένας καὶ διδασκάλους, πρὸς τὸν καταρτισμὸν τῶν ἁγίων εἰς ἔργον διακονίας, εἰς οἰκοδομὴν τοῦ σώματος τοῦ Χριστοῦ, μέχρι καταντήσωμεν οἱ πάντες εἰς τὴν ἑνότητα τῆς πίστεως καὶ τῆς ἐπιγνώσεως τοῦ υἱοῦ τοῦ θεοῦ, εἰς ἄνδρα τέλειον, εἰς μέτρον ἡλικίας τοῦ πληρώματος τοῦ Χριστοῦ, ἵνα μηκέτι ὦμεν νήπιοι, κλυδωνιζόμενοι καὶ περιφερόμενοι παντὶ ἀνέμῳ τῆς διδασκαλίας ἐν τῇ κυβείᾳ τῶν ἀνθρώπων, ἐν πανουργίᾳ πρὸς τὴν μεθοδείαν τῆς πλάνης, ἀληθεύοντες δὲ ἐν ἀγάπῃ αὐξήσωμεν εἰς αὐτὸν τὰ πάντα, ὅς ἐστιν ἡ κεφαλή, Χριστός, ἐξ οὗ πᾶν τὸ σῶμα συναρμολογούμενον καὶ συμβιβαζόμενον διὰ πάσης ἁφῆς τῆς ἐπιχορηγίας κατ' ἐνέργειαν ἐν μέτρῳ ἑνὸς ἑκάστου μέρους τὴν αὔξησιν τοῦ σώματος ποιεῖται εἰς οἰκοδομὴν ἑαυτοῦ ἐν ἀγάπῃ.[155]

---

153 Mounce, *Romans,* 232.

154 Ibid., 232–233. Mounce describes the nature and characteristics of a mind that is set on the things of God.

> By nature our thoughts tend to dwell on the ephemeral. But that which passes quickly is normally inconsequential. As Paul said in another place, "What is seen is temporary, but what is unseen is eternal" (2 Cor 4:18). The mind renewed enables us to discern the will of God. Released from the control of the world around us, we can come to know what God has in mind for us. We will find that his will is "good, pleasing and perfect." It is good because it brings about moral and spiritual growth. It is pleasing to God because it is an expression of his nature. It is perfect in that no one could possibly improve on what God desires to happen.

A renewed mind has a radically different perspective than the world's system. It can discern God's will for one's life and ultimately is pleasing to God because it reveals sensitivity to God's leading.

155 Kurt Aland et al., Eph 4:11–16.

"And He gave some *as* apostles, and some *as* prophets, and some *as* evangelists, and some *as* pastors and teachers, for the equipping of the saints for the work of service, to the building up of the body of Christ; until we all attain to the unity of the faith, and of the knowledge of the Son of God, to a mature man, to the measure of the stature which belongs to the fullness of Christ. As a result, we are no longer to be children, tossed here and there by waves and carried about by every wind of doctrine, by the trickery of men, by craftiness in deceitful scheming; but speaking the truth in love, we are to grow up in all *aspects* into Him who is the head, *even* Christ, from whom the whole body, being fitted and held together by what every joint supplies, according to the proper working of each individual part, causes the growth of the body for the building up of itself in love."

In Ephesians 4:11–16, Paul describes to the church at Ephesus the "gifts" that God has given to the church to help believers reach the potential that God has for them. These "gifts" are individuals who God has uniquely gifted and prepared to help believers grow to maturity. After Paul describes the "gifts," he states the reason that the "gifts" were given to the church. Disciples are to reach a level of maturity, and no excuse can be given, because God has provided the necessary "gifts" to help them reach this maturity.

A Description of the Gifts

Apostles

The first "gift" that God has provided for the church is the "apostles." An apostle was an official delegate of Jesus Christ. He was commissioned by Jesus to proclaim authoritatively the Gospel in oral and written form.[156] In addition, a secondary function of an apostle was to establish churches in areas that have not been reached by others (Rom 15:20). They were God's ambassadors to open new regions with the message of Jesus Christ.[157]

---

156 Harold W. Hoehner, *Ephesians: An Exegetical Commentary* (Grand Rapids, MI: Baker Academic, 2002), 541.

157 Ibid., 542.

Prophets

The prophet had a unique spiritual function. The prophet was endowed by the Holy Spirit with the gift of prophecy (involving foretelling and forth telling) for the purposes of edification, comfort, and encouragement. In the church age, the prophet would aid in the understanding and communicating of the mysteries and revelation of God to the church.[158]

Evangelists

Evangelists went everywhere preaching the gospel. The function of the prophets was to speak on the occasions that required special revelation. However, the evangelists continually spoke the message of salvation. In the 21st century, their function would resemble that of a missionary who brings the Gospel to new territories.[159]

Pastor and Teachers

There has been debate as to whether the final classification describes a single office (pastor/teacher) or two offices (pastor and teacher). The reason for the debate is that the terms "pastors" and "teachers" are linked by a single definite article in the Greek. The definite article, which has been listed before each of the three "gifts" mentioned previously in the text, is repeated before "pastors" but omitted before "teachers." Some have claimed that the omission of the definite article indicates that the two groups are identical.[160]

Other commentators have suggested that this omission of the definite article indicates a close relationship between two groups who minister within one congregation.[161] Daniel Wallace describes the distinctive

---

158 Ibid., 542.

159 Ibid., 542–543.

160 Andrew T. Lincoln, *WBC: Ephesians* (Waco, TX: Word Books, 1990), 250. Lincoln goes on to write that he does not believe that the omission of the definite article indicates this function but rather "it is doubtful whether that is enough to demonstrate that the two ministries were always exercised by the same people. It is more likely that they were overlapping functions, but that while almost all pastors are also teachers, not all teachers were also pastors."

161 Peter T. O'Brien, *The Letter to the Ephesians* (Grand Rapids, MI: W.B. Eerdmans Publishing Co., 1999), 300. "Although some argue that the two positions describe one office, it is more likely that the terms describe overlapping but different functions."

yet overlapping function that these two offices possess. "All pastors were to be teachers, though not all teachers were to be pastors."[162]

The role of both pastor and teacher was to teach the Word of God to the believers within the churches. With regular corporate instruction by both pastors and teachers, believers would be challenged to grow spiritually.[163]

---

162 Daniel B. Wallace, *Greek Grammar Beyond the Basics: An Exegetical Syntax of the New Testament with Scripture, Subject, and Greek Word Indexes* (Grand Rapids, MI: Zondervan, 1996), 284.

163 In Acts 2 the church begins on the Day of Pentecost as the Holy Spirit descends and fills the believers as they repent and accept Jesus as their Savior. At the birth of the church and throughout its existence, corporate education has played a vital part in the teaching, growth, edifying, and equipping of the saints for the work of the ministry (Eph. 4). God has used the corporate education of the church throughout the centuries in the sanctification process of the individual believer.

In Acts 2:42, immediately after the Day of Pentecost, the importance of corporate education is revealed through the ministry of the apostles. The early church community was constituted based on the apostolic teaching. This apostolic (corporate) teaching was authoritative because it was the teaching of the Lord communicated through the apostles in the power of the Spirit. F. F. Bruce, *The Book of the Acts* (Grand Rapids, MI: William B. Eerdmans Publishing Co., 1988), 73. Richard Longenecker emphasizes the critical role of the teaching ministry of the apostles: "Undoubtedly the early congregation at Jerusalem, amid differences of perspective and along with a lively eschatological expectation, had a general 'sense of center' provided by the historical and doctrinal teaching of the apostles. And this, Luke tells us, was preeminently the raison d'eter ('reason for being') and the focus of the early Christian community." Richard N. Longenecker, *EBC: John–Acts* (Grand Rapids, MI: Zondervan Pub. House, 1981), 289.

The early church, at its conception, understood the importance of the role of corporate education in the life of the believer. Acts 2:42 reveals that the church continually "devoted" themselves to listening and learning as the apostles instructed these new believers in God's Word. It was upon this corporate teaching that individuals and the church grew both spiritually and numerically, respectively.

The importance of corporate education in the New Testament is further revealed in the ministry of the Apostle Paul. Paul, arguably the greatest pastor/missionary/evangelist of the church age, revealed the importance of the teaching ministry to which he was called. Paul described himself as "a preacher and an apostle and a teacher" (2 Tim. 1:11). In 1 Corinthians 15:1–8, Paul stated to the believers in Corinth that he delivered (preached) to them what he had received from Christ regarding the gospel. It was upon this truth that they were to stand firm during hardship and doubt. In Colossians 1:25–29, Paul stated that he was a minister "according to the stewardship from God bestowed on me for your benefit, so that I might fully carry out the preaching of the word of God" (v. 26). Paul believed that the function of proclamation or teaching was a critical aspect of his ministry. Paul's message to the lost was Christ. The method of proclamation was teaching with wisdom so that all might be presented complete in Christ (v.

Pastors and teachers did not simply convey information, but rather they urged the hearers to live by what they had been taught (Eph. 4:20–21).[164]

The Reason for the Gifts

Once Paul has established the importance of these "gifts" to the church, he provides the reason that they were given to the church. These "gifts" were to challenge and prepare believers to do God's work and to lead believers to a level of maturity that they would be unable to attain without the ministry of these "gifts."

Equipping the Saints to do the Work of the Ministry

$Καταρτισμος$ (equipping) refers to that which is "fit, is restored to its original condition, or is made complete." The word was used in nautical settings to describe "refitting a ship" or in medical situations for the "setting of bones."[165] The term indicates in Ephesians 4:12 that the "gifts" are provided to "fit out" saints to do God's service. Paul's language, "for the equipping of the saints for the work of service," indicates that it is not the "gifts" who are to do all of the work of service.[166] Obviously the "gifts" share in doing the work of the ministry, but God's basic design is for the saints to be equipped so that they can serve each other effectively.[167]

---

28). Teaching was required because the mysteries of Christ require explanation and instruction. It was Paul's practice to proclaim the gospel in a new region and then remain in that region to teach the new believers the mysteries of Christ so that their lives would be conformed into the image of the Savior. Perry G. Downs, *Teaching for Spiritual Growth* (Grand Rapids, MI: Zondervan Pub. House, 1994), 28.

164 O'Brien, *The Letter to the Ephesians*, 300–301.

165 Vincent, *Word Studies of the New Testament*, 390.

166 John MacArthur, *Ephesians* (Chicago, IL: Moody Press, 1986), 155. MacArthur explains that the pastors themselves cannot do all the work of the ministry.

> No pastor, or even a large group of pastors, can do everything a church needs to do. No matter how gifted, talented, and dedicated a pastor may be, the work to be done where he is called to minister will always vastly exceed his time and abilities. His purpose in God's plan is not to try to meet all those needs himself but to equip the people given into his care to meet those needs (cf. v. 16, where this idea is emphasized).

In contrast to the pastors doing all the work in a church, these leaders are to train the believers of the church to help carry out the work of the ministry.

167 Ibid., 155.

Clinton Arnold clarifies, "Christ has given gifted leaders to the church not merely to do the ministry, but to invest their time heavily in developing and preparing fellow believers to engage in ministry to the body."[168] The model Paul is proposing to the church is of mutual service and not of professionals serving a group of consumers.[169]

In conclusion, Christ gave gifts to the church for the immediate purpose of preparing all the saints for service to build up the entire body of Christ. As each believer carries out his/her work, the church will be built up. The idea that the ministry belongs to the clergy and not to the saints is foreign to this context because every saint is involved in the ministry.[170]

---

168 Clinton E. Arnold, *Ephesians: Zondervan Exegetical Commentary on the New Testament* (Grand Rapids, MI: Zondervan, 2010), 262.

169 Ibid., 262–263. Arnold clarifies his point by explaining the debate over the prepositional phrases in Ephesians 4:12.

> There has been much debate over how to interpret the relationship between the three prepositional phrases in this verse. The implications are profound, with one view leading to a strong clergy/laity distinction and the other view pointing the direction toward the concept of the priesthood of all believers. The first view contends that all three prepositional phrases are coordinate and describe the ministry responsibilities of the five gifted leaders. This view is expressed in the KJV and is held by Roman Catholic scholars as well as many high church leaders [Muddiman, MacDonald, Lincoln, Schnackenburg]. The alternative view argues that the second and third prepositional phrases are dependent on the first and that it is the entire church that is responsible for the work of the ministry. This view is expressed in most contemporary English language translations and is held by Protestants in a wide variety of denominations [Hoehner, Best, O'Brien, Bruce, Barclay].
>
> The evidence appears to lean strongly in favor of the second view. (1) The Second view takes into better account the change of prepositions (from πρoς to εις) .... (2) The object of the first preposition has the article whereas the objects of the second two prepositions do not.... (3) Ernest Best has correctly observed that if the three phrases were parallel, it would have made more sense for Paul to begin with the more general (v. 12b: "for the work of service") and then to develop it with the other two phrases (12a: "for equipping of the saints"; v. 12c: "for the building up of the body of Christ") (Best, p. 397–398).... (4) The first view depends on an unlikely meaning for the noun "equipping" (καταρτισμος) .... (5) Finally, the first prepositional phrase (beginning with πρoς) provides the most natural completion to the idea of equipping.

170 Hoehner, *Ephesians*, 551.

Leading the Saints to Maturity in Their Spiritual Walks

Once Paul establishes that the gifted people were given to the church for the immediate purpose of preparing all the saints to minister for the building up of the body of Christ, he explains the need for the process that believers mature to the measure of the fullness of Christ. The adjective τελειος means "having reached its end, complete, or accomplished."[171] The term is used of sacrifices that are "perfect, without spot/blemish," of animals that are "fully grown," and of a person who is "fully grown" or "matured" as opposed to an infant or child.[172]

In contrast, the term νηπιος refers to "infants or very young children."[173] The term suggests not only physical age but childish understanding, foolishness, inexperience, or lack of insight.[174] NT writers use the term "infants" to represent spiritual immaturity.[175] The nature of the children's immaturity is graphically pictured in the following clauses and phrases in Ephesians 4:14. These infants are unstable, lacking in direction, vacillating, and open to manipulation. Like a small, rudderless boat, they are tossed back and forth by the waves. They are continually driven back and forth by the different winds of teaching.

---

171 BDAG, s.v. τελειος, 809.

172 Hoehner, *Ephesians*, 554.

173 BDAG, s.v. νηπιος, 537.

174 Hoehner, *Ephesians*, 560.

175 F. F. Bruce, *NICNT: The Epistle to the Colossians, to Philemon, and to the Ephesians* (Grand Rapids, MI: Eerdmans, 1984), 351. Bruce describes this spiritual infancy as:

> [A]n immaturity which is culpable when sufficient time has passed for those so described to have grown out of infancy. Paul tells the Corinthian Christians that, for all their cultivation of "knowledge," he could not address them as spiritual men and women but as "infants in Christ," still needing to be fed with milk rather than solid food (1 Cor. 3: 1–2). Infants are defenseless, unable to protect themselves; in the spiritual life they are an easy prey for false teachers and others who would like to lead them astray from the true path. Like ships at sea without adequate means of steering, they are tossed about by the waves and carried this way and that according to the prevailing wind. Maturity brings with it the capacity to evaluate various forms of teaching, to accept what is true and reject what is false.

Spiritual infants, according to Bruce, lack the discernment to adequately determine spiritual decisions and truths.

It is important to examine the participles that described the infants. "Being tossed back and forth by the waves and carried about by every wind of doctrine"—these two participles further describe one who is childish and lacks stability. The first participle, κλυδωνιζομενοι, implies that they are being thrown around by the waves of the sea and being cast into confusion. The meaning of Ephesians 4:14 reflects that this spiritually immature believer is easily confused in their thinking and easily influenced by other teachers.[176] The second participle, περιφερομενοι, "turn around or make dizzy," indicates a level of confusion by the spiritually immature believer. Both participles are passive, indicating that an outside force—"false teachers" or "false teaching"—is causing the confusion.[177]

"Every wind of doctrine" indicates false teaching that stands against the unity of faith and knowledge contained within the Scriptures (v. 13). Paul's reference is best understood as the various religious philosophies and systems which threatened to undermine or dilute the gospel message.[178] "Every wind" is followed by τησ διδασκαλιας, which is most likely a genitive of content.[179] The teaching that is causing the confusion is false teaching designed to counteract that of the pastors and teachers (v. 11).[180] The pastors and teachers bring stability and unity, whereas these

---

176 Hoehner, *Ephesians*, 561.

177 Ibid., 561.

178 O'Brien, *Ephesians*, 308–309.

179 Hoehner, *Ephesians*, 561.

180 O'Brien, *Ephesians*, 309. O'Brien describes the source of this false teaching that is counteracting the teaching of the church leaders.

> Behind this dangerous and misleading teaching by which immature believers are tossed to and fro are deceitful people who seek to manipulate them by evil trickery. Paul's language is graphic, if not forthright. The false teaching which causes so much strife is promoted by the cunning of men. Cunning literally refers to dice-playing and comes to be used metaphorically of a trickery that results from craftiness, while the qualifier of men (as in Col. 2:8, 22) depicts it as human—that, and nothing more—and therefore opposed to Christ and his teaching.

These false teachers were evil in that they through cunning words sought to derail the lives of believers.

teachings bring confusion, turmoil, and disunity. The false teaching is meant to confuse and swirl one around violently, causing dizziness.[181]

Paul provides this important text for the church to reveal the "gifts" that God has given to the saints to enable them to serve Him. God provided these gifted individuals to the church to equip the saints to do His work, to bring unity to the body, to bring believers from infancy to maturity, and to establish believers so they are not tossed about by false teaching. True disciples of Christ reveal that they are established and grounded in God's Word and are actively participating in the work of the ministry.

Discipleship Principles:

Disciples are actively involved in ministry.

Disciples are grounded in the truth and are not persuaded to follow false teaching.

2 Timothy 2:2: The Pattern of Discipleship

καὶ ἃ ἤκουσας παρ' ἐμοῦ διὰ πολλῶν μαρτύρων, ταῦτα παράθου πιστοῖς ἀνθρώποις, οἵτινες ἱκανοὶ ἔσονται καὶ ἑτέρους διδάξαι.[182]

"The things which you have heard from me in the presence of many witnesses, entrust these to faithful men who will be able to teach others also."

What has Timothy Learned?

Paul urges Timothy to entrust "things which you heard from me" to faithful men who teach those "things" to others. What is it that Timothy has learned from Paul? What Timothy is to pass along to "faithful men" appears to be first mentioned in 2 Timothy 1:13–14: "Retain the standard of sound words which you have heard from me, in the faith and love which are in Christ Jesus. Guard, through the Holy Spirit who dwells in us, the treasure which has been entrusted to *you*." The "sound words" mentioned in 1:13 and the "things" mentioned again in 2:2 are the foundational truths of the gospel.[183] The preeminence of the gospel

---

181 Hoehner, *Ephesians*, 561–562.

182 Kurt Aland et al., 2 Tim 2:2.

183 Thomas D. Lea and Hayne P. Griffin, *NAC: 1, 2 Timothy, Titus* (Nashville, TN:

in Paul's preaching is a common thread that is seen throughout Paul's writings. From his first letter on, the gospel has become the central focus of his preaching.[184] Timothy is to entrust the treasure of gospel truths to others.[185]

Though the gospel is clearly a component of the "things" Paul is describing in 2 Timothy 2:2, Paul appears to have in mind an additional component as well. Dibelius, Conzelmann, Knight, and others suggest that "what you have heard" (ἤκουσας) refers to a formulated summary of his teachings (1 Cor 15:3ff).[186] Paul wants Timothy to entrust to others the "traditions" that he has received from Paul (cf. 2 Thess 2:15).[187] Timothy has received teaching from Paul over a period of several years. Through his extensive travel with Paul and his ministry alongside of Paul at Ephesus, Timothy has been taught foundational truths.[188]

There is debate as to the interpretation of the phrase "in the presence of many witnesses." The debate is centered around the usage of διᾳ, generally translated as *"through."* The NIV's and NASB's translation "in the presence of many witnesses" suggests that the things Timothy heard was

---

Broadman Press, 1992), 201.

184 Gordon D. Fee, *NIBC: 1 and 2 Timothy, Titus* (Peabody, MA: Hendrickson Publishers, 1988), 240.

185 Lea and Griffin, *1, 2 Timothy, Titus,* 201. "The command 'entrust' (παρατιθημι) comes from the same word family as the noun 'deposit' (παραθηκη) of 1:14. The clear reference to the gospel in that verse makes it likely that Paul here conveys the same idea."

186 Martin Dibelius and Hans Conzelmann, *The Pastoral Epistles: A Commentary on the Pastoral Epistles* (Philadelphia, PA: Fortress Press, 1972), 108.

187 George W. Knight, *The Pastoral Epistles: A Commentary on the Greek Text* (Grand Rapids, MI: W.B. Eerdmans, 1992), 390. Knight describes what Paul has entrusted to Timothy.

> Paul refers to this message with the indefinite plural relative pronoun α, which is appropriately rendered by the broad and indefinite terms "what" (RSV) or "the things [which]" (NIV, NASB) and which includes all his teaching (cf. 1:13–14). He has made explicit this sense of the authority and permanent significance of his words on several earlier occasions (cf. 1 Thess 2:13). He speaks of his teaching as "tradition(s)" (παραδοσις) received from him and to be held and followed by Christians (2 Thess 2:15; 3:6–7) and commends the Corinthians for holding firmly to the "traditions" just as he delivered them (1 Cor 11:2).

Paul has entrusted "traditions" to Timothy which includes the teachings of Paul.

188 John MacArthur, *2 Timothy* (Chicago, IL: Moody Press, 1995), 40.

in conjunction with his ordination or baptism.[189] The witnesses would have then heard the "things" (charges or admonitions) that Paul gave to Timothy.[190] However, if δια is translated as "through,"[191] the interpretation would lend itself to the fact that many witnesses joined in communicating the truth to Timothy.[192] If this interpretation is correct, it reveals that the foundational truths taught to Timothy had content that was publicly acknowledged as being valuable (a core of content that would prove valuable to pass along to others) by the testimonies of many others. Lea and Griffin clarify that "this emphasis on a widespread knowledge of the truth fits well in Ephesus, which had been riddled with enervating heresy."[193]

What is Timothy to do with the Learning?

Timothy is commanded to take "the things" and entrust them to faithful men who will then teach "the things" to others. Timothy is commanded to "entrust" (παραθου) the deposit made by Paul to faithful people who will then teach others. The chain of teaching, the "tradition," is therefore continued generation to generation.[194] This passage reveals that Paul was concerned that the foundational truths of the gospel were both guarded[195] and accurately transmitted from one generation of Christians to

189 Dibelius and Conzelmann, *The Pastoral Epistles*, 108. "The reference must be to baptism, or rather 'ordination,' which provided the occasion on which the 'deposit' (παραθηκη) was transmitted to Timothy."

190 Lea and Griffin, *1, 2 Timothy, Titus*, 202.

191 BDAG, s.v. δια, 179.

192 The list of individuals who would have helped teach Timothy would include Barnabas, his mother and grandmother, and other Christian leaders (apostles).

193 Lea and Griffin, *1, 2 Timothy, Titus*, 202.

194 Risto Saarinen, *The Pastoral Epistles with Philemon & Jude* (Grand Rapids, MI: Brazos Press, 2008), 134.

195 Donald A. Carson, Douglas J. Moo, and Leon Morris, *An Introduction to the New Testament*, 2nd ed. (Grand Rapids, MI: Zondervan, 2005), 581.

> There is a "given" about the Christian faith; it is something inherited from the very beginning of God's action for our salvation, and it is to be passed on as long as this world lasts. Paul is not arguing that believers should be insensitive to currents of thought and action in the world about them, nor is he saying that the Christian is a kind of antiquarian, interested in antiquity for its own sake. He is saying that there is that about the essence of the Christian faith that

another (2 Tim 1:13–14). However, Paul was not describing a type of apostolic succession.[196] The NT neither teaches nor supports the idea of apostolic succession. The truths taught in this passage reveal the gospel is to be transmitted from generation to generation.[197]

William Barclay states, "The teacher is a link in the living chain which stretches unbroken from this present moment back to Jesus Christ. The glory of teaching is that it links the present with the earthly life of Jesus Christ."[198] The first stage in the spiritual "relay" was "these things" being handed from Paul to Timothy. Timothy's obligation was to "run the second lap" in which he was to entrust the things he had been taught by Paul to faithful men.[199] "Entrusting" these foundational truths of the gospel was not simply tapping another believer on the shoulder and providing basic encouragement. Rather, it would require Timothy to teach and to model the faith before others who in turn would teach and model the faith before others.[200]

For this teaching to pass from generation to generation, it is essential that people of character continue to teach the true gospel. It is imperative

---

is not open to negotiation. God has said and done certain things, and Christians must stand by those things whatever the cost.

It is essential that believers guard those sacred truths of the Christian faith no matter what the cost.

196 Lea and Griffin, *1, 2 Timothy, Titus,* 202. "We do not find Paul's discussion of apostles in their relationship to overseers and deacons. What we find are Paul's instructions to Timothy concerning the importance of holding to the truth of the gospel message. Paul's 'interest is in the reliability rather than the status of the men Timothy will select.'"

197 MacArthur, *2 Timothy,* 39. "Jesus, of course, was the Master Teacher. He taught the apostles, who then taught others, who taught others, who are still teaching others, and so on throughout the church age."

198 William Barclay, *The Letters to Timothy, Titus, and Philemon* (Philadelphia, PA: Westminster, 1957), 182.

199 MacArthur, *2 Timothy,* 41. "That which he was to carefully guard (1:14: cf. 1 Tim. 6:20) he also was to carefully teach. The truth Paul is talking about here is beyond the basic gospel message of salvation, which is to be preached to all who will hear. He is rather talking about the careful, systematic training of church leaders who will teach and disciple other believers in the fullness of God's Word."

200 Philip H. Towner, *NICNT: The Letters to Timothy and Titus* (Grand Rapids, MI: William B. Eerdmans Pub. Co., 2006), 491.

that Timothy identify these men and entrust the gospel to them before he departs. By identifying "faithful men," he will ensure the integrity of the gospel message as it is passed on.[201] Another quality of these individuals who are to pass on these foundational truths is that they have the ability to teach others.[202] They had to be "qualified to teach others." They had to "be able and competent in turn to pass on to others this treasure by their ability and willingness to teach."[203] Paul is urging Timothy to entrust the foundational truths of the gospel in a systematic way to faithful people who can teach others.

The Pattern of Replication

2 Timothy 2:2 provides the pattern of replication in discipleship: entrust the foundational truths of the gospel to faithful people, who in turn will entrust the truths to other faithful people. This pattern of replication is expressed clearly in the book of Acts. In Acts 9 and 11, Barnabas encouraged a new believer, Paul, introducing him to believers at Jerusalem who were reticent to get close to Paul because of his former reputation. Barnabas had a discipling/mentoring relationship with Paul. Later in the book of Acts, an established believer, Paul, entrusted to young believers, Aquila and Priscilla, the truths of Scripture (Acts 18). Aquila and Priscilla, after reaching maturity, taught the truths they learned from Paul to Apollos (Acts 18:24–26). This pattern, which is explained in 2 Timothy 2:2 and revealed in Acts, provides us the ongoing pattern of discipleship: the church is to train young believers to maturity, who will then continue to teach and train other young believers.

Discipleship Principle:

Disciples replicate themselves into the spiritual lives of others.

---

201 William D. Mounce, *WBC: Pastoral Epistles* (Waco, TX: Word Books, 2000), 504.

202 George W. Knight, *The Pastoral Epistles: A Commentary on the Greek Text* (Grand Rapids, MI: W.B. Eerdmans, 1992), 392.

203 Lea and Griffin, *1, 2 Timothy, Titus,* 201.

Discipleship Principles from Select NT Passages

This section presented several principles of discipleship that can be gleaned from select NT passages. These NT passages provide a foundation for discipleship in the church age.[204] The principles that were gleaned from the NT provided the basis for the catechumenate (first educational/discipleship program for the church). An examination of NT instruction regarding discipleship is essential to understanding post-apostolic discipleship as well as discipleship in 21st-century church settings. Twelve discipleship principles have been garnered from Matthew 28:19–20, Luke 6:40, Luke 14:26–27, John 13:34–35, John 15:7–8, Romans 12:1–2, Ephesians 4:11–16, and 2 Timothy 2:2.

1. Disciples are commanded to make disciples of all peoples.
2. The means by which disciples are made is by baptizing (initiation) and teaching (instruction).
3. Disciples of Christ strive to be like their Master not just cognitively but also in conduct.
4. Disciples are singular in their allegiance to Christ.
5. Disciples must be willing to sacrifice all for Christ.
6. Disciples display genuine love to fellow believers.
7. Disciples are characterized by an intimate relationship with Jesus Christ, a passion for the Bible, a consistent prayer life, and a heart for ministry and service.
8. Disciples dedicate their lives as a consistent, blameless sacrifice to God.
9. Disciples consistently allow themselves to be transformed through meditation on the Word of God.
10. Disciples are actively involved in ministry.
11. Disciples are grounded in the truth and are not persuaded to follow false teaching.
12. Disciples replicate themselves into the spiritual lives of others.

---

204 The church age covers the timeframe from Acts 2 until the present.

Conclusion

As the post-apostolic church prepared to train individuals for member-ship to their community, it based its foundation for theological teaching and personal commitment upon the instruction of the NT Scriptures. The principles that were gleaned from the NT provided the basis for the catechumenate. This section examined select NT passages to provide an understanding of key principles in the development of NT disciples. From these NT passages, twelve discipleship principles were proposed that should be practiced by disciples and disciple-making systems.

CHAPTER 3

Catalysts for the Catechumenate

The first official Christian education program for the church was the catechumenate. The catechumenate, from κατηχεω meaning "to teach" or "instruct"[1] was designed for the education of adult converts prior to joining the church through baptism. A question is posed as to whether these individuals who entered the catechumenate were believers or unbelievers. At the beginning of the *Apostolic Tradition* (an accumulation of material from different sources from a variety of geographical regions dating to the mid-second century A.D.) the following statement appears which provides insight into the question of whether the individuals entering the catechumenal process were believers: "Concerning newcomers, those who will give their assent to the faith."[2] The initial interviewing teacher was further instructed: "Let them be asked the reason why they have given their assent to the faith."[3] One can infer from these statements that the new people coming to the church and entering the catechumenal process have a rudimentary level of faith. They have heard the gospel message and have exercised faith in that message. These individuals, after a profession of faith, now desire to join the community of believers

---

1 Walter Bauer, William F. Arndt, Wilbur Gingrich, and Fredrick W. Danker, *A Greek-English Lexicon of the New Testament and Other Early Christian Literature,* 2nd ed. (Chicago, IL: University of Chicago Press, 1979), 423.

2 Paul F. Bradshaw, Maxwell E. Johnson, L. Edward Phillips, and Harold W. Attridge, *The Apostolic Tradition: A Commentary* (Minneapolis, MN: Fortress Press, 2002), 82.

3 Ibid., 82.

by giving themselves to a period of rigorous study and preparation for baptism.[4]

A question can be posed as to whether the catechumenate was a necessary step for the ancient church. Why catechize before baptism? Didn't the early church baptize individuals directly after conversion (Acts 2:38—Pentecost; 8:26–40—Ethiopian Eunuch; 16:27–34—Philippian Jailer)? Is Jesus providing a procedural order in Matthew 28 ("baptizing" in vs. 19, "teaching" in vs. 20)? In the first century, it appears that baptism preceded catechism, but by the second century the process had been reversed; now the catechumenate was a necessary step before baptism and church membership. Why the change? Alan Kreider proposed several reasons:

1. Early converts in the first century were primarily Jewish or God-fearers who understood the Jewish story, morality, and worldview. By contrast converts in the second century were primarily ex-pagans, who needed instruction and re-socialization.

2. The theological disputes present in the second century demanded extended biblical instruction.

3. The need to screen possible spies and informers in an age of persecution.

4. Pastoral experience indicated that the teachings of Jesus were strenuous and demanded a process of re-socialization for both Jew and Greek.[5]

In addition to Lynch and Kreider's proposal, Michel Dujarier suggests that the early church fathers argued that fundamental elements were conveyed to both the Ethiopian Eunuch and at Pentecost that would later be taught in extended form in the catechumenate. Dujarier argues that Tertullian, Ambrose, and Augustine each taught that instruction was provided both prior to baptism of the Ethiopian Eunuch and at the day

---

4 Clinton E. Arnold, "Early Church Catechesis and New Christians' Classes in Contemporary Evangelicalism," *JETS 47* (2004), 42.

5 Alan Kreider, "Baptism, Catechism and the Eclipse of Jesus' Teaching in Early Christianity," *Tyndale Bulletin 47(2)*, 318. The first two of these points Kreider draws from Joseph H. Lynch, *Godparents and Kinship in Early Medieval Europe* (Princeton, NJ: Princeton University Press, 1986), 86–87.

of Pentecost.[6] Whatever the rationale by the early church fathers, by the second century A.D., the catechumenate was established as a standard for introduction to the church and was a necessary criterion for baptism.

The impetus behind the development of the catechumenate derived from the second part of Jesus' Great Commission to his disciples. Jesus states to His followers that as they make disciples they were to be "teaching them to observe all that I commanded you" (Matt. 28:20). Alan Kreider asserts the following regarding this phrase: "In saying this Jesus, in keeping with the emphases throughout Matthew's gospel, underscored the importance of a lived practical response to his teachings."[7] The desire was to instruct and teach these new followers in the areas of Scripture and theology to produce disciples. As the church moves into the post-apostolic period, there develops widespread testimony of a focused, coherent plan to instruct new believers: the catechumenate.[8] What influences impacted the church which ultimately provided a motivation to begin the catechumenal process?

Pre-Christian Religious Influences

Following the apostolic era, the early church experienced influence from the religious traditions of the Essenes and the Jews. The catechumenal process resembled in many ways the process of initiation to both the Essene and Jewish communities. Many from the Essene community became followers of Christ after the persecution and subsequent destruction of Jerusalem in A.D. 70. Dujarier contends that as they joined this new religious system (Christianity), they brought with them the influences that had helped form and shape the Essene community. The Essene influence helped to shape the church as it evolved its programs to minister to believers.[9]

Historical evidence indicates that the Essene and Jewish traditions influenced the process of baptism and membership into the early Christian church. Baptism no longer immediately followed salvation as was seen

---

6 Michel Dujarier, *A History of the Catechumenate: The First Six Centuries* (New York, NY: William H. Sadlier Inc., 1979), 15–17.

7 Kreider, *Tyndale Bulletin*, 316.

8 Arnold, *JETS*, 43.

9 Dujarier, *A History of the Catechumenate*, 22.

at times in Scripture (Acts 2:41; 8:38). Following the influence from the Essene and Jewish traditions, the early church began a process of education and preparation for both baptism and membership into the Christian community.

Essene Community

History provides little evidence regarding the origin and early development of the Essene community. Historical experts agree that the beginning of the Essene sect was roughly around 110 B.C.[10] Due to the characteristics of the group, as evidenced through first-century historians as well as writings from the Essenes themselves, one can gather that the group was like, yet distinct from, the Pharisees and Sadducees.[11] Josephus claims that at the time of his writing there were three sects of the Jews. "The one was called the sect of the Pharisees, another the sect of the Sadducees, and the other the sect of the Essenes."[12] The sects of the Jews were established to promote purity among the people of Israel (purity that had been neglected during the inter-testamental period). However, the Pharisees focused on Levitical and legal purity, whereas the Essenes emphasized absolute purity from material things.[13]

In addition, the Essenes separated themselves from the masses because they viewed them as impure and impious. Marcel Simon, French specialist in the history of religions—particularly relations between Christianity and Judaism in antiquity—states the following about the Essenes' isolation from the other Jewish sects at the time of Christ.

> They were separated from the Sadducees who, in their eyes, represented an illegitimate priesthood. They were separated from the Pharisees, despite certain affinities of spirit, practice, and doctrine, because in general they exceeded the Pharisees in the strictness and the completeness of their observance of the law. They were separated from the Zealots, despite certain belated

---

10 Duncan Howlett, *The Essenes and Christianity* (New York, NY: Harper and Brothers Publishers, 1957), 48.

11 Alfred Edersheim, *The Life and Times of Jesus the Messiah, Vol. 1* (Grand Rapids, MI: WM. B. Eerdmans Publishing Co., 1883), 825.

12 Flavius Josephus, *The Works of Josephus: Complete and Unabridged* (Peabody, MA: Hendrickson Publishers, 1987), 346.

13 Edersheim, *The Life and Times of Jesus the Messiah*, 325.

convergences ... because Essenism by nature was not at all a manifestation of militant nationalism. Indeed, the Essenes were separated from the totality of the Jews, because they constituted a closed society with secret rites and esoteric teaching.[14]

The Essenes then were a sect of the Jews that practiced purity to the OT law by remaining isolated from society and materialism.

There has been debate as to the meaning of the name "Essene." Philo used the Greek (*Essaioi*) for the Essenes and offers that the name means "holiness" or "purity."[15] Josephus similarly uses the Greek words *Essaioi* and *Essenoi* and offers that the name means "the venerable."[16] By contrast, an argument has been made that the term "Essene" derives from the Aramaic *hosios* or *hasya*. *Hasya* is the equivalent of the Hebrew term *hasidim* and would translate "pious."[17] Another alternative has been postulated by Andrew Dupont-Sommer that the term "Essene" derives from the Hebrew term *ezah*, meaning a "council" or "party."[18] Though there is dispute as to the origin of the term "Essene," the idea behind the term is that this was a "party" or group within Judaism which sought a "pious" lifestyle, and they were revered by first-century historians.

Characteristics of the Essene Community

Edouard Schuré, French author, writes the following regarding the characteristics of the Essene Community.[19]

---

14 Marcel Simon, *Jewish Sects at the Time of Jesus* (Philadelphia, PA: Fortress Press, 1967), 47–48.

15 Philo, *Apology*, in Eusebius, *Praeparatio Evangelica*, trans. E.H. Gifford (1903), accessed June 9, 2014, http://www.tertullian.org/fathers/eusebius_ pe_08_book8. htm#13.

16 Simon, *Jewish Sects at the Time of Jesus*, 49.

17 Ibid., 49.

18 Andre Dupont-Sommer, *The Essene Writings from Qumran* (Cleveland, OH: Meridian Books, 1962), 21 and 43.

19 Edouard Schuré, *Jesus, The Last Great Initiate* (Chicago, IL: Yogi Publication Society, 1908), 40. Schuré (42–45) argues that Jesus and John the Baptist were trained by the Order of the Essenes prior to public ministry.

> Indifferent to the outward pomp of worship at Jerusalem, repelled by the harshness of the Sadducees, and the prayers of the Pharisees, as well as by the pedantry of the synagogue, Jesus was attracted towards the Essenes by natural affinity. The premature death of Joseph set entirely free Mary's son, now

The Order of the Essenes constituted in the time of Jesus the final remnant of those brotherhoods of prophets organized by Samuel. The despotism of the rulers of Palestine, the jealousy of an ambitious and servile priesthood, had forced them to take refuge in silence and solitude. They no longer struggled as did their predecessors, but contented themselves with preserving their traditions. They had two principal centers, one in Egypt, on the banks of Lake Maoris, the other in Palestine, at Engaddi, near the Dead Sea. The name of Essenes they had adopted came from the Syrian word 'Asaya,' physician—in Greek, therapeutes; for their only acknowledged ministry with regard to the public was that of healing disease, both physical and moral.[20]

The Essene community, located primarily in Egypt and Palestine, was a Jewish sect that emphasized moral separation.

Philo, Hellenistic Jewish philosopher who lived in Alexandria, Egypt from 20 B.C. until A.D. 50, highlights several features of the Essene community.

---

grown into a man. His brothers could continue the father's trade and supply all family needs, so Mary gave him permission to leave secretly for Engaddi [*sic*]. Welcomed as a brother and one of the elect, he rapidly acquired over his very masters an invincible ascendancy, by reason of his superior faculties, his ardent love, and an indescribable divine element manifested throughout his entire being. From the Essenes he received what they alone could give him: the esoteric tradition of the prophets, and by its means, his own historical and religious tendency or trend. He came to understand how wide a gulf separated the official Jewish doctrine from the ancient wisdom of the initiates, the veritable mother of religions, though ever persecuted by Satan, *i.e.*, by the spirit of evil, of egoism, hatred, and denial, allied with absolute political power and priestly imposture.... Jesus passed a series of years among the Essenes.

Schuré continues to write that the Essenes supported Jesus in his earthly ministry; therefore, as he travelled during his public ministry, he had financial and physical support. It is beyond the scope of this dissertation to argue for or against Jesus being an Essene by education and tradition. However, this writer has not discovered sufficient evidence to prove that Jesus was trained in the Essene tradition. The evidence in support of Jesus being an Essene appears to be developed out of inferences from Jesus' teachings and lifestyle. However, these inferences do not provide sufficient proof to declare emphatically that Jesus was an Essene. But Schuré's work does in fact provide helpful insights into the traditions and practices of the Essenes at the time of Christ that can serve as a basis for understanding this important community.

20 Schuré, *Jesus*, 40.

1. There were nearly 4000 Essenes living in Palestine around the time of Christ.
2. They were people of great piety.
3. They devoted themselves to God and refrained from immoral influences.
4. They participated in communal living without slaves among them.
5. They considered the seventh day as sacred and refrained from work on this day.
6. They studied the "holy volume" and lived by its standards of faith and morality.
7. They were people of great wisdom and virtue.[21]

Schuré provided several features regarding the character of the members of the Essene community.

Among the Essenes, the brothers, properly so called, lived under a community of property, and in a condition of celibacy, cultivating the ground, and, at times, educating the children of strangers: The married Essenes formed a class affiliated and under subjection to the other. Silent, gentle, and grave, they were to be met with here and there, cultivating the arts of peace. Carpenters, weavers, vine-planters, or gardeners, never gunsmiths or merchants. Scattered in small groups about the whole of Palestine, and in Egypt, even as far as Mount Horeb, they offered one another the most complete hospitality.[22]

Titus Flavius Josephus, first-century Roman-Jewish scholar, historian, and hagiographer, wrote that the Essenes were of high moral character.

They dispense their anger after a just manner, and restrain their passion. They are eminent for fidelity, and are the ministers of peace; whatsoever they say also is firmer than an oath; but swearing is avoided by them, and they esteem it worse than perjury; for they

---

21 Philo, *The Works of Philo*, trans. C. D. Yonge (Peabody, MA: Hendrickson, 1993), 689–690. For further examination of Philo's explanation of the Essene community see Appendix 2.

22 Schuré, *Jesus*, 42.

say, that he who cannot be believed without [swearing by] God, is already condemned.[23]

Initiation Process

The Essene initiation process was unique as compared to the requirements of all other Jewish groups in the Second Temple times.[24] The Essenes utilized a multi-year initiation process to test and teach the proselytes who desired entrance into the sect. It appears that the reason for this multi-year initiation process was for both the group and the prospective candidate to determine if they were in fact right for each other. It was understood that more candidates may seek entrance to the sect than were willing to persist to become members of the Essenes.[25] Schuré describes the duration of the initiation process into the Essene community.

> The rules of the Order were strict; in order to enter, a year's novitiate was necessary. If one had given sufficient proofs of temperance, he was admitted to the ablutions, though without entering into relations with the masters of the Order. Tests, extending over

---

23 Josephus, *The Works of Josephus*, 605–606.

24 Hartmut Stegemann, "The Qumran Essenes—Local Members of the Main Jewish Union in Late Second Temple Times," *The Madrid Qumran Congress: Proceedings of the International Congress on the Dead Sea Scrolls, Madrid, 18–21 March 1991*. Edited by Julio C. Barrera and Luis Montaner (Leiden, The Netherlands: E. J. Brill, 1992), 112. Stegemann highlights the difference between Essene initiation and the Pharisee initiation process.

> The Pharisees only demanded that new members of their group should bind themselves to the strictest observation of their purity regulations, and this binding promise should be uttered in the presence of three witnesses. One may not exclude the possibility that some time of instruction on the laws of purity, or on other teachings of the Pharisees, may sometimes have preceded the final step of admission. But there is no hint of a time span of several years, or of stages of admission similar to those of the Essenes. Perhaps the binding promise of new members of the Pharisees was not basically different from the binding oath of new Essene members at their final admission. But at least the long period of teaching and testing of new members with its different stages of admission was again specific to the Essenes, not comparable to customs of other Jewish groups in Second Temple times.

Stegemann explained the Essenes and Pharisees, though both sects of the Jews, were very different in their perspectives.

25 Albert L. Baumgarten, *The Flourishing of Jewish Sects in the Maccabean Era: An Interpretation* (Leiden, the Netherlands: Brill, 1997), 53.

another two years, were necessary before being received into the brotherhood. They swore "by terrible oaths" to observe the rules of the Order and to betray none of its secrets. Then only did they participate in the common repasts, which were celebrated with great solemnity and constituted the inner worship of the Essenes.[26]

According to Schuré, initiation into the Essene community lasted three years. During this time the candidate was evaluated and assessed by the community before membership was granted.

The Essene community had a specific initiation process that is described by Josephus. The first year of entrance into the Essene community was a period of probation. During the first year, the candidate lived outside the community. The candidate was given a hatchet, a loincloth, and a white garment. During this first year, they were to provide for themselves. In addition, they were required to take oaths of loyalty to the community and to demonstrate dedication to God. During the next two years, the candidate was admitted to the community slowly and deliberately as they were allowed to partake in additional rites. As they became aware of the requirements for full membership into the community, their character was assessed, and if they were deemed worthy, they would be admitted into the community.[27]

---

26 Schuré, *Jesus*, 40–41.

27 Josephus, *The Works of Josephus*, 606. Josephus provides a description of the level of commitment that was necessary to join the Essene community.

> But now if any one hath a mind to come over to their sect, he is not immediately admitted, but he is prescribed the same method of living which they use for a year, while he continues excluded; and they give him also a small hatchet, and the fore-mentioned girdle, and the white garment. And when he hath given evidence, during that time, that he can observe their continence, he approaches nearer to their way of living, and is made a partaker of the waters of purification; yet is he not even now admitted to live with them; for after this demonstration of his fortitude, his temper is tried two more years; and if he appear to be worthy, they then admit him into their society. And before he is allowed to touch their common food, he is obliged to take tremendous oaths, that, in the first place, he will exercise piety towards God, and then that he will observe justice towards men, and that he will do no harm to any one, either of his own accord, or by the command of others; that he will always hate the wicked, and be assistant to the righteous; that he will ever show fidelity to all men, and especially to those in authority, because no one obtains the government without God's assistance; and that if he be in authority, he will at no time whatever abuse his authority, nor endeavor to outshine his subjects either in his garments,

Alfred Edersheim, Jewish convert to Christianity and biblical scholar, states the following about the initiation process of the Essene community:

> Admission to the order was only granted to adults, and after a novitiate which lasted three years. On entering, the novice received the three symbols of purity: an axe, or rather a spade, with which to dig a pit, a foot deep, to cover up the excrements; an apron, to bind round the loins in bathing; and a white dress, which was always worn, the festive garment at meals being of linen. At the end of the first year the novice was admitted to the lustrations. He had now entered on the second grade, in which he remained for another year. After its lapse, he was advanced to the third grade, but still continued a novice until, at the close of the third year of his probation, he was admitted to the fourth grade—that of full member, when, for the first time, he was admitted to the sacrifice of the common meals.[28]

Similarly, the Qumran community enumerated the criteria for initiation in the *Rule of the Community* (1 QS 6. 13–23).[29]

> or any other finery; that he will be perpetually a lover of truth, and propose to himself to reprove those that tell lies; that he will keep his hands clear from theft, and his soul from unlawful gains; and that he will neither conceal anything from those of his own sect, nor discover any of their doctrines to others, no, not though anyone should compel him so to do at the hazard of his life. Moreover, he swears to communicate their doctrines to no one any otherwise than as he received them himself; that he will abstain from robbery, and will equally preserve the books belonging to their sect, and the names of the angels [or messengers]. These are the oaths by which they secure their proselytes to themselves. *War of the Jews*, II, 8, 7.

According to Josephus, the Essene initiation practices were lengthy and a strenuous test.

28 Alfred Edersheim, *The Life and Times of Jesus the Messiah. Vol. 1* (Grand Rapids, MI: WM. B. Eerdmans Publishing Co., 1883), 327–328.

29 James H. Charlesworth, *The Dead Sea Scrolls, Vol. 1, Rule of the Community and Related Documents* (Louisville, KY: Westminster John Knox Press, 1994), 29.

> And (regarding) each one who freely offers himself from Israel to join the Council of the Community, the Overseer at the head of the Many shall examine him with respect to his insight and his works. If he is suited to the discipline he shall permit him to enter into the covenant to turn to the truth and depart from all deceit; he shall instruct him in all the precepts of the Community. And later, when he enters to stand before the Many, then they shall all be asked concerning his affairs, and as the lot comes out according to the counsel of the

Recently, the Essene-Qumran hypothesis has undergone debate.[30] However, Todd Beall, OT scholar and linguist, provides several points of similarity between the *Rule of the Community* (*Manual of Discipline*) and Josephus' discussion of Essene initiation procedures.

Many, he shall approach or withdraw. When he approaches the Council of the Community he must not touch the pure-food of the Many, until he has been examined concerning his spirit and his work until one full year is completed, nor shall he have any share in the property of the Many. When he has completed one year within the Community, the Many shall be asked about his affairs with regards to his insight and his works in Torah. If the lot should go out to him that he should approach the assembly of the Community according to the priests and the multitude of the men of their covenant, then both his property and his possessions shall be given to the hand of the man (who is) the Examiner over the possessions of the Many. And he shall register it into the account with his hand, and he must not bring it forth for the Many. He must not touch the drink of the Many until he has completed a second year among the·men of the Community. When that second year has been completed he shall be examined according to the Many. If the lot goes out to him to approach the Community, he shall be registered in the order of his rank among his brothers, for Torah, judgment, and purity, and his property shall be assimilated (into that of the Many). His counsel and his judgment shall belong to the Community.

30 Stegemann, *The Qumran Essenes*, 83–166. Stegemann agrees that most scholars hold to a Qumran-Essene hypothesis (that the writers of the Dead Sea Scrolls at Qumran were Essenes). However, Stegemann highlights in detailed fashion that recently scholarship has challenged this hypothesis. Steve Mason highlights the faulty basis for a Qumran-Essene hypothesis.

Recent vigorous disagreement about the identity of the Qumran community exposes in part the faulty method by which conclusions were initially drawn and permitted to ossify. Once the site of Qumran had been hypothetically identified as an Essene installment and the Dead Sea Scrolls as Essene productions, this nexus imposed constraints upon interpreters of the DSS, on the one hand, and of the Greek and Latin texts that purport to describe Essenes, on the other. Exegesis of both had now to fit the theory.

Steve Mason, *Josephus, Judea, and Christian Origins: Methods and Categories* (Peabody, MA: Hendrickson Publishers, 2009), 239. See also Norman Golb, *Who Wrote the Dead Sea Scrolls? The Search of the Secret of Qumran* (New York, NY: Scribner, 1995); Lena Cansdale, *Qumran and the Essenes: a Re-Evaluation of the Evidence* (Tubingen, Germany: J. C. B. Mohr and Paul Siebeck, 1997). In contrast however, Joseph Fitzmyer states the following in relationship to the current debate over the identity of the members of the Qumran community. "The best identification of the Qumran community is still that which early students of the Dead Sea Scrolls have always proposed, namely, the Essene identification." Joseph A. Fitzmyer, *The Dead Sea Scrolls and Christian Origins* (Grand Rapids, MI: William B. Eerdmans Publishing Company, 2000), 260.

1. The joining of the community was a voluntary decision.
2. There was a period spent outside the sect.
3. The language used to describe the novice after the one-year period is similar between the two texts.
4. There was a two-year period of initiation within the community itself.
5. The novice participated in purification baths during the two-year period.
6. The novice was not allowed to participate in the community meal.
7. After a further examination following the two-year period, the candidate was admitted into the community with full rights and privileges.[31]

The process of joining the Essene community was a progressive process in which tests were given to the candidates to assess their morals and lifestyles. To join the community, the candidate had to be approved by the entire community. A group of members were assigned the task of examining the candidate. Upon adequately proving knowledge of specific criteria and demonstrating an appropriate lifestyle, the candidate was approved to join the community.[32]

Influence on Christianity and the Catechumenate

No historical phenomenon or religious system originates and develops in isolation. Christianity (and specifically the church) is not an exception to this truth. Though God's plan is clearly revealed in both the OT and the NT, factors influenced the beginning of the church. Clearly, the Essenes and the primitive Church of the first century were two very different entities. However, as the Essene community exited the historical stage and Christianity entered it, there is every reason to believe that the Essenes had an impact on the early church, especially in areas of initiation and recruitment.[33]

---

31 Todd S. Beall, *Josephus' Description of the Essenes Illustrated by the Dead Sea Scrolls* (Cambridge, England: Cambridge University Press, 1988), 74–75.

32 Dujarier, *A History of the Catechumenate*, 23.

33 Simon, *Jewish Sects at the Time of Jesus*, 145.

Several similarities between the Essene community and early Christianity have been postulated by historians. Though the basis for Jesus and John the Baptist being Essenes is highly questionable—and significant distinctions are evident as one studies Essene theology in contrast to the teachings of Jesus[34]—there is still much in common between the teachings of the Essenes and the early church. Christian Ginsburg, British scholar and student of the Masoretic tradition in Judaism, provides several parallels in beliefs and practices of the Essenes and Christianity. The following are clear examples of similarity between the two groups in content of teaching:

1. The Essenes urged their disciples to seek first the kingdom of God and his righteousness; so did Jesus Christ (Matt 6:33; Luke 12:31).
2. The Essenes prohibited the laying up of treasures on earth; so did Jesus Christ (Matt 6:19–21).
3. The Essenes required that candidates sell their possessions and divide off the profits to help the poor brethren; Jesus taught something like this to the rich young ruler (Matt 19:21), and this practice was highlighted in the early church (Acts 4:36–37).
4. The Essenes practiced communal living; the early church practiced a type of communal living (Acts 2:44–45).
5. The Essenes did not show favoritism among members but encouraged mutual service; so did the early church (Mark 9:35–37; 10:42–45; James 2:1–13).
6. The Essenes commanded their disciples to call no man master upon the earth; so did Jesus Christ (Matt 23:8–10).
7. The Essenes placed great emphasis on being meek and lowly in spirit; so did Jesus Christ (Matt 5:5; 11:29).
8. The Essenes commended their followers for being poor in spirit, for desiring righteousness, for being merciful, for being pure of heart, and for being peacemakers; so did Jesus Christ (Matt 5).

---

34 Reference chapters 13–15 of Duncan Howlett's book, *The Essenes and Christianity*, 145–163.

9. The Essenes required that their followers not swear oaths but rather let your yes be yes and your no be no; so did Jesus Christ (Matt 5:37; James 5:12).

10. The Essenes adopted a philosophy when they started a mission of mercy; this philosophy parallels Jesus' instruction to his disciples as they went forth on mission (Matt 10:9–10; Luke 22:36).

11. The Essenes did not offer animal sacrifices (as did the rest of Judaism) but rather taught the presentation of the body as a living sacrifice; this directive is clearly taught by the Apostle Paul (Rom 12:1–2).[35]

The greatest similarity between the Essene community and the early church was the initiation process of the candidates for membership. Historians contend that after the destruction of the temple in A.D. 70 (and the subsequent ending of the Essene movement) there was an influx of Essenes entering the early church. With this entrance they brought with them the customs of their initiation process.[36] As will be delineated in chapter four, the process of initiation (duration, manner of instruction, level of involvement, increased participation during later stages, and graduation ceremonies) was remarkably similar between the Essene community and the Post-Apostolic Church.

Michel Dujarier contends that two important observations must be made regarding the similarities between the Essene community's initiation process and that of the early church's catechumenal process. 1) Both communities are focused upon a progressive initiation. 2) Both communities viewed the stages as a time of formation and examination (one had to be tested regarding morality and lifestyle).[37] Both communities required a multi-year candidacy process (teaching) before baptism (entrance) into their communities. It appears that the Essene community influenced early

---

35 Christian D. Ginsburg, *The Essenes: Their History and Doctrines* (London, England: Routledge & Kegan Paul LTD, 1956), 23–24.

36 Edward Buchanan, "The Catechumenate of the Early Church with Implication for the Church of the 21st Century" (Valley Forge, PA: ETS Annual Conference, 2005), 5.

37 Dujarier, *A History of the Catechumenate*, 23.

Christianity in relation to initiation practices when the Church became compelled to adopt more structured forms.[38]

Jewish Community

In addition to the Essene community, many of the original Christians came to Christ from the broader Jewish faith. It appears that the Jewish initiation process impacted the Christian community as well.

Proselyte Initiation Process

Judaism began an intentional missionary effort earlier than 100 B.C. when "apostles" were sent through the Roman Empire to collect the temple taxes and to proclaim the message of the Scriptures.[39] Upon acceptance of this missionary message a proselyte to Judaism progressed through a multi-stage initiation process.

The Jewish proselyte went through a four-step process to become a full member of the Jewish community. In the first step, the proselyte had to declare his desire to become a Jew. The Rabbi would ask the candidate why he wanted to be become a Jew because the Jews were a persecuted people. If he still desired to become a Jew, he was advanced to the next step. In the second step, he was instructed in the commandments and the law. In the third step, if the proselyte was a man, he was circumcised. Once he was healed from his circumcision, he was advanced to the fourth step which was baptism. Following the baptism, the proselyte was accepted as a full member of Judaism.[40] According to Dujarier the four

---

38 Ibid., 22.

39 Lewis J. Sherrill, *The Rise of Christian Education* (New York, NY: The Macmillan Company, 1950), 66.

40 Dujarier, *A History of the Catechumenate*, 24–26. Rabbi I. Epstein records the questions and subsequent instruction that occurred between the rabbi and the proselyte.

> Our Rabbis taught: If at the present time a man desires to become a proselyte, he is to be addressed as follows: "What reason have you for desiring to become a proselyte; do you not know that Israel at the present time are persecuted and oppressed, despised, harassed and overcome by afflictions"? If he replies, "I know and yet am unworthy", he is accepted forthwith, and is given instruction in some of the minor and some of the major commandments. He is informed of the sin [of the neglect of the commandments of] Gleanings, the Forgotten Sheaf, the Corner and the Poor Man's Tithe. He is also told of the punishment for the transgression of the commandments. Furthermore, he is addressed thus: "Be it known to you that before you came to this condition, if you had

stages of proselyte initiation are as follows: 1) Declaration of intent, 2) Instruction, 3) Circumcision, and 4) Baptism.[41]

Instruction of Proselytes

Lewis Sherrill, pioneer in Christian Education, emphasized the instructional component in his description of the four-stage Jewish proselyte initiation process.

> A proselyte to Judaism was required to pass through four steps or stages. The first was his presentation and examination. He was asked, "What reason have you for desiring to become a proselyte; do you not know that Israel at the present time are persecuted and oppressed, despised, harassed, and overcome by afflictions?" If he replied, "I know and yet am unworthy," he was to be accepted forthwith. The second stage of the ritual consisted of "instruction in some of the minor and some of the major commandments." The third stage was circumcision if the candidate were a man, and the final stage was baptism. In the case of a man, "Two learned men must stand by his side and acquaint him with some of the minor commandments and with some of the major ones," at this time when he was taking upon himself "the yoke of the commandments." In the case of a woman proselyte, she must "sit in the water up to her neck, while two learned men stand outside and give

eaten suet you would not have been punishable with *kareth*, if you had profaned the Sabbath you would not have been punishable with stoning; but now were you to eat suet you would be punished with *kareth*; were you to profane the Sabbath you would be punished with stoning". And as he is informed of the punishment for the transgression of the commandments, so is he informed of the reward granted for their fulfillment. He is told, "Be it known to you that the world to come was made only for the righteous, and that Israel at the present time are unable to bear either too much prosperity or too much suffering". He is not, however, to be persuaded or dissuaded too much. If he accepted, he is circumcised forthwith. Should any shreds which render the circumcision invalid remain, he is to be circumcised a second time. As soon as he is healed arrangements are made for his immediate ablution, when two learned men must stand by his side and acquaint him with some of the minor commandments and with some of the major ones. When he comes up after his ablution he is deemed to be an Israelite in all respects.

Rabbi I. Epstein, "Yebamoth: Folio 47 a–b." *Soncino Babylonian Talmud* (London, England: Soncino Press, 1948).

41 Dujarier, *A History of the Catechumenate*, 24–26.

her instruction in some of the minor commandments and some of the major ones."[42]

However, the content of the "minor and major commandments" appears to be unknown. From the Yebamoth folio #47 of the Talmud, the instruction of proselytes included instruction in "six hundred and thirteen commandments."[43] It is important to note that whatever content comprised these commandments it was not to the level of instruction that was provided to a Jewish-born individual.[44]

Though the content of the instruction is undetermined, the implication from the Talmud is that "systematic instruction had taken place."[45] Two German works by Alfred Seeberg (*Die Didache des Judentums und der Urchristenheit*) and Gottlieb Klein (*Der älteste christliche Katechismus und die jüdische Propaganda-Literatur*) have formulated a proposal regarding the form and content of the Jewish proselyte instruction. The focus of the instruction, according to Seeberg, was in three areas: dogmatic instruction about God, ethical instruction regarding vice and virtue, and eschatological instruction.[46]

Though an extensive treatise regarding the content of the Jewish proselyte instructional content is not available to modern scholars, several features regarding proselyte instruction surface.

1. Proselyte instruction was an important step in the initiation process.
2. Proselyte instruction occurred over an extended period.
3. Proselyte instruction followed a systematic approach in the education of an individual.
4. Proselyte instruction occurred before baptism and acceptance into the Jewish community.

---

42 Sherrill, *The Rise of Christian Education*, 66–67.

43 Rabbi I. Epstein, "Yebamoth: Folio 47 b."

44 Rabbi I. Epstein, "Yebamoth: Folio 48 b." The rabbis stated that proselytes "are not so well acquainted with the details of the commandments as the Israelites."

45 Frank S. B. Gavin, *The Jewish Antecedents of the Christian Sacraments* (New York, NY: Cosimo Inc., 2005), 38.

46 Alfred Seeberg, *Die Didache des Judentums und der Urchristenheit* (Leipzig, Germany: Georg Bohme, 1908), 1.

The similarities between the catechumenate and the Jewish proselyte initiation process will be presented in chapter four. However, it appears that the catechumenate gleaned structure and content regarding instruction from the Jewish proselyte process. Because many of the earliest Christians came from Judaism, it appears that the early church replicated aspects of the Jewish custom of initiating proselytes. An influence that became a catalyst for the early church to begin the catechumenate was the impact of both the Essene community and broader Judaism regarding the initiation process into their respective communities and religious systems. In addition to religious influences, there appears to be sociological influences that served as a catalyst for the early church to develop the catechumenal process.

Sociological Influences

As the church sought to educate and prepare those interested in joining their community, they created a program (catechumenate) that answered and addressed the sociological influences of society on Christian individuals and the church at large. If a believer intended to join the church, he or she must be prepared to live according to a different ethical standard than was presented in society. One also needed to be prepared to suffer and possibly die for one's commitment to the church and ultimately Jesus Christ. Ottorino Pasquato provides the perceived need for instruction prior to baptism in the 2nd and 3rd centuries A.D. as opposed to baptism described in Acts.

> We note that admission to baptism was more cautious than in the NT period. In fact, in this period, as an antidote to the moral decadence of the Christian communities and to cases of apostasy in the period of persecution, there was the introduction of a twofold examination, the first in the initial phase of orientation toward Christianity, the second at the act of enrollment for baptism. The phase of preparation for baptism was designed to last 2–3 years.[47]

Therefore, the church created the catechumenate that prepared individuals to address the sociological influences of their day. The following

---

47 Ottorino Pasquato, *Encyclopedia of Ancient Christianity, A–E: Catechumenate-Discipleship* (Downers Grove, IL: Intervarsity Press, 2014), 460.

is an examination of apparent sociological influences that affected the development of the catechumenate for the early church.

Persecution

The initial step of the catechumenate was to evaluate whether a believer was prepared to face the persecution that so often accompanied the joining of the early church. Persecution of Christians was the norm in the early centuries A.D. After the great fire of Rome that was blamed upon the Christians, the following quotation reveals the persecution that the Christians faced:

> First, then, the confessed members of the sect were arrested; next, on their disclosures, vast numbers were convicted, not so much on the count of arson as for hatred of the human race. And derision accompanied their end: they were covered with wild beasts' skins and torn to death by dogs; or they were fastened on crosses, and, when daylight failed were burned to serve as lamps by night. Nero had offered his Gardens for the spectacle, and gave an exhibition in his Circus, mixing with the crowd in the habit of a charioteer, or mounted on his car.[48]

Early believers, during Nero's reign, faced extensive persecution as they lived their lives seeking to please their Savior Jesus Christ.

Although the Roman Empire began to persecute Christians from the time of Nero, the details of those persecutions are scarce. However, by the second century, records begin to reveal the magnitude and gravity of the persecutions that the Christians faced. The "Act of the Martyrs" retells in dramatic and graphic fashion the arrest, trial, and death of various martyrs. The records are so extensively detailed that many argue they are taken, at least in part, from official court records. Among the list of Christian martyrs, Polycarp and Ignatius of Antioch stand out for the extent of the records of their persecution, their importance within the Empire, and their resolve during their death.[49]

During Marcus Aurelius' reign (A.D. 161–180), there were an endless string of invasions, floods, epidemics, and other diseases. Soon the

---

48 Tacitus, "Annals," *Loeb Classical Library edition of Tacitus, Vol. 5, Book 15* (Cambridge, MA: Harvard University Press, 1937), 15.44.

49 Justo L. González, *The Story of Christianity* (Peabody, MA: Prince Press, 1999), 38–45.

explanation was presented that it was the Christians who were to blame for the various calamities. Aurelius, though it is uncertain he believed the charges, allowed the full-scale persecution of Christians.[50]

During the entire second century, Christians were in a precarious position. At times, they were persecuted. At times, there was a lapse in the persecutions they faced. However, Christians knew that it was highly probable that they would face physical persecution. The church developed a process (catechumenate) that vetted and prepared these individuals to face possible persecution and death.

Immorality

In addition to the catechumenate preparing a new believer to face persecution, the catechumenate also addressed the purity by which a new believer (and ultimately a member of the early church) needed to live one's life. Secular culture surrounding the early church was a perverse blend of hedonism, sexual immorality, unrestrained appetites, and cruelty to others. One popular Roman Graffito of that day read, "Baths, wine and love-making destroy our bodies, yet love-making, wine and baths make life worth living."[51] The philosophical systems of that day shaped the moral compass of the Roman society. The Epicureans argued that a young man could choose immediate pleasure in preference to ultimate happiness, if he cared to assume the risks involved. The Stoics argued that morality was linked to a person's reason. To make wise/ethical choices, the individual needed to consult his reason which would guide him to the right path. However, if one's reason permits a specific course of action, who can argue with his reason?[52]

According to Edersheim, the Roman culture was driven by these two philosophical viewpoints. The one (Stoicism) emphasized an individual's pride. The other (Epicureanism) emphasized its sensuality. Both approaches led the individual to despair: the one by turning all aspirations

---

50 Ibid., 46.

51 James S. Jeffers, *The Greco-Roman World of the New Testament Era, Exploring the Background of Early Christianity* (Downers Grove, IL: Intervarsity Pr., 1999), 29.

52 Tenney Frank, *A History of Rome* (New York, NY: Henry Hold and Company, 1923), 318–319.

self-ward, the other by quenching future aspirations for the enjoyment of the moment.[53]

The Roman culture was in a state of extraordinary moral degeneration. Two thousand lords in Rome had 1,300,000 slaves. In the Roman Empire, there were more than 6,000,000 slaves, and these were often treated with great cruelty.[54] Within the home, marriage and chastity were the exception while divorce and immorality were the rule. The emperors were monsters of crime. Thousands of lives were sacrificed in the arena to furnish the entertainment for the emperor. Seneca testified that children were considered with great disfavor and infant exposure was prevalent. Tacitus said that the spirit of the times was "to corrupt and to be corrupted."[55]

The decline in morals, especially in the rich upper classes, nobility, and the emperors, had a devastating impact on the Romans. Immoral and promiscuous sexual behavior often was associated with public orgies. Emperors such as Tiberius kept groups of young boys for his pleasure. Elagabalus forced a Vestal Virgin into marriage. Commodus, with his harems of concubines, enraged Romans by sitting in the theatre or at the games dressed in a woman's garments.[56] These Emperors were to be examples to the populous, but with their immorality, they influenced the masses in a negative way. The decline in morals also affected the lower classes and slaves. Religious festivals, such as Saturnalia and Bacchanalia, included lewd acts and sexual promiscuity. Bestiality and other lewd and sexually explicit acts were exhibited in the Colosseum arena to amuse the mob. Brothels and forced prostitution flourished. Widespread gambling on the chariot races and gladiatorial combats were the norm.[57]

Edward Gibbon, noted Roman historian, states the following about the immorality that was present in Antioch around A.D. 360:

---

53 Edersheim, *The Life and Times of Jesus the Messiah*, 257.

54 John W. Shephard, *The Christ of the Gospels* (Grand Rapids, MI: WM. B. Eerdmans Publishing Company, 1947), xv.

55 Ibid., xv.

56 Linda Alcin, "Causes for the Fall of the Roman Empire," accessed July 28, 2014, from, http://www.tribunesandtriumphs.org/roman-empire/causes-for-the-fall-of-the-roman-empire.htm.

57 Ibid.

The warmth of the climate disposed the natives to the most intemperate enjoyment of tranquility and opulence; and the lively licentiousness of the Greeks was blended with the hereditary softness of the Syrians. Fashion was the only law, pleasure the only pursuit, and the splendor of dress and furniture was the only distinction of the citizens of Antioch. The arts of luxury were honored; the serious and manly virtues were the subject of ridicule; and the contempt for female modesty and reverent age announced the universal corruption of the capital of the East. The love of spectacles was the taste, or rather passion, of the Syrians; the most skillful artists were procured from the adjacent cities; a considerable share of the revenue was devoted to the public amusements; and the magnificence of the games of the theatre and circus was considered as the happiness and as the glory of Antioch.[58]

In Antioch during this period, individuals sought sensual pursuits to gratify their lusts. The goal was pleasure, and immorality was the norm.

The moral degradation that was on display through popular "spectacles" of the pagan world was criticized by early Christian moralists and apologists.[59] Tertullian in *Against Marcion* states the following regarding the three main "spectacles" of that day: "absent yourself from those popular pleasures, the excitement of the race-course, the savagery of the wild beast show, the lechery of the stage."[60] These three main forms of entertainment (amphitheaters/circuses, the athletic arenas, and the theatre) displayed nudity, hedonism, and murder and were a way to enflame the savage and perverse lusts of the populace.

Describing the theatre, Everett Ferguson explains that by the time that Christianity began the Greek drama had long past from the stage. The most popular theatrical performances were the charades, mimes, and parodies that described everyday life.[61] Most of the performances quickly digressed into vulgar and sexual displays to obtain laughs from the audience. Christian moralists and apologists exhorted the church

58 Edward Gibbon, *Decline and Fall of the Roman Empire, Vol. 2, Ch XXIV,* Accessed July 28, 2014, from http://sacred-texts.com/cla/gibbon/02/daf02043.htm.

59 Everett Ferguson, *Backgrounds of Early Christianity* (Grand Rapids, MI: W. B. Eerdmans Pub. Co., 2003), 97.

60 Tertullian, *Tertullian: Adversus Marcionem,* Translated by Ernest Evans (Oxford: Oxford University Press, 1972), 78.

61 Ferguson, *Backgrounds of Early Christianity,* 99.

against attending such performances. John Chrysostom, Archbishop of Constantinople—an important Early Church Father—stated the following in a homily against the theatre:

> Why do I talk about the theatre? Often if we meet a woman in the marketplace, we are alarmed. But you sit in your upper seat, where there is such an invitation to outrageous behavior, and see a woman, a prostitute, entering bareheaded and with a complete lack of shame, dressed in golden garments, flirting coquettishly and singing harlots' songs with seductive tunes, and uttering disgraceful words. She behaves so shamelessly that if you watch her and give consideration, you will bow your head in shame. ... Therefore, I make this proclamation, in a clear and loud voice, that if anyone after this exhortation and teaching deserts back to the unlawful disgrace of the theatre, I shall not receive him within these precincts, I will not let him share in the sacraments, I will not let him touch the sacred table. Just as shepherds separate the sheep that are afflicted by mange from the healthy sheep, so as to prevent the rest from catching the disease, so I shall act in the same way.[62]

Chrysostom believed that the sensual displays that were a part of the production of the theatre led believers into adulterous thoughts. The theatre, according to Chrysostom and other Christian apologists, had no place within the life of a believer in Christ.

In addition to the theatre, the athletic arena was another "spectacle" that was criticized by Christianity because of its lewd displays. Professional athletes before and around the time of Christ received financial rewards and were revered by audiences in a similar way as athletes are revered in present times.[63] However, the Greeks (more so than the Romans) exercised and competed in the nude. The nudity that was on display during these athletic events shocked the Jews and later Christians. Though earlier than Christian origins, writings from the Maccabean period described the immoral displays that were present during athletic competitions. In 2

---

62 John Chrysostom, *Against the Circuses and Theatre: Homily of St. John Chrysostom, Archbishop of Constantinople, our Sainted Father: Against Those who have Abandoned the Church and Deserted it for Hippodromes and Theatres*, Translated by Mark Vermes, Accessed July 29, 2014, from http://www.tertullian.org/fathers/chrysostom_against_theatres_and_circuses.html.

63 Ferguson, *Backgrounds of Early Christianity*, 101.

Maccabees 4:7–17, Jason introduced Hellenistic games and athletic events to the Jews and their priests. The athletic activity is described as "unlawful proceedings" and "disdaining the honors prized by their fathers." This neglect of their Jewish heritage and practice led them to "heavy disaster."[64] Later, after the establishment of Christianity, these same displays of nudity were common practices during athletic events. This "spectacle" of the athletic arena was criticized by early Christian moralists.

A final "spectacle" that was criticized by Christian apologists and moralists was the arenas or amphitheaters. The best known of these arenas was the Colosseum (the Flavian Amphitheatre). The Colosseum could hold nearly 50,000 spectators and was used to display "plays, gladiatorial combats, or wild animal shows; it could be flooded for mock sea battles."[65] The Colosseum, like other amphitheaters, was used to gratify the blood-thirsty appetites of the masses. Roland Auguet in his book, *Cruelty and Civilization: The Roman Games*, describes for modern readers the impact of the games on life in the Roman Empire.

> Because of the almost mythical character which these games have assumed for us, it is difficult for us today to realize to what extent they became one of the most familiar aspects of everyday life. One might even say that they pervaded life. They imposed their rhythm on existence and provided nourishment for the passions. The spectacle was awaited with impatience; everyone discussed it, some applauded and others booed frantically. Goaded by habit, by idleness, by fanaticism, an entire people crowded on to the tiers of the circus or the amphitheatre, as to a temple which had a ritual peculiar to it. In Rome there was undoubtedly an emotion special

---

64 2 Maccabees 4:12–16:

> For with alacrity he founded a gymnasium right under the citadel, and he the noblest of the young men to wear the Greek hat. 13 There was such an extreme of Hellenization and increase in the adoption of foreign ways because of the surpassing wickedness of Jason, who was ungodly and no high priest, 14 that the priests were no longer intent upon their service at the altar. Despising the sanctuary and neglecting the sacrifices, they hastened to take part in the unlawful proceedings in the wrestling arena after the call to the discus, 15 disdaining the honors prized by their fathers and putting the highest value upon Greek forms of prestige. 16 For this reason heavy disaster overtook them, and those whose ways of living they admired and wished to imitate completely became their enemies and punished them.

65 Ferguson, *Backgrounds of Early Christianity*, 102.

to the amphitheatre, even as there exists amongst us a quite special pleasure on entering a cinema, regardless of the film which is to be shown.[66]

The arenas and amphitheaters served as an amusement to the vast array of social classes by depicting grotesque battles between gladiator–gladiator, gladiator–wild beast, gladiator–slave, beast–slave, beast–criminal, and beast–Christian.[67] Baker describes the bloodlust of the people of Rome for the battles of the arenas.

> The ancient Romans loved gladiators. They loved the men, the weapons, the fighting and the bloodshed. They also loved the death. Bathed in the fierce heat of the Mediterranean sun, the Romans rejoiced in the blood of the dead and the dying, for in so doing they showed the qualities that had made their civilization great and powerful. They demonstrated their utter contempt for suffering and death. The great amphitheatres of Rome and her provinces were routinely packed with spectators, who watched men fight bloody battles, both with each other and with a dazzling array of wild and dangerous animals. Awful violence stalked the arenas in the form of sword, arrow, trident, tooth and claw, of an intensity that we can barely now imagine.[68]

François-René de Chateaubriand, French writer, politician, diplomat and historian, sought to depict the brutality and moral debauchery of the arenas.

> The people in the meantime were assembled at the amphitheatre of Vespasian: all Rome flocked hither to drink the blood of the martyrs. ... A hippopotamus and several crocodiles floated on the surface of a canal which surrounded the arena; five hundred lions, forty elephants, tigers, panthers, bulls, and bears, trained to rend men in pieces, shook with their terrific roar the dens of the amphitheatre. A body of gladiators, not less ferocious than the beasts, were preparing themselves for the sports of blood. Near these

---

66 Roland Auguet, *Cruelty and Civilization: The Roman Games* (New York, NY: Routledge, 1994), 15.

67 Alan Baker, *The Gladiator: The Secret History of Rome's Warrior Slaves* (Cambridge, MA: Da Capo Press, 2000), 3–10.

68 Ibid., 2.

caves of death were the places of public prostitution: a number of courtesans, and Roman ladies of the first rank, augmented, as in the days of Nero, the horror of the spectacle, and came, the rivals of death, to dispute with each other the favor of an expiring prince.[69]

The arena was a place of untold suffering and death. The sport of blood was the appeal to the masses. In droves, the populace came to the arenas to witness the torture and violence that led to the death of many.

In addition to the three main "spectacles" described by Tertullian (arenas, games, and theatre) the Roman Empire was known for its public baths. It was within these structures that the masses turned from spectators to participants in the entertainment. Historians believe that every town had at least one public bathing establishment (larger cities with multiple establishments).[70] Everett Ferguson describes the atmosphere of these public baths as well as their importance to society.

> The atmosphere was somewhat that of a country club combined with a community center. Here one came to meet with friends, converse, and have a snack of food and drink. Here one could read, exercise, get a massage, listen to philosophers or poets, as well as bathe.[71]

It appears from architecture that initially men and women had separate bathing areas. However, by the 1st century A.D. women and men were bathing together.[72] Nicarchus, 1st century Greek poet and writer, describes in an epigram that Onesimus went to the baths and left his child at home. Nicarchus proposed that when Onesimus returned home he would be the father of two more children.[73] The obvious assumption

---

69 François-René de Chateaubriand, *The Martyrs* (New York, NY: Derby and Jackson, 1859), 436.

70 Ferguson, *Backgrounds of Early Christianity*, 105.

71 Ibid., 105

72 Roy B. Ward, "Women in Roman Baths," *Harvard Theological Review*. Vol. 85, No. 2 (April, 1992), 134.

73 Nicarchus, "Anthologia Graeca, 11.243," *Greek Anthropology, Vo. 4*. Edited by W.R. Paton, Accessed July 30, 2014, from http://www.perseus.tufts.edu/hopper/text?doc=Perseus%3Atext%3A2008.01.0475%3Abook%3D11%3Achapter%3D243. λούσασθαι πεπόρευται Ὀνήσιμος εἰς βαλανεῖον δωδεκάτῃ δύστρου μηνός, ἐπ᾽ Ἀντιφίλου,

is that women were bathing with men which would provide Onesimus the opportunity to procreate at the bath. Pliny the Elder, 1st century Roman author, naturalist, and natural philosopher, also made a clear assertion that women and men bathed nude together.[74] Several lines from surviving graffiti from Roman baths indicate clearly that fornication and explicit sexual activity took place at the public bath houses in the 1st century.[75]

Many of the early church moralists and apologists wrote against the vices of the public bath houses. Clement of Alexandria, 2nd century A.D. Christian theologian, stated the following about the detestable nature of the bath houses.

And of what sort are their baths? Houses skillfully construct-ed, compact, portable, transparent, covered with fine linen. And gold-plated chairs, and silver ones, too, and ten thousand vessels of gold and silver, some for drinking, some for eating, some for bathing, are carried about with them. Besides these, there are even braziers of coals; for they have arrived at such a pitch of self-in-dulgence, that they sup and get drunk while bathing. And articles of silver with which they make a show, they ostentatiously set out in the baths, and thus display perchance their wealth out of ex-cessive pride, but chiefly the capricious ignorance, through which they brand effeminate men, who have been vanquished by women; proving at least that they themselves cannot meet and cannot sweat without a multitude of vessels, although poor women who have no display equally enjoy their baths. The dirt of wealth, then, has an abundant covering of censure. With this, as with a bait, they hook the miserable creatures that gape at the glitter of gold. For dazzling thus those fond of display, they artfully try to win the admiration of their lovers, who after a little insult them naked. They will scarce strip before their own husbands affecting a plausible pretense of modesty; but any others who wish, may see them at home shut up naked in their baths. For there they are not ashamed to strip before spectators, as if exposing their persons for sale. But Hesiod advises "Not to wash the skin in the women's bath." The baths are

παῖδα λιπὼν οἴκοις ἐπιτίτθιον, ὃν δύο τέκνων ἄλλων εὑρήσει λουσάμενος πατέρα. ἥξειν δ᾽ εἰς ὥρας ἡμῖν γράφει· οἱ βαλανεῖς γὰρ εἰς τότε τάσσονται τὴν πυρίαν καθελεῖν.

74 Pliny, *Natural History*, 29.26, 33.153. Accessed July 30, 2014, from http://penelo-pe.uchicago.edu/Thayer/L/Roman/Texts/Pliny_the_Elder/29*.html.

75 Ward, *HTR*, 138.

opened promiscuously to men and women; and there they strip for licentious indulgence (for from looking, men get to loving), as if their modesty had been washed away in the bath. Those who have not become utterly destitute of modesty shut out strangers; but bathe with their own servants, and strip naked before their slaves, and are rubbed by them; giving to the crouching menial liberty to lust, by permitting fearless handling. For those who are introduced before their naked mistresses while in the bath, study to strip themselves in order to audacity in lust, casting off fear in consequence of the wicked custom. The ancient athletes, ashamed to exhibit a man naked, preserved their modesty by going through the contest in drawers; but these women, divesting themselves of their modesty along with their tunic, wish to appear beautiful, but contrary to their wish are simply proved to be wicked. For through the body itself the wantonness of lust shines clearly; as in the case of dropsical people, the water covered by the skin. Disease in both is known from the look. Men, therefore, affording to women a noble example of truth, ought to be ashamed at their stripping before them, and guard against these dangerous sights; "for he who has looked curiously," it is said, "has sinned already" Matthew 5:28. At home, therefore, they ought to regard with modesty parents and domestics; in the ways, those they meet; in the baths, women; in solitude, themselves; and everywhere the Word, who is everywhere, "and without Him was not anything" John 1:3. For so only shall one remain without falling, if he regard God as ever present with him.[76]

Similarly, in *Didascalia Apostolorum*, Christian treatise from the 3rd century A.D., the following quotation provides an admonition to Christian women in relations to the public baths of that day.

And take heed that thou bathe not in a bath with men. For when there is a women's bath in the city or in the village, a believing woman may not bathe in a bath with men. For if thou coverest thy face from strange men with a veil of modesty, how then canst thou go in with strange men to a bath? But if there is no women's bath, and thou art constrained to bathe in a bath of men and women,— which indeed is unfitting—bathe with modesty and shame, and with bashfulness and moderation: and not at all times, nor every

---

76 Clement of Alexandria, *Paedagogos*, 3.5. Translated by William Wilson. Accessed July 30, 2014, from http://www.newadvent.org/fathers/02093.htm.

day, and not at midday; but let there be an appointed season for thee to bathe at, (to wit) at the tenth hour. For it behoves thee, as a believing woman, by every means to fly from the vain and curious gaze of the many which is met with in a bath.[77]

Due to the moral depravity of culture during the early life of the church, the leaders of the church determined that moral instruction was critical for believers (especially new believers who were beginning a Christian walk apart from the norms of culture).

It was within this morally degenerate society that the Christian church began and flourished. Many of the believers who came to faith in Christ were saved out of this wicked lifestyle. It was imperative that the church teach and train these new converts to obey and live a radically different lifestyle from the previous style they exhibited. Key passages from *Apostolic Constitutions*, *Canons of Hippolytus*, and *Testamentum Domini* address the examination of new believers regarding their occupations. If the candidates were part of these occupations, they were instructed to either quit their present job or limit their involvement. It was critically important for the candidate to understand the moral lifestyle that Christ was calling the new believer to follow. Instructions to new believers from *Apostolic Constitutions*:

If anyone is a brothel keeper, either let him stop his pimping or be rejected. Let a prostitute who comes either stop or be rejected. Let an idol maker who comes either stop or be rejected. If any of them belongs to the theater, whether man, woman, charioteer, gladiator, stadium runner, trainer of athletes, one who participates in the Olympic Games, or one who accompanies the chorus on flute, lute, or lyre, or who puts on a display of dancing or is a fraudulent trader, let them either stop or be rejected. Let a soldier who comes be taught to do no injustice or to extort money, but to be content with his given wages. Let the one who objects be rejected. A doer of unmentionable things, a lustful person, a lascivious person, a magician, a mob leader, a charmer, an astrologer, a diviner, a charmer of wild beasts, a pimp, a maker of charms, one who purifies by applying objects, a fortuneteller, an interpreter of oracles, an

---

77 R. Hugh Connolly, *Didascalia Apostolorum*, (Oxford, England: Clarendon Press, 1929). Accessed July 30, 2014, from http://www.earlychristianwritings.com/text/didascalia.html.

interpreter of bodily vibrations, one who, upon encountering them, observes defects of eyes or feet or birds, or cats, or loud noises, or significant chance remarks—let them be examined for a time, for the evil is hard to wash out. Then, let those who stop be received, but let those not persuaded be rejected.[78]

Similarly, the *Canons of Hippolytus* contain moral instruction to be provided to new believers:

Every craftsman is to be told not to make any image, or any idol, whether he is a sculptor, silversmith, or painter, or of any other art. If they happen after baptism to make any such thing, except what the people need, they are to be excluded until they repent. Whoever becomes director of a theater, or a wrestler, or a runner, or teaches music, or plays before the processions, or teaches the art of the gladiator, or a hunter, or a hairdresser, or a fighter with savage beasts, or a priest of idols, all these, one is not to reveal to them any of the Holy Word, until they are purified first from these impure occupations. Then, during forty days they are to hear the Word, and if they are worthy they are to be baptized. The teacher of the church is the one who judges this matter.[79]

The *Testamentum Domini* also exhorts the leadership of the church to have strict rules related to new believers who are involved in certain occupations.

If a fornicatress, or a brothel keeper, or a drunkard, or a maker of idols, or a painter, or one engaged in shows, or a charioteer, or a wrestler, or one who goes to the contest, or a combatant [in the games], or one who teaches wrestling, or a public huntsman, or a priest of idols, or a keeper of them, be [among those that come], let him not be received. If any such desires to become faithful, let him cease from these [things]; and being indeed faithful, and being baptized, let him be received and let him partake. And if he does not cease, let him be rejected.[80]

---

78 Paul F. Bradshaw, Maxwell E. Johnson, L. Edward Phillips, and Harold W. Attridge, "Apostolic Constitutions," *The Apostolic Tradition: A Commentary* (Minneapolis, MN: Fortress Press, 2002), 89.

79 Ibid., "Canons of Hippolytus," 89.

80 Ibid., "Testamentum Domini," 89.

Although this list of occupations includes jobs that may not appear offensive in 21st-century contexts, the early church was responding to immorality (at least perceived immorality in some cases) and was seeking to educate candidates regarding moral living before entrance into the church community.

The catechumenate was developed to teach and mentor individuals to cast off vice and replace it with virtue. In addition to the spiritual instruction, the catechumens were discipled/mentored by mature believers. Before baptism, a "scrutiny" was made of the individual's lifestyle to verify that he/she was qualified to join the church. Upon finishing the "scrutiny," the new believers were taken through a multi-level educational process over a lengthy period to teach virtuous living in a degenerate culture.

Doctrinal Influences

As the church dealt with ethical issues and persecution, another issue arose during the expansion of the church. Doctrinal heresies began to surface, which challenged the very fabric of Christian teaching. Justo Gonzalez explains the theological climate of the early church.

> The many converts who joined the early church came from a wide variety of backgrounds. This variety enriched the church and gave witness to the universality of its message. But it also resulted in widely differing interpretations of that message, some of which threatened its integrity. The danger was increased by the syncretism of the time, which sought truth, not by adhering to a single system of doctrine, but by taking bits and pieces from various systems. The result was that, while many claimed the name of Christ, some interpreted that name in such a manner that the very core of his message seemed to be obscured or even denied.[81]

The catechumenate sought to educate individuals in theology and apologetics to be able to respond to the doctrinal heresies presented from both within and outside the church.

---

81 Justo L. González, *The Story of Christianity* (Peabody, MA: Prince Press, 1999), 58.

Gnosticism

One major group that doctrinally challenged the early church was the Gnostics. Gnosticism was a very diverse and complex movement like the New Age movement of modern times. Gnosticism posed a major problem for the early church because it was like Christianity in certain points but interpreted Scripture passages in a heretical way that posed questions that needed to be answered by the early church leaders.[82] Gnosticism reached its height of influence from about A.D. 135 to 160, though it continued to have influence long after these dates. It provided the early church its gravest crisis since the Pauline battle for freedom from the law.[83]

Christian tradition has posited the founder of Gnosticism as Simon Magus from Acts 8:9–11. Irenaeus, 2nd century church father and apologist, asserted that Simon was the founder. "Now this Simon of Samaria, from whom all sorts of heresies derive their origin."[84] In addition, Justin Martyr asserted that Simon Magus was the founder of the heresy that would be later known as Gnosticism.[85] However, historically those who were the clear leaders of the Gnostics were Satornilus of Antioch (before A.D. 150), Basilides (Alexandria—A.D. 130), and Valentinus (Rome, between A.D. 135–165).[86]

The name "Gnosticism" derives from the Greek word *gnosis*, which means "knowledge." The Gnostics believed that they possessed a special, mystical knowledge which was the secret key to salvation.[87] To the Gnostic, salvation was achieving a special kind of knowledge that was not generally known by Christians. This *gnosis*, knowledge, involved an awareness of the unknowable God and his messenger, Jesus, who came immaterially

---

82 Alister E. McGrath, *Historical Theology: An Introduction to the History of Christian Thought* (Malden, MA: Blackwell Publishing, 1998), 29.

83 Williston Walker, *A History of the Christian Church* (New York, NY: Charles Scribner's Sons, 1970), 51.

84 Irenaeus, *Against Heresies*, I.23.2, translated by Alexander Roberts and William Rambaut, Accessed July 31, 2014, from http://www.newadvent.org/fathers/0103123.htm.

85 Justin Martyr, *First Apology, Ch. 26*, translated by Marcus Dods and George Reith. Accessed July 31, 2014, from http://www.newadvent.org/fathers/0126.htm.

86 Walker, *A History of the Christian Church*, 53.

87 González, *The Story of Christianity*, 58–59.

to this earth to recapture the "sparks" trapped in material bodies. Frend explains the Gnostic view of salvation.

> The "self" or "I" of the Gnostic, however, belonged to the divine world. It was a "spark of God." At some stage in its existence it had fallen into the visible world and had become imprisoned and drugged into slumber by it. It could be freed only by accepting the call of a "Divine Messenger" (Christ) and, thus enlightened and emancipated, would return to its true heavenly home at the end of time.[88]

Gnostics believed that Jesus only appeared to be human.[89] Williston Walker explains the Gnostic view regarding Jesus Christ:

> Since the material world is evil, Christ could not have had a real incarnation, and the Gnostics explained His appearance either as Docetic and ghostly, or as a temporary indwelling of the man Jesus, or as an apparent birth from a virgin mother without partaking of material nature.[90]

According to Gnosticism, Jesus Christ was not the God-Man of orthodox Christianity but rather a deity who "appeared" to be man.

Gnostics believed that matter/body is an evil prison dragging down the good soul of the human person. The spirit/soul is a divine "spark of God" dwelling in the tomb of the body. Because the body serves as a prison of the spirit/soul it is therefore evil. To the Gnostic the eventual goal is to escape the body and ultimately the material world in which our soul has been exiled.[91] The question arises then, "if all matter is evil, why did God create a physical world and a material body?" The Gnostics stated that all reality was originally spiritual. God never intended to create a physical realm, but an "eon" (spiritual being) fell into error and created the physical world.[92] The present goal of all "sparks" (spiritual part of

---

88 W. H. C. Frend, *The Rise of Christianity* (Philadelphia, PA: Fortress Press, 1984), 198.

89 Roger E. Olson, *The Story of Christian Theology, Twenty Centuries of Tradition & Reform* (Downers Grove, IL: Intervarsity Pr., 1999), 29.

90 Walker, *A History of the Christian Church*, 52.

91 González, *The Story of Christianity*, 59.

92 Ibid., 59.

every person's being) is to wake up from this "dream" and break free from this material world. So how does one break free? How is one to live one's life? Justo Gonzalez explains the two Gnostic views regarding these important questions:

> Gnostics gave two divergent answers. Most declared that, since the body is the prison of the spirit, one must control the body and its passions and thus weaken its power over the spirit. But there were also some who held that, since the spirit is by nature good and cannot be destroyed, what we are to do is to leave the body to its own devices and let it follow the guidance of its own passions. Thus, while some Gnostics were extreme ascetics, others were libertines.[93]

According to Gonzalez, Gnostics responded differently to the question, "how is one to live their life?" revealing that there were divisions within Gnostic thought.

Several doctrinal issues needed to be addressed by the early church to counteract the teachings of Gnosticism.

1. Who was Jesus Christ and what did his incarnation entail?
2. Was the God of the OT (the creator of heaven and earth) the Supreme Being?
3. What did God create?
4. What role does the body play in personhood?
5. How were Christians to live their lives spiritually in a secular, "physical" world?

The catechumenate was viewed by early church leaders as the necessary tool to address and teach critical theological issues. As will be discussed in chapter 4 of this book, many of the topics that were taught during the catechumenate addressed these doctrinal issues raised by Gnosticism.

Montanism

Another source of heresy came from Montanus. While the second-century church leaders saw a great danger in Gnosticism, another group confronted the church from within. Unlike Gnosticism which was a religion of syncretism (blending elements of various religions into one

---

93 Ibid., 60.

or at least a multi-faceted philosophy), Montanism was a movement that started within Christianity itself.[94] This fanatical movement saw itself as the "New Revelation" and the "New Prophecy" which came to be known as Montanism, from its chief prophet Montanus. Montanus believed that the church was spiritually dead and called for "new prophecy" with all the signs and wonders of the church at Pentecost.[95]

The problem for the leaders of the early church was not Montanus's critique of the spiritual life of the church but rather his self-identification as God's spokesman without equal. He referred to himself as the "Mouthpiece of the Holy Spirit." Walker describes Montanus's view of his relationship to God:

> About 156 Montanus proclaimed himself the passive instrument through whom the Holy Spirit spoke. In this new revelation Montanus declared the promise of Christ fulfilled, and the dispensation of the Holy Spirit begun. To him were soon joined two prophetesses, Prisca and Maximilla. They now affirmed, as mouthpieces of the Spirit, that the end of the world was at hand, and that the heavenly Jerusalem was about to be established in Phrygia, whither believers should betake themselves.[96]

He vehemently opposed the church's viewpoint that inspiration had ended with the closing of the apostolic writings. In contrast, he argued that the Holy Spirit was continually providing revelation from inspired utterances. Montanus claimed he was the chief vessel used by the Holy Spirit to convey these inspired teachings.[97]

The church was forced to respond to this heretical viewpoint regarding both eschatology and special revelation. Was Montanus ushering in the future kingdom? Was he truly a mouthpiece of God being given special revelation? The church responded by stating that the supernatural utterances such as tongues and prophecies and other miraculous gifts (signs and wonders) had ceased. Like Gnosticisim, Montanism challenged the early church to think and respond theologically to the heretical claims

---

94 Walker, *A History of the Christian Church*, 55.

95 Olson, *The Story of Christian Theology*, 31.

96 Walker, *A History of the Christian Church*, 56.

97 Olson, *The Story of Christian Theology*, 31.

pronounced by leaders regarding doctrine (inspiration and authority) which was taught to new believers through the catechumenate.

Teachings of Marcion

Another source of heresy that the early church encountered was from Marcion. In many ways, Marcion presented a greater threat to the early church than did the Gnostics and Montanus. For nearly a century after Marcion's death (A.D. 160), he was considered by the Church Fathers to be the "arch-heretic." He was condemned in the writings of Justin, Irenaeus, Clement, Tertullian, Hippolytus, Bardesanes, and Origen.[98]

Marcion was convinced that the world was in fact evil. Therefore, he concluded that its creator must be either evil or ignorant.[99] Marcion asserted that the vindictive God of the OT (who created the world and gave the OT law) was different from the God revealed in the NT (Jesus—unknown good God of mercy).[100] Marcion argued that God, the Father of Jesus, is not the same as Jehovah, the God of the Old Testament. According to Marcion, it was Jehovah, the God of the OT, who created this world. By contrast, Marcion taught that it was God, the Father of Jesus, who desired to create only a spiritual world. However, Jehovah, the God of the OT, made this wicked world and placed humanity within it.[101] For Marcion, there were far too many instances in which the OT actions of Jehovah contradicted the loving and merciful actions of God, the Father of Jesus, in the NT.[102]

Marcion went on to teach that in contrast to the vindictive Jehovah of the OT, God, the Father of Jesus, is the Father of Christians and loves His children. For Marcion, Jesus came to us to reveal the Father God to us in contrast to Jehovah revealed in the OT. As a result of this perspective, this "good" God requires nothing of Christians, but rather gives freely to His children (including salvation).[103] Marcion laid aside Old Testament Scriptures and started his own church emphasizing the New Testament writings.

---

98 Frend, *The Rise of Christianity*, 212.

99 Gonzalez, *The Story of Christianity*, 61.

100 Walker, *A History of the Christian Church*, 54.

101 Gonzalez, *The Story of Christianity*, 61.

102 Frend, *The Rise of Christianity*, 215.

103 Gonzalez, *The Story of Christianity*, 61.

Orthodox Christianity was forced to examine several key doctrinal issues. 1) Was the church founded upon the foundation of Israel? 2) Is the OT Scripture, and is it relevant for NT saints? 3) Are there two Gods who act independently from one another? 4) How do we reconcile the OT portrayal of God with the NT teachings of Christ regarding the Father? The church was forced to address these issues, and the catechumenate provided teaching (specifically concerning the Trinity) regarding these heavily contested theological interpretations.

Arianism

Arianism reached its pinnacle of influence in the later stages of the catechumenate. However, the roots of Arianism began much earlier than the time of Constantine and developed out of a misinterpretation regarding the nature of God and the Logos.[104] The catechumenate spent ample

104 Ibid., 159–161. Gonzalez writes the following about the foundational roots of Arianism.

> The roots of the Arian controversy are to be found in theological developments that took place long before the time of Constantine. Indeed, the controversy was a direct result of the manner in which Christians came to think of the nature of God, thanks to the work of Justin, Clement of Alexandria, Origen, and others. When the first Christians set out to preach their message throughout the Empire, they were taken for ignorant atheists, for they had no visible gods. In response, some learned Christians appealed to the authority of those who antiquity considered eminently wise, the classical philosophers. The best pagan philosophers had taught that above the entire cosmos there was a supreme being, and some had even declared that the pagan gods were human creations. Appealing to such respected authorities, Christians argued they believed in the supreme being of the philosophers, and that this was what they meant when they spoke of God. Such an argument was very convincing, and there is no doubt that it contributed to the acceptance of Christianity among the intelligentsia. Two means were found to bring together what the Bible says about God and the classical notion of the supreme being as impassible and fixed. These two means were allegorical interpretation of scriptural passages, and the doctrine of the Logos. Allegorical interpretation was fairly simple to apply. Wherever Scripture says something "unworthy" of God—that is, something that is not worthy of the perfection of the supreme being—such words are not to be taken literally. Thus, for instance, if the Bible says that God walked in the garden, or that God spoke, one is to remember that an immutable being does not really walk or speak. Intellectually, this satisfied many minds. But emotionally it left much to be desired, for the life of the church was based on the faith that it was possible to have a direct relationship with a personal God, and the supreme being of the philosophers was in no way personal.

time addressing the nature of God and the concept of Trinitarianism. Therefore, the roots of Arianism had great impact on the topics that were addressed within catechumenal instruction.

At the time of the Arian controversy, Arius was advanced in years and was a highly respected leader in his church. The actual controversy began in Alexandria, about A.D. 320. The main dispute started between Arius and his bishop, Alexander.[105] The center of the debate appears to be an overemphasis by both Arian and Alexander on different aspects of Origen's teachings regarding Christ. To Arius, Jesus was of the same substance as God but was made like other creatures out of "nothing" and therefore was not eternal with the Father. By contrast, Bishop Alexander was influenced by the other side of Origen's teaching. To Alexander, Jesus was not only eternal but was also of the same essence as the Father and wholly uncreated.[106]

A main point of clarification that led Arius to this understanding of Jesus was the absolute uniqueness and transcendence of God.[107] To

---

There was another way to resolve the conflict between the philosophical idea of a supreme being and the witness of Scripture. This was the doctrine of the Logos, as developed by Justin, Clement, Origen, and others. According to this view, although it is true that the supreme being—the "Father"—is immutable, impassible, and so on, there is also a Logos, Word, or Reason of God, and this is personal, capable of direct relations with the world and with humans. Thus, according to Justin, when the Bible says that God spoke to Moses, what it means is that the Logos of God spoke to him. Due to the influence of Origen and his disciples, these views had become widespread in the Eastern wing of the church—that is, that portion of the church that spoke Greek rather than Latin. The generally accepted view was that, between the immutable One and the mutable world, there was the Word or Logos of God. It was within this context that the Arian controversy took place.

Gonzalez's examination of the history of the foundation of Arianism is important to understand as one develops a context for which Arius developed his teachings.

105 Walker, *A History of the Christian Church*, 107.

106 Ibid., 107.

107 Arius, *Confession of Faith of Arius and his Followers to Bishop Alexander of Alexandria*, Accessed August 11, 2014, from http://www.fourthcentury.com/index.php/urkunde-6.

Our faith from our forefathers, which also we learned from you, Blessed Father, is this: We acknowledge One God, alone unbegotten, alone everlasting, alone without beginning, alone true, alone having immortality, alone wise, alone good, alone sovereign, judge, governor, and provider of all, unalterable and unchangeable, just and good, God of the Law and the Prophets and the New

Arius, God the Father is the one source of all things. Therefore, He is the only uncreated being in the universe. Because of this interpretation, God cannot share his being or essence with anyone else.[108] Jesus then,

Testament; who begat an only-begotten Son before time and the ages, through whom he made both the ages [Heb 1:2] and all that was made; who begot Him not in appearance, but in reality; and that he made him subsist at his own will, unalterable and unchangeable, the perfect creature (*ktisma*) of God, but not as one of the creatures; offspring, but not as one of the other things begotten; nor as Valentinus pronounced that the offspring of the Father was an emanation (*probolē*); nor as the Manicheans taught that the offspring was a one-in-essence-portion (*meros homoousion*) of the Father; nor as Sabellius, dividing the Monad, speaks of a Son-Father; nor as Hieracas speaks of one torch [lit] from another, or as a lamp divided into two; nor that he who existed before was later generated or created anew into a Son, as you yourself, O blessed Father, have often condemned both in church services and in council meetings; but, as we say, he was created at the will of God, before time and before the ages, and came to life and being from the Father, and the glories which coexist in him are from the Father.

For when giving to him [the Son] the inheritance of all things [Heb 1:2], the Father did not deprive himself of what he has without beginning in himself; for he is the source of all things. Thus there are three subsisting realities (*hypostaseis*). And God, being the cause of all that happens, is absolutely alone without beginning; but the Son, begotten apart from time by the Father, and created (*ktistheis*) and founded before the ages, was not in existence before his generation, but was begotten apart from time before all things, and he alone came into existence (*hypestē*) from the Father. For he is neither eternal nor co-eternal nor co-unbegotten with the Father, nor does he have his being together with the Father, as some speak of relations, introducing two unbegotten beginnings. But God is before all things as monad and beginning of all. Therefore he is also before the Son, as we have learned also from your public preaching in the church.

Therefore he thus has his being from God; and glories, and life, and all things have been given over to him; in this way God is his beginning. For he is over him, as his God and being before him. But if the expressions *from him* [Rom. 11:36] and *from the womb* [Ps. 109:3 (LXX), 110:3 English] and *I came from the Father, and I have come* [John 16:28], are understood by some to mean that he is part of him [the Father], one in essence or as an emanation, then the Father is, according to them, compounded and divisible and alterable and material, and, as far as their belief goes, the incorporeal God endures a body.

This letter provides a basis for understanding Arius's belief related to Jesus and God.

108 Millard J. Erickson, *Christian Theology* (Grand Rapids, MI: Baker Books, 1998), 712.

according to Arius, was in no way equal with the Father in either essence or eternality.

In a letter to Eusebius of Nicomedia in A.D. 318, Arius clarified his view on the nature of the Son in response to Alexander's "ravaging and persecuting."

> Before he was begotten, or created, or defined, or established, he did not exist. For he was not unbegotten. But we are persecuted because we have said the Son has a beginning but God has no beginning. We are persecuted because of that and for saying he came from non-being. But we said this since he is not a portion of God nor of anything in existence.[109]

Arius believed that Jesus was begotten or created by God and therefore was not eternal. To Arius, Jesus had a point of beginning.

So, what happened at the incarnation of Christ? Arius believed that the Logos entered a human body replacing the normal human reasoning spirit. Therefore, Christ was neither fully God nor fully man, but a *tertium quid* between.[110] Millard Erickson describes Arius' viewpoint on the relationship between the created Jesus and the Father:

> While the Word is a perfect creature, not really in the same class with the other creatures, he is not self-existent. From this, two other conceptions regarding the Word followed. First, the Word must have had a beginning at some finite point. The Arians' slogan therefore became, "There was a time when he was not." It seemed to the Arians that if the Word were coeternal with the Father, there would be two self-existent principles. This would be irreconcilable with monotheism, the one absolute tenet of their theology. Second, the Son has no communion with or even direct knowledge of the Father. Although he is God's Word and Wisdom, he is not of the very essence of God; being a creature, he bears these titles only because he participates in the Word and Wisdom of the Father.[111]

---

109 Arius, *Letter of Arius to Eusebius of Nicomedia*, Accessed August 11, 2014, from http://www.fourthcentury.com/index.php/urkunde-1.

110 Walker, *A History of the Christian Church*, 107.

111 Erickson, *Christian Theology*, 712.

But, what about the passages that describe the deity of Christ? Arius argued that those biblical passages which elevate Jesus to the status of divinity were simply using language in an honorific manner.[112]

Arius' position can therefore be summarized in the following manner:

1. The Son is a creature who, like all other creatures, derives from the will of God.

2. The term "Son" is thus a metaphor, an honorific term intended to underscore the rank of the Son among other creatures. It does not imply that Father and Son share the same being or status.

3. The status of the Son is itself a consequence of the will of the Father; it is not a consequence of the nature of the Son, but of the will of the Father.[113]

Arius's viewpoint was highly contested among believers in the fourth century. He was condemned as a heretic in synods in Egypt and Antioch and defended at synods in Bithynia and Caesarea.[114] Eventually Constantine called together a council in Nicea to settle the dispute among the church.

Nearly 230 bishops arrived at the Council of Nicea. The proceedings opened on May 20, 325.[115] At the beginning of the council, the Arians presented a creed that was quickly rejected. Eusebius of Caesarea presented a creed that was used at his church which predated the Council of Nicea. This Caesarean creed was amended by adding the phrases "begotten, not made" and "of one essence (ὁμοούσιον) with the Father" and by the specific rejection of Arian formulae such as "there was a time when He was not" and "He was made of things that were not." Terms such as "essence" or "substance" (ουσια) and "hypostasis" (υποστασις) were used to describe Christ's relationship with the Father.[116] The original Nicene Creed of 325 reads as follows:

---

112 Alister E. McGrath, *Historical Theology: An Introduction to the History of Christian Thought* (Malden, MA: Blackwell Publishing, 1998), 49.

113 Ibid., 49.

114 Susan A. Harvey and David G. Hunter, *The Oxford Handbook of Early Christian Studies* (Oxford, UK: Oxford University Press, 2008), 245.

115 Frend, *The Rise of Christianity*, 498.

116 Walker, *A History of the Christian Church*, 108.

We believe in one God, the Father Almighty, Maker of all things visible and invisible. And in one Lord Jesus Christ, the Son of God, begotten of the Father [the only-begotten; that is, of the essence of the Father, God of God], Light of Light, very God of very God, begotten, not made, being of one substance (ὁμοούσιον) with the Father; by whom all things were made [both in heaven and on earth]; who for us men, and for our salvation, came down and was incarnate and was made man; he suffered, and the third day he rose again, ascended into heaven; from thence he shall come to judge the quick and the dead. And in the Holy Ghost. [But those who say: "There was a time when he was not;" and "He was not before he was made;" and "He was made out of nothing," or "He is of another substance" or "essence," or "The Son of God is created," or "changeable," or "alterable"—they are condemned by the holy catholic and apostolic Church.][117]

This creed was presented at the council to be accepted by Orthodoxy. At the conclusion of the Council of Nicca, all but two members of the council signed the new statement. Arius and the two bishops who did not sign were banished by Constantine.[118] Arius was condemned as a heretic and exiled. However, the council did not turn out to be the stabilizing consensus that Constantine had hoped for. Following the Council, debates raged over "modalism" and the term *homoousios*. The debate over the essence of Christ would rage for over 200 years following the Council of Nicea.[119] The Arian controversy was a divisive issue that forced the early church to address theological disputes regarding the person and character of Christ. The catechumenate addressed this theological issue by providing biblical instruction regarding the person and essence of Christ.

Teachings of Celsus

Celsus provided another doctrinal challenge to the early church. The Gnostics, Montanists, Marcion, and Arius presented threats to the church and demanded that the church address theological heresies. However, the

---

117 Philip Schaff, *Creeds and Cristendom*, Accessed August 11, 2014, from http://www.ccel.org/ccel/schaff/creeds1.iv.iii.html.

118 Walker, *A History of the Christian Church*, 109.

119 Harvey and Hunter, *The Oxford Handbook of Early Christian Studies*, 246.

church also faced heretical threats from pagan scholars/orators as well. The challenges arose from men like Fronto, Tacitus, Lucian, Prophyry, and primarily Celsus.[120] At a time when rumors and false accusations regarding Christians were rampant, Celsus provided a stunningly articulate critique of Christian belief. He did not engage with rumors about Christians, but simply highlighted what appeared to be inconsistencies and superstitious elements of Christian doctrine. For instance, in response to the Christian's worship of Jesus, Celsus wrote the following:

> It cannot be the case that God came down to earth, since in so doing he would have undergone an alteration of his nature. To be blunt: Either God really does change as they suggest into a human being (and this, as noted, is an impossibility), or else he does not change, but rather makes them who see him think that he is only mortal, and so deceives them, and tells lies—which is not the nature of a god to do.[121]

This argument presented by Celsus forced the early church to make coherent two seemingly conflicting claims. Christians were faced with a choice. They could either ignore Celsus and critics like him or rise to the challenge and develop cogent doctrines that would reconcile a monotheistic claim and the deity of Jesus Christ.[122] A major component to the catechumenate was the theological instruction that answered the charges and questions that surfaced from doctrinal heresies presented to the early church.

In addition to the prominent heretical teachings stated above, other influential heresies provided the early church with difficulties. The following heresies were present during the time of the catechumenate: Manicheism (combination of Zoroastrianism, Buddhism, and ideals from Bardesanes and Marcion),[123] Ebionism (severe asceticism that rejected the divinity of Christ),[124] Apollinarianism (Apollinarius rejected the

---

120 Olson, *The Story of Christian Theology*, 33.

121 R. Joseph Hoffman, "Translation of Celsus," *On the True Doctrine, A Discourse Against the Christians* (USA: Oxford University Press, 1987), 78.

122 Olson, *The Story of Christian Theology*, 35.

123 Frend, *The Rise of Christianity*, 314.

124 F. L. Cross and E. A. Livingstone, "Ebionites," *Dictionary of the Christian Church* (Peabody, MA: Hendrickson Publishers, 1997), 523. Little evidence from history has survived regarding the Ebionites. However, from what remains they were a Jewish

presence of a human mind, will, and personality in Jesus),[125] Nestorian-ism (Nestorius emphasized the disunity between the human and divine natures of Jesus),[126] and Pelagianism (major controversy during the 5th century regarding original sin, grace, and soteriological issues).[127]

Heretical teachings needed to be addressed and answered by the early church. One primary way of addressing these heretical issues with new believers, who are typically more susceptible to erroneous teachings, was to have an instructional program in which Scriptural refutation was pro-vided to new converts. The catechumenate served as that instructional program for the early church.

Conclusion

The catechumenate was the first intentional, systematic training of new believers conducted by the post-apostolic church. Several influences were a catalyst for the development of catechumenal instruction. Among these influences were pre-Christian religious influences (the Essene com-munity and the Jewish proselyte initiation process), sociological influenc-es (immorality and persecution), and doctrinal influences (Gnosticism, Montanism, teachings of Marcion, Arianism, the teaching of Celsus). Because of the pagan culture in which the early church began, church leaders found it necessary to train believers to forsake vice and seek

---

Christian sect who practiced severe asceticism mainly east of the Jordan River. Their two primary tenets were 1) that Jesus was not divine but rather the human son of Jo-seph and Mary and 2) that NT believers should practice the characteristics of Mosaic Law.

125 Olson, *The Story of Christian Theology*, 188–190. According to Apollinarius, the flesh of Jesus was like a human shell in which the Logos took up earthly residence. Thus, Logos is the interiority of Christ, the God-man. In Jesus there was no human psychology, no human intelligence, no human mind, no human will. The interior of Je-sus was the Logos that had become fused with the flesh.

126 Ibid., 211–231. Nestorius rejected the term *theotokos* (Mary's being the moth-er of God) in favor of a view that argued for Mary as the mother of the humanity of Jesus only. Cyril of Alexandria entered the debate with Nestorius and the issue was ad-dressed in both the First Council of Ephesus in A.D. 431 and the Council of Chalce-don in A.D. 451.

127 Frend, *The Rise of Christianity*, 673–683. The center of the dispute was between Pelagius and Augustine. However, the issue came to the forefront at the end of the cate-chumenate and therefore did not have great impact on the catechumenal system.

virtue as well as be prepared to answer the theological disputes of early Christianity. This catechumenal process was a multi-year training period in discipleship.

CHAPTER 4

Characteristics of the Catechumenal Process

The Importance and Role of Corporate Education

Education is both the process of acquiring significant learning experiences as well as the product of a desired change of personality and behavior. Throughout history, teaching has played a vital role in the development of the student/learner to progress from novice to expert, from immaturity to maturity. Spiritually, God's desire has been that corporate education be used as a critical component in training individuals to learn who He is and what He desires of them as they study and are instructed by Scripture. An important link within the educational chain is corporate education/teaching for the instruction of the whole (Israel and the Church) and the person (individually).

Corporate Education in the Old Testament

In the Old Testament, the purpose of teaching was to challenge Israel to learn God's laws so that their position as the people of God would become evident to the nations and that God would be glorified through them.[1] The teacher was assigned the important task of teaching the people not simply to know the commands of God but to obey them. Knowledge was linked to action within the Hebrew mindset. To *know* God's law was to *do* God's law (Deut 4:1, 5–6). Parents, specifically fathers, were

---

1 Perry G. Downs, *Teaching for Spiritual Growth* (Grand Rapids, MI: Zondervan Pub. House, 1994), 24.

primarily responsible for instructing their children in the knowledge and commands of God (Deut 6:4–9).

The book of Deuteronomy was Moses' opportunity to convey to the new generation of Israelites the importance of obeying God's commands as he rehearsed the Law of God with them. In Deuteronomy 6, Moses uses the literary tool of a "merism" to demonstrate God's specific command to the parents of the children of Israel. "These words, which I am commanding you today, shall be on your heart. You shall teach them diligently to your sons and shall talk of them when you sit in your house and when you walk by the way and when you lie down and when you rise up" (Deut 6:6–7 NAU). A "merism" provides two extremes and implies everything in between.[2] In this example parents are commanded to repeatedly teach the Word of God to their children. The emphasis is on the repeated action of teaching God's commands and words so that the next generation will continue in obedience to the Lord. Speaking is the activity involved in the second clause. The curriculum that is to be spoken is God's Word. In Deuteronomy 6:7, Moses specifically instructs parents that they are responsible to continue the instruction that has been placed before them. Parents are commanded to repeatedly teach and speak the words of God to their children in every action, place, and time. Thus, each aspect of life, represented in these verses as a pair of extremes (sitting and walking, rising and lying), implies that the teaching should occur during all of life between them.

In addition to the parent-child instruction, the leaders of the nation were also exhorted to teach the commands of God to the people of Israel (corporate education). Deuteronomy 31:10–13 explains that during the Festival of Booths, in the sabbatical year, the nation of Israel was to devote themselves to a detailed study of the Torah. The Old Testament reveals two instances when this corporate instruction occurred: during the reign of King Josiah (2 Kgs 23:1–3) and in the time of Ezra (Neh 7:73–9:37). The consistent neglect of this corporate instruction was a contributing factor to the involvement of the nation of Israel in idolatry and ruin. Hosea stated that the people were destroyed because of their lack of knowledge of God and His Word (Hos 4:6).[3]

---

2 Tremper Longman III and Peter Enns, *Dictionary of the Old Testament: Wisdom, Poetry & Writings* (Downers Grove, IL: InterVarsity Press, 2008), 464.

3 Duane L. Christensen, *Word Biblical Commentary: Deuteronomy* (Nashville, TN:

During the sabbatical year, the nation was to study the Word of God. Moses entrusted the Law to the priests and elders of the nation for the purpose of reading the Law in the presence of the people at the Feast of Tabernacles (Festival of Booths) during the year of release (Sabbatical year). Moses entrusted the reading of the Law to the priests and the college of elders as the spiritual leaders of the congregation of Israel.[4] The task to study the Law was not strictly for the men of the nation, but rather it was to be the task of "men and women and little ones," as Deuteronomy 31:12 suggests.

This study of the Torah included two basic elements. First, the people were to listen to the commands of God. Most of the nation was illiterate, therefore instruction often involved an oral recitation of God's laws; however, listening is not the same as learning. Therefore, secondly, the nation was to learn from the Law of God, which would culminate in the fear of God. Perry Downs states the following regarding Moses' command to learn: "The word translated 'learn' (*lamath*) is the most common Hebrew word for learning. It implies a subjective assimilation of the truth being learned, an integration of the truth into life."[5] This learning or "truth in action" resulted in a change of attitude and a change of action. This type of learning resulted in a fear of God. This fear of God implied two concepts: a literal fear of Him as God and a proper respect for his authority in one's life.[6] A proper fear of God resulted in obedience to His commands and a change of one's behavior to align with the instructions provided by God.

Nehemiah 8 provides a clear example of this corporate teaching during the Feast of Tabernacles. Several elements surface as one reads the text of Nehemiah. First, Ezra was summoned to read the Law to the nation (vv. 1–4). Second, as the Law was read, it was also interpreted so that all could understand (v. 8). Third, the people were challenged regarding their sin as they heard the Law read to them (v. 9). Fensham states the following regarding the impact of the teaching of the Law to the people: "The reading of the law and its explanation to the people had its effect.

Thomas Nelson, 2002), 766.

4 Carl F. Keil and Franz Delitzsch, *Commentary on the Old Testament: The Pentateuch* (Grand Rapids, MI: Eerdmans, 1975), 456.

5 Downs, *Teaching for Spiritual Growth*, 25.

6 Ibid., 25.

They became aware of their sins and wept. Instead of a joyous gathering, they were mourning. This reaction is not according to the character of the festival, which should be an occasion of joy."[7] Fourth, the festival was designed as a joyous occasion, but the nation was struck with grief as they understood God's commands to them (vv. 9–12). Breneman asserts, "the people realized that the Babylonian captivity was a result of disobedience. Only genuine repentance before God could bring about a real change in the community."[8] Fifth, the nation gathered the next day to study the Law to understand God's direction for them (v. 13). Breneman emphasizes the role the leaders had during this second day of instruction: "Leaders pointed out God's mercy to the people. Those who teach must show God's justice and the need for repentance but must not forget to emphasize God's love and mercy."[9] Sixth, a proper understanding of the Law led to decisive action by the nation to obey God's directives concerning the Feast of Booths (vv. 14–18). This corporate education involved the reading and explanation of the Word of God. The result of this teaching was a change of heart within the nation of Israel which produced the action of returning to the practice of worshipping God.

Second Chronicles 17:7–9 reveals another important aspect regarding corporate education within the nation of Israel—the roles of the priests, Levites, and officials (laymen) within the education of the nation. After the time of Moses, the priests played an integral role in the corporate education of the nation of Israel. The priests and Levites became the professional teachers for Israel.[10] The priests communicated the letter and meaning of the Law and were responsible to deliver to the people knowledge of both religious rituals and the history of the nation.[11] Later, during the monarchial period of Israel, there emerged a larger group of corporate teachers to assist the priests and Levites. These individuals were laymen and would eventually develop into a new class—scribes and

---

7 F. Charles Fensham, *The New International Commentary on the Old Testament: Ezra and Nehemiah* (Grand Rapids, MI: W. B. Eerdmans, 1982), 218–219.

8 Mervin Breneman, *New American Commentary: Ezra, Nehemiah, Esther* (Nashville, TN: Broadman & Holman Publishers, 1993), 227.

9 Ibid., 227.

10 Downs, *Teaching for Spiritual Growth, 25.*

11 Kenneth O. Gangel and Warren S. Benson, *Christian Education: Its History and Philosophy* (Chicago, IL: Moody Press, 1983), 24.

teachers of the law. Roland de Vaux describes this new developing class and their function within the corporate education of Israel: "Teaching was given quite apart from worship, in the synagogues, and a new class arose, of scribes and teachers of the Law. This class was open to all; priests and Levites and layfolk alike, and eventually it displaced the priestly caste in the work of teaching."[12]

Second Chronicles 17:7–9 describes the itinerate function of the officials, priests, and Levites in the corporate instruction of the people of Israel. During the reign of Jehoshaphat, groups of teaching officials were sent throughout the kingdom to educate and teach the people. Jehoshaphat's teaching mission was led by five officials (laymen) and ten religious' leaders (eight Levites and two priests). These individuals travelled from city to city within Judah teaching the people and renewing/ nurturing the faith of the Israelites.[13]

Corporate Education in the New Testament

In Acts 2 the church begins on the Day of Pentecost as the Holy Spirit descends and fills the believers as they repent and accept Jesus as their Savior. At the birth of the church and throughout its existence, corporate education has played a vital part in the teaching, growth, edifying, and equipping of the saints for the work of the ministry (Eph 4). God has used the corporate education of the church throughout the centuries in the sanctification process of the individual believer.

In Acts 2:42, immediately after the Day of Pentecost, the importance of corporate education is revealed through the ministry of the apostles. The early church community was constituted based on the apostolic teaching. This apostolic (corporate) teaching was authoritative because it was the teaching of the Lord communicated through the apostles in the power of the Spirit.[14] Richard Longenecker emphasizes the critical role of the teaching ministry of the apostles:

---

12 Roland de Vaux, *Ancient Israel: Its Life and Institutions* (London, England: McGraw Hill Book Company, 1961), 355.

13 J. A. Thompson, *New American Commentary: 1, 2 Chronicles* (Nashville, TN: Broadman & Holman, 1994), 279–280.

14 F. F. Bruce, *The Book of the Acts* (Grand Rapids, MI: Eerdmans Publishing Co, 1988), 73.

Undoubtedly the early congregation at Jerusalem, amid differences of perspective and along with a lively eschatological expectation, had a general "sense of center" provided by the historical and doctrinal teaching of the apostles. And this, Luke tells us, was pre-eminently the *raison d'eter* ("reason for being") and the focus of the early Christian community.[15]

The early church, at its inception, understood the importance of the role of corporate education in the life of the believer. Acts 2:42 reveals that the church continually "devoted" themselves to listening and learning as the apostles instructed these new believers in God's Word. It was upon this corporate teaching that individuals and the church grew both spiritually and numerically, respectively.

The importance of corporate education in the New Testament is further revealed in the ministry of the Apostle Paul. Paul, arguably the greatest pastor/missionary/evangelist of the church age, revealed the importance of the teaching ministry to which he was called. Paul described himself as "a preacher and an apostle and a teacher" (2 Tim 1:11). In 1 Corinthians 15:1–8, Paul stated to the believers in Corinth that he delivered (preached) to them that which he had received from Christ regarding the gospel. It was upon this truth that they were to stand firm during hardship and doubt. In Colossians 1:25–29, Paul stated that he was a minister "according to the stewardship from God bestowed on me for your benefit, so that I might fully carry out the *preaching of* the word of God" (v. 26). Paul believed that the function of proclamation or teaching was a critical aspect of his ministry. Paul's message to the lost was Christ. The method of proclamation was teaching with wisdom so that all might be presented complete in Christ (v. 28). Teaching was required because the mysteries of Christ require explanation and instruction. It was Paul's practice to proclaim the gospel in a new region and then remain in that region to teach the new believers the mysteries of Christ so that their lives would be conformed into the image of the Savior.[16]

Not only did Paul exemplify his passion for corporate teaching, but he also commanded Timothy to train men who would be able to continue corporate education in new churches. In 2 Timothy 2:2, Paul exhorted

---

15 Richard N. Longenecker, *EBC: John–Acts* (Grand Rapids, MI: Zondervan, 1981), 289.

16 Downs, *Teaching for Spiritual Growth,* 28.

Timothy to take the teaching that he received from Paul and "entrust these to faithful men who will be able to teach others also." Paul's concern was not to pass beliefs through proper ecclesiastical channels but rather to convey the truth of the gospel to those living in Ephesus. Paul's desire was that Timothy pass gospel truths to faithful/reliable men who would protect the church from doctrinal heresy. The "things" that are to be conveyed are the foundational truths of the gospel.[17] Paul instructed Timothy on the importance of finding reliable men who would continue the corporate education of the gospel in Ephesus after Timothy left to rejoin Paul.

The role these "faithful" men played within the education of the church can be clearly seen in Ephesians 4:11–16. God "gifted" to the church apostles, prophets, evangelists, pastors, and teachers for the equipping of the saints, for the work of the ministry, and for the building of the body of Christ (vv. 11–12). As examined in chapter 2, the pastors and teachers are linked by a single definite article in the Greek which suggests a close relationship between two groups who minister within one congregation. Although some argue that the two positions describe one office, it is more likely that the terms describe overlapping but different functions.[18] Daniel Wallace further clarifies, "All pastors were to be teachers, though not all teachers were to be pastors."[19] The role of both pastor and teacher was to feed God's flock with His Word. With regular corporate teaching by both pastor and teacher, believers would be challenged to grow spiritually.

Teachers did not simply impart information but also urged the hearers to live by what they heard (Eph 4:20–21). The resulting outcome of this faithful teaching was the equipping of the saints to perform the work of the ministry. Their teaching and exhortation would "equip, prepare, complete, train, and disciple" the body to do the work that God has called the church to perform.[20] Harold Hoehner explains the ultimate goal of these

---

17 Thomas D. Lea and Hayne P. Griffin, *NAC: 1, 2 Timothy, Titus* (Nashville, TN: Broadman Press, 1992), 201.

18 Peter T. O'Brien, *The Letter to the Ephesians* (Grand Rapids, MI: W.B. Eerdmans Publishing Co., 1999), 300.

19 Daniel B. Wallace, *Greek Grammar Beyond the Basics: An Exegetical Syntax of the New Testament with Scripture, Subject, and Greek Word Indexes* (Grand Rapids, MI: Zondervan, 1996), 284.

20 O'Brien, *The Letter to the Ephesians*, 301–304.

teachers and their teaching ministry: "Having established that the gifted people were given to the church for the immediate purpose of preparing all the saints to minister for the building up of the body of Christ, Paul explains the need for the process to continue until attaining the goal that believers mature to the measure of the fullness of Christ."[21] The result of these gifted teachers and their teachings is the preparing of the members of the body to perform the work that God has called the church to do. In addition, the corporate education of the body should continue until believers reach maturity, the measure of Christ (i.e., this teaching work does not stop until glorification).

As one examines both the corporate education of the Old Testament and New Testament periods, it is critical to note the important role that corporate teaching had on Israel and the church. In both periods, the emphasis in corporate education was on obedience to God and His Word. This obedience emerged from knowledge of God's commands and truths and an implementation of this knowledge into life and action. The Scriptures demand that corporate education be used as a vital tool in leading people to spiritual maturity.

The Catechumenate's Place within the Corporate Education of the Early Church

The first official Christian education program for the church was the catechumenate. The catechumenate, from κατηχεω (in the active meaning "to teach" or "instruct"[22] but in the passive meaning "to listen"[23]) was designed for the education of adult converts prior to joining the church through baptism. Pasquato describes the catechumenate as a critical component in Christian initiation and discipleship.

> By catechumenate, from the neo-Latin *catechumenatus* and its modern derivation from *catechumenus* (*katechoumenos*), is meant the process of formation in the church's *forma vitae*; in the ancient church

---

21 Harold W. Hoehner, *Ephesians: An Exegetical Commentary* (Grand Rapids, MI.: Baker Academic, 2002), 551.

22 Walter Bauer, William F. Arndt, Wilbur Gingrich, and Fredrick W. Danker. *A Greek-English Lexicon of the New Testament and Other Early Christian Literature* (2d. ed.; Chicago, IL: University of Chicago Press, 1979), 423.

23 Ottorino Pasquato, *Encyclopedia of Ancient Christianity, A–E: Catechumenate-Discipleship* (Downers Grove, IL: Intervarsity Press, 2014), 458.

it pertained to the reception of the three sacraments of Christian initiation [baptism, confirmation, and Eucharist], in view of Christian discipleship.[24]

The catechumenate then involved a period of instruction in which new believers were discipled and initiated into the Christian community.

Pasquato describes this important process of catechumenate as a critical step in preparing individuals for baptism and entrance into the church body.

> Initiation (typical of every religion) in primitive Christianity was aimed at introducing persons coming from paganism or Judaism to Christian discipleship. ... The catechumenate was a basic part of Christian initiation. The early church's effort in selecting and preparing candidates for baptism was substantial: a process of initiation, growth and apprenticeship through which the whole person was transformed, orienting his life in a radically new way toward the God of Jesus Christ and the church community.[25]

The goal then of the catechumenate was to take a new convert to Christianity through a process of initiation into the church family.

Three intended purposes are noticeable as the church created this Christian educational program. The first purpose was to help develop a disciplined lifestyle among new believers. A second purpose was to acquaint the catechumen (an individual in the catechumenal process) with the Christian tradition. The final purpose was to create a profound devotion to the Christian faith and way of life.[26] Individuals passed through stages of increasingly intimate fellowship and participation within the Christian community. As they progressed through these stages, the catechumens would be introduced to deeper instruction until they were admitted to baptism and then participation in the Lord's Supper. Cyril of Jerusalem provides insight as to why a process of systematic education was important.

---

24 Ibid., 458.

25 Pasquato, *Encyclopedia of Ancient Christianity, A-E: Catechumenate-Discipleship*, 459.

26 Lewis J. Sherrill, *The Rise of Christian Education* (New York, NY: The Macmillan Company, 1950), 186.

Suppose, pray, that the Catechising is a kind of building: if we do not bind the house together by regular bonds in the building, lest some gap be found, and the building become unsound, even our former labour is of no use. But stone must follow stone by course, and corner match with corner, and by our smoothing off inequalities the building must thus rise evenly. In like manner we are bringing to thee stones, as it were, of knowledge.[27]

The desire of the catechumenal process was to equip and "build" new believers through an understanding of God's Word, moral teachings from Scripture, and theological truths derived from the Bible.

The church in the first through sixth centuries lived in a pagan, immoral, and hostile world. This community of Christians had sworn loyalty to Christ and pledged themselves to obey and follow His will. Christians considered themselves soldiers of Christ and fellow soldiers with other believers. At their baptism they were "enlisted" in Christ's army. Their baptism served as a *sacramentum*, or pledge, which would be the equivalent of a military oath. They were members of the camp of Christ, and His Word served as their orders.[28] The catechumenal process prepared them to enter this militant Christian lifestyle.

A History of the Catechumenate from A.D. 150 to A.D. 420

The impetus behind the development of the catechumenate derived from the second part of Jesus' Great Commission to his disciples. Jesus states to His followers that as they make disciples, they are to be "teaching them to observe all that I commanded you" (Matt. 28:20). Alan Kreider asserts the following regarding this phrase: "In saying this, Jesus, in keeping with the emphases throughout Matthew's gospel, underscored the importance of a lived practical response to his teachings."[29] The desire was to instruct and teach these new followers in the areas of Scripture and theology in order to produce disciples. As the church moved into the post-apostolic period, there developed widespread testimony of a focused,

27 Philip Schaff, *Nicene, and Post-Nicene Fathers of the Christian Church: Cyril of Jerusalem and Gregory Nazianzen. Vol. VII* (Grand Rapids, MI: Eerdmans, 1978), 3.

28 Sherrill, *The Rise of Christian Education*, 187.

29 Alan Kreider, "Baptism, Catechism and the Eclipse of Jesus' Teaching in Early Christianity," *Tyndale Bulletin, 47(2)* (Nov. 1996), 316.

coherent plan which lasted for several years to instruct new believers: the catechumenate.[30]

Recent scholarship has challenged the idea that the catechumenate was a universal multi-year catechesis of catechumens in preparation for baptism.[31] As Bradshaw illuminates, the duration of time in the early churches of Rome, Jerusalem, and Syria indicate three-week prebaptismal catechesis.[32] Subsequently however, the question is raised by Bradshaw that this three-week period may describe the final period immediately preceding baptism and not the full duration catechesis which would be significantly longer (2–3 years).[33] Either way, the study of the rites of Christian initiation in the first five centuries of the church is really a study in diversity.[34] As Maxwell Johnson highlights, several traditions, in various regions, were active during this early church period.

> To study the rites of Christian initiation in the early church is to encounter not one but several liturgical traditions in development, each with its own unique ritual patterns, structures, and theologies: the early Aramaic or Syriac-speaking Christians centered in Edessa and, later, Nisibis, Syria (modern-day Iraq, Iran, and portions of Turkey); the Greek-speaking Syrian Christians centered in Antioch of Syria and in the Jerusalem of Syro-Palestine, and from the beginning of the fourth century, also in Armenia; the Greek-speaking Christians of Lower Egypt and the Coptic-speaking Christians of Upper Egypt, where already by the third century both liturgy and scripture had been translated into Coptic; the Latin-speaking members of the North African churches; and the, undoubtedly, multi-linguistic groups which made up the Christian communities living in Rome and elsewhere in the West. Further, these distinct

---

30 Clinton E. Arnold, "Early Church Catechesis and New Christians' Classes in Contemporary Evangelicalism," *JETS, 47* (2004), 43.

31 For further study on the differentiation of the duration of the catechumenal period see Maxwell E. Johnson, "From Three Weeks to Forty Days: Baptismal Preparation and the Origins of Lent," in *Living Water, Sealing Spirit* (Collegeville, MN: The Liturgical Press, 1995), 118–136.

32 Paul F. Bradshaw, Maxwell E. Johnson, L. Edward Phillips, and Harold W. Attridge, *The Apostolic Tradition: A Commentary* (Minneapolis, MN: Fortress Press, 2002), 98.

33 Ibid., 98.

34 Maxwell E. Johnson, "Christian Initiation," in *The Oxford Handbook of Early Christian Studies* (New York: Oxford University Press, 2008), 693.

ecclesial, linguistic, and cultural traditions will themselves come to be expressed, especially in the centuries immediately after Constantine, in those various families called "rites", those unique ways of being Christian still existing as Armenian, Byzantine, Coptic, East Syrian, Ethiopic, Maronite, and West Syrian in the Christian East, and Ambrosian (Milanese), Mozarabic (Visigothic), and Roman in the West.[35]

Within this diverse context, it is important to understand the historical development of the catechumenate from A.D. 150 until A.D. 420.

Catechumenate 2nd—3rd Century A.D. (Prior to A.D. 313)

During the period beginning in A.D. 150 until A.D. 313, the catechumenate reached its pinnacle of influence. This period is often referred to as the golden age of the catechumenate.[36] Unlike the NT period, admission to baptism was more cautious among the churches due to persecution, immorality, and doctrinal heresies that were prevalent during this period of church history.[37] Though there is dispute among scholars, early evidence indicates that the catechumenal process took between 2–3 years as the catechumens began preparation for baptism and entrance into the community of believers. Several key texts and individuals provide a picture of the catechumenal process during this period.

The *Didache*, or "The Teaching of the Lord to the Gentiles through the Apostles," dates from the late first century A.D. to the early second century A.D. This Greek text provided directions for the worship and structure of the early Christian church.[38] The first six chapters of the *Didache* serve as instructions for pre-baptismal catechesis in the "Two Ways" (of death and life). *Didache 7* provides instruction for those who have gone through this catechesis period.

> But concerning baptism, thus baptize ye: having first recited all these precepts, baptize in the name of the Father, and of the Son, and of the Holy Spirit, in running water; but if thou hast not

---

35 Ibid., 693.

36 Pasquato, *Encyclopedia of Ancient Christianity, A–E: Catechumenate-Discipleship*, 460.

37 Ibid., 460.

38 Maxwell E. Johnson, *The Rites of Christian Initiation: Their Evolution and Interpretation* (Collegeville, MN: The Liturgical Press, 2007), 43.

running water, baptize in some other water, and if thou canst not baptize in cold, in warm water; but if thou hast neither, pour water three times on the head, in the name of the Father, and of the Son, and of the Holy Spirit. But before the baptism, let him who baptizeth and him who is baptized fast previously, and any others who may be able. And thou shalt command him who is baptized to fast one or two days before.[39]

According to Maxwell Johnson, scholar on Christian initiation, the following features emerge from the *Didache* as steps in the catechesis process.

1. There is a period of pre-baptismal catechesis, but the duration is not indicated.
2. There is a one or two day fast immediately preceding baptism by the catechumens.
3. The rite of baptism followed the Trinitarian formula delineated in Matthew 28:20 and involved immersion.
4. Participation in the Eucharist (Lord's Supper) functioned as the culmination of the baptismal rite.[40]

Though the above features are prominent in the *Didache*, there is a great deal of information that the *Didache* does not reveal regarding the catechumenal process.[41]

The *Shepherd of Hermas*, a Christian literary work of the 2nd century (roughly A.D. 140) and highly regarded by early Christians including Irenaeus, describes several baptismal requirements. In addition, it highlights the seriousness of the baptismal requirements when it states,

---

39 C. H. Hoole, *Didache,* Accessed March 22, 2012, from http://www.earlychristian-writings.com/text/didache-hoole.html.

40 Johnson, *The Rites of Christian Initiation*, 45.

41 Modern scholarship has challenged the validity of the *Didache* regarding theological disputes that contradict teachings from the NT. For further examination of these disputes see Wayne Grudem, *Systematic Theology* (Leicester, England: InterVarsity Press, 1994). However, most historians value the *Didache* as a support document for early Christian studies because it provides insight into early Christian practices. Whether or not the *Didache* is theologically accurate is not the point in this dissertation. The *Didache* was used by the early church in the catechumenate as an important document in the instruction of new believers.

> But the others, which are near the waters and yet cannot roll into the water, wouldest thou know who are they? These are they that heard the word and would be baptized unto the name of the Lord. Then, when they call to their remembrance the purity of the truth, they change their minds, and go back again after their evil desires.[42]

This text indicates that there was a period of instruction prior to baptism. In addition, certain individuals would turn away from baptism due to the serious requirements that were involved in following this rite. The inference can be drawn that a period of baptismal preparation was in place before A.D. 150 and was rigorous for those who entered the baptismal rite.

Clement of Alexandria. The works of Clement of Alexandria, A.D. 150–215, a Christian theologian who taught at the Catechetical School of Alexandria, were the first to utilize the term *catechumen.* Though candidates for baptism existed prior to Clement, he provided the name that would be used into the future.[43] By the end of the 2nd century A.D., baptismal preparation was becoming institutionalized. Clement highlighted three categories of individuals in relationship to the church: those who were baptized, those in catechetical formation prior to baptism, and those who were outside the church.[44]

According to Clement, the catechetical instruction of candidates for baptism should last for three years.[45] Four features surface from Clement regarding catechetical instruction.

---

42 J. B. Lightfoot, *The Shepherd of Hermas,* Accessed August 27, 2014, from http://www.earlychristianwritings.com/text/shepherd-lightfoot.html.

43 Paul Turner, *Hallelujah Highway: A History of the Catechumenate* (Chicago: IL: Liturgy Training Publications, 2000), 23.

44 Clement of Alexandria, *The Instructor 1.6,* Accessed August 27, 2014, from http://www.ccel.org/ccel/schaff/anf02.vi.iii.i.vi.html.

45 Clement of Alexandria, *The Stromata 2:18,* Accessed August 27, 2014, from http://www.ccel.org/ccel/schaff/anf02.vi.iv.ii.xviii.html. Clement used the imagery of husbandry to describe this three-year catechetical training.

> For it orders newly planted trees to be nourished three years in succession, and the superfluous growths to be cut off, to prevent them being loaded and pressed down; and to prevent their strength being exhausted from want, by the nutriment being frittered away, enjoins tilling and digging round them, so that [the tree] may not, by sending out suckers, hinder its growth. And it does not allow imperfect fruit to be plucked from immature trees, but after three years,

1. Participation in catechetical instruction should last three years.

2. Those participating are identified as *catechumens*.

3. Preparation for baptism included preaching about Christ and instruction related to spiritual formation.

4. *Catechumens* were expected to denounce their former manner of life (behavior).[46]

Origen, A.D. 185–253, a scholar and early Christian theologian, also participated in the catechesis of candidates for baptism. His writings highlighted several features in catechetical instruction not found in previous works by Church Fathers. Origen distinguished between groups of catechumens. In other words, there were levels within the group of candidates for baptism. Origen states,

> The Christians, however, having previously, so far as possible, tested the souls of those who wish to become their hearers, and having previously instructed them in private, when they appear (before entering the community) to have sufficiently evinced their desire towards a virtuous life, introduce them then, and not before, privately forming one class of those who are beginners, and are receiving admission, but who have not yet obtained the mark of complete purification; and another of those who have manifested to the best of their ability their intention to desire no other things than are approved by Christians; and among these there are certain persons appointed to make inquiries regarding the lives and behaviour of those who join them, in order that they may prevent those who commit acts of infamy from coming into their public assembly, while those of a different character they receive with their whole heart, in order that they may daily make them better.[47]

---

in the fourth year; dedicating the first-fruits to God after the tree has attained maturity. This type of husbandry may serve as a mode of instruction, teaching that we must cut the growths of sins, and the useless weeds of the mind that spring up round the vital fruit, till the shoot of faith is perfected and becomes strong.

46 Turner, *Hallelujah Highway,* 25.

47 Origen, *Against Celsus 3:51*, Translated by Frederick Crombie, Accessed August 27, 2014, from http://www.newadvent.org/fathers/04163.htm.

In addition to different levels within catechesis, Paul Turner highlighted several features taught by Origen regarding catechesis and baptism.

1. Entrance to the catechesis involved a renunciation of idols.
2. Instruction included extensive doctrinal and moral formation.
3. Exorcisms were a regular part of the catechesis process.
4. The length and duration of catechesis was not predetermined.
5. The community offered the invitation to baptism based upon the testimony of believers (this may be the first introduction of "godparents" that will be later seen with the catechumenal process) within the church.
6. Candidates for baptism renounced Satan and proclaimed allegiance to God.
7. Candidates were anointed with oil either before or after baptism.[48]

During the 3rd and 4th century A.D., the catechumenate reached its golden age when the church established clear guidelines for the training of *catechumens*. The works of Hippolytus of Rome (Christian theologian and scholar from A.D. 170–235), as they appear in *The Apostolic Tradition*, are some of the most extensive explanations regarding the catechumenal process.[49] During the 3rd century A.D., the catechumenal process leading to baptism became very elaborate and specific. The catechumenal procedures during this period will be described in the next section; however, several features are highlighted by Paul Turner that derive from *The Apostolic Tradition*.

1. A member of the church presented the candidate to the church leaders for entrance into the catechumenate.
2. Church leaders conducted an inquiry into the candidate's conversion and background.
3. The catechumenate lasted for 3 years but could be adapted depending on level of faith.

---

48 Turner, *The Hallelujah Highway*, 35.

49 See Bradshaw, et. al., "Canons of Hippolytus" in *The Apostolic Tradition*.

4. Instruction involved doctrine, Scriptures, moral living, prayer, and hand laying.

5. Catechumens were mentored by "godparents" throughout the catechesis.

6. The catechumens were called upon to perform good works.

7. Those preparing for baptism were described as the "chosen."

8. This group underwent a second examination regarding their behavior and conduct.

9. The catechumens underwent special practices during the week leading to baptism and the night prior to baptism.

10. After baptism they were welcomed into the church family and took their first Eucharist.[50]

This period of the catechumenate ended with the clearest delineation of catechetical practices and procedures. By the end of the 3rd century and into the beginning of the 4th century A.D., the catechumenate reached its zenith regarding procedures and influence. The catechumenate would be radically altered at the beginning of the 4th century due to the "Constantinian turn" in A.D. 313.[51]

Catechumenate 4th–5th Century AD (A.D. 313–420)

Dramatic changes to the catechumenate occurred after Constantine stopped persecutions against Christians and legalized Christianity throughout the empire in A.D. 313. William Harmless highlights several cultural shifts that occurred with the "Constantinian turn" which dramatically impacted the catechumenate. First, the church ceased experiencing fierce persecutions and began a new privileged status among society. Second, due to this increased status, the church experienced an influx of new converts.[52] Third, the church experienced a series of bitter theological

---

50 Turner, *The Hallelujah Highway*, 42–43.

51 Pasquato, *Encyclopedia of Ancient Christianity, A–E: Catechumenate-Discipleship*, 463.

52 William Harmless, *Augustine and the Catechumenate*, 53. Harmless summarizes several key points from Arnold Hugh Martin Jones as to why there was an influx of converts to Christianity after Constantine's conversion: 1) The new tolerance allowed evangelical campaigns to flourish without government opposition. 2) The conversion of Constantine the emperor gave Christianity considerable publicity. 3) Constantine lavished the church with benefits which made them public centers. 4) Due to the favors

controversies. Fourth, the church witnessed the rise of several extraordinary Christian thinkers that reshaped Christian beliefs. Fifth, there was a shift in the church from the few, pure believers in Christ to a church of many (many who had not professed a true faith in Jesus Christ).[53] These shifts dramatically impacted the catechumenate that was established in the 3rd century.

David Knowles described the impact that Constantine's conversion had on Christianity and subsequently upon the catechumenate of the late 4th and 5th centuries A.D.

> ... the conversion of Constantine [produces] the swift transformation of the Church from a persecuted and fervent sect into a ruling and rapidly increasing body, favoured and directed by the emperor, membership of which was a material advantage. In the sequel, the standards of life and the level of austerity were lowered and the Christian Church became what it has in large measure remained ever since, a large body in which a few are exceptionally devout, while many are sincere believers without any pretension to fervor, and a sizeable number, perhaps even a majority, are either on their way to losing the faith, or retain it in spite of a life which neither obeys in all respects the commands of Christ nor shares in the devotional and sacramental life of the Church with regularity.[54]

Though at the end of the 5th century the catechumenate was a remnant of the institution that helped shape the church of the 2nd and 3rd centuries, several individuals continued to dramatically impact believers through the catechumenal instruction during the 4th and 5th centuries A.D. Among these were Cyril of Jerusalem, John Chrysostom, Theodore of Mopseuestia, and Augustine of Hippo.

Cyril of Jerusalem. Cyril was bishop of Jerusalem from A.D. 350–387. Cyril has provided for the church an abundance of information related to catechetical instruction. In Philip Schaff's work, *Nicene and Post-Nicene*

Constantine gave to Christians, it became popular in governmental and military circles to become a Christian. 5) Pagan cults faced mounting legislation that made it more difficult for them to practice their beliefs. Arnold Hugh Martin Jones, *The Later Roman Empire, 284–602: A Social, Economic, and Administrative Survey* (Baltimore, MD: Johns Hopkins Press, 1986), 89–97.

53 Harmless, *Augustine and the Catechumenate*, 52–55.

54 David Knowles, *Christian Monasticism* (New York, NY: McGraw-Hill, 1969), 12.

Fathers: Cyril of Jerusalem and Gregory Nazianzen, there are recorded a series of catechetical lectures by Cyril. Contained in these lectures are both lectures during catechesis as well as a series of lectures related to the "mysteries" of the church, *Mystagogical Catechesis*.[55] Cyril of Jerusalem provided insight as to why a process of systematic education was important.

> Suppose, pray, that the Catechising is a kind of building: if we do not bind the house together by regular bonds in the building, lest some gap be found, and the building become unsound, even our former labour is of no use. But stone must follow stone by course, and corner match with corner, and by our smoothing off inequalities the building must thus rise evenly. In like manner we are bringing to thee stones, as it were, of knowledge.[56]

The desire of the catechumenal process was to equip and "build" new believers through an understanding of God's Word, moral teachings from Scripture, and theological truths derived from the Bible.

From Cyril's lectures, several features regarding the catechumenate surface as Cyril taught the catechumens regarding preparation for baptism, baptism process, and post-baptismal actions and lifestyle.[57]

1. *Penitence.* The candidates were required to be diligent in attending the catechetical instruction and to live a life of strict devotion and penitential discipline during catechesis.

2. *Confession.* Cyril placed stress on the necessity of sincere inward repentance and upon open confession. To Cyril, these confessions involved two areas. First, the confession should be an inward regular confession before God.[58] Second, the confession should also involve private confession before your fellow man. Cyril attached a high value on confession. Whether these confessions were made in the privacy of solitude, or openly before the ministers of the church and the congregation, the key was to be in right standing with God.

---

55 Philip Schaff, *Nicene, and Post-Nicene Fathers of the Christian Church: Cyril of Jerusalem and Gregory Nazianzen*, Vol. VII (Grand Rapid, MI: WM. B. Eerdmans Publishing Company, 1978), 94–401.

56 Ibid., 99.

57 The following list is summarized from Schaff, *Cyril of Jerusalem*, 30–44.

58 Ibid., *Cat, 2.20*, 118.

3. *Exorcism.* Cyril enforced the duty of performing exorcisms at multiple times throughout catechesis.

4. *Renunciation.* Cyril called those who were to be baptized to renounce Satan.[59]

5. *Profession of Faith.* After the renunciation of Satan, the candidate turned to the east and professed faith and commitment to Christ.[60]

6. *Baptism by Triple Immersion.* Once the profession of faith was made, the candidate was baptized by triple immersion.[61]

7. *Chrism.* Chrism was the custom of anointing the baptized with consecrated ointment representing the anointing of Jesus by the Spirit at His Baptism.[62]

8. *First Communion.* When the rites of Baptism and Chrism were completed, the new member of the community was robed in white and participated in his/her first communion.

Cyril's lectures provided great insight into the content of instruction directed toward the catechumens at various stages in preparation. In addition, his lectures revealed that the catechumenate that was inherited from the 3rd century was still in effect from A.D. 350–387 after the "Constantinian turn" of A.D. 313.

John Chrysostom (c. A.D. 347–407), Archbishop of Constantinople, was an important early Church Father known for his preaching and public speaking. His views on the catechumenate appeared to be like Cyril of Jerusalem (specifically regarding renunciation of Satan, profession of Christ, and baptismal process). Chrysostom declared a unique perspective related to the commitment that candidates were making during catechesis. This view may have been in place in previous centuries (it most likely was), but Chrysostom highlighted this commitment to the Savior.

> After the contract of renunciation and attachment, after you have confessed His sovereignty and by the words you spoke have attached yourself to Christ, in the next place, as if you were a

---

59 Ibid., *Myst. 1.2,* 374.

60 Ibid., *Myst 1.9,* 378.

61 Ibid., *Myst 2.4,* 381.

62 Ibid., *Myst. 3.4,* 386.

combatant chosen for the spiritual arena, the priest anoints you on the forehead with the oil of the Spirit and signs you .... Henceforth from that day there is strife and counterstrife with him [Satan], and on this account the priest leads you into the spiritual arena as athletes of Christ.[63]

To Chrysostom this commitment to Christ was equated with being a soldier or gladiator in the spiritual arena. The catechumens needed to view this catechesis and ultimate membership into the community of Christ as a spiritual war with Satan.

Theodore of Mopsuestia. Theodore was bishop of Mopsuestia from A.D. 392 to 428. His homilies related to catechesis are like John Chrysostom's writing. However, Theodore of Mopsuestia gave great importance to the role of the "godfather" or "godparents" in the life of a candidate for baptism. These individuals were assigned to the candidate from the beginning and were actively involved throughout catechesis. They mentored individuals in the teachings that they had learned through lectures by the church leaders. They also attested to the growth that the *catechumens* had experienced throughout catechesis.

He, therefore, who is desirous of drawing near to baptism comes to the Church of God through which he expects to reach that life of the heavenly abode. He ought to think that he is coming to be the citizen of a new and great city, and he should, therefore, show great care in everything that is required of him before his enrolment in it. He comes to the Church of God where he is received by a duly appointed person—as there is a habit to register those who draw near to baptism—who will question him about his mode of life in order to find out whether it possesses all the requisites of the citizenship of that great city. After he has abjured all the evil found in this world and cast it completely out of his mind, he has to show that he is worthy of the citizenship of the city and of his enrolment in it. This is the reason why, as if he were a stranger to the city and to its citizenship, a specially appointed person, who is from the city in which he is going to be enrolled and who is well versed in its mode of life, conducts him to the registrar and testifies for him to the effect that he is worthy of the city and of its citizenship and that, as he is not versed in the life of the city or in the knowledge

---

63 John Chrysostom, *Baptismal Instructions, 2:22–23* (Mahwah, NJ: Paulist Press, 1963), 51–52.

of how to behave in it, he himself would be willing to act as a guide to his inexperience. This rite is performed for those who are baptized by the person called godfather, who, however, does not make himself responsible for them in connection with future sins, as each one of us answers for his own sins before God. He only bears witness to what the catechumen has done and to the fact that he has prepared himself in the past to be worthy of the city and of its citizenship. He is justly called a sponsor because by his words (the catechumen) is deemed worthy to receive baptism. When in this world there is an order of the Government for a census of countries and of people who are in them, it is right for those who are registered in particular countries to obtain a title which would assure for them the cultivation of the fields which are registered in their name, and to pay readily the land taxes to the king. The same thing is required of the one who is enrolled in the heavenly city and in its citizenship, as "our conversation is in heaven." Indeed he ought to reject all earthly things, as is suitable to the one who is inscribed in heaven, and to do only the things that fit the life and conversation in heaven. He will also, if he is wise, pay perpetual taxes to the king and live a life which is consonant with baptism. ... It is for this reason that as regards you also who draw near to the gift of baptism, a duly appointed person inscribes your name in the Church book, together with that of your godfather, who answers for you and becomes your guide in the city and the leader of your citizenship therein. This is done in order that you may know that you are, long before the time and while still on the earth, enrolled in heaven, and that your godfather who is in it is possessed of great diligence to teach you, who are a stranger and a newcomer to that great city, all the things that pertain to it and to its citizenship, so that you should be conversant with its life without any trouble and anxiety.[64]

For Theodore of Mopseuestia, the "godparents" played an important role in catechesis. They attested to the spiritual growth of their assigned catechumen prior to baptism. From this example, mentorship was an important aspect in catechesis.

---

64 Theodore of Mopseustia, *Commentary on the Lord's Prayer, Baptism and the Eucharist*, Translated by Alphonse Mingana, 1933, Accessed August 28, 2014 from http://www.ccel.org/ccel/pearse/morefathers/files/theodore_of_mopsuestia_lordsprayer_02_text.htm#3.

Augustine of Hippo. The impact that Augustine of Hippo (A.D. 354–430) had upon Western Christianity and continues to have on current theology cannot be overstated.[65] Augustine followed the example of those Church Fathers before him in relationship to the catechumenate. However, Augustine paid significant attention to theological truths in the education of catechumens, especially in relationship to sin.[66] In addition, Augustine placed great emphasis on the "scrutinies" of the catechumens. Thomas Finn provided a glimpse into a scrutiny that occurred in North Africa (the region in which Augustine ministered). This may provide insight into the level of commitment that Augustine alluded to in his "scrutinies."

> In the eerie light of first dawn the candidates stood barefoot on the course animal skins (*cilicium*), naked and with head bowed. Invoking the power of Christ and the Trinity, voicing vituperative biblical condemnations of Satan, and imposing hands, the exorcist hissed in the faces of competentes, peremptorily commanding the Evil One to depart. There followed a physical examination to determine whether any of the competentes showed evidence of a disease, which signaled the continued inhabitation of Satan. Granted that they passed scrutiny, the competentes, each in her or his own voice, then renounced Satan, his pomps, and his service.[67]

Along with the scrutinies, Augustine urged moral formation. He stated, "I instruct by discourses: do you advance in good works. I scatter the teaching of the word; do you render the fruit of faith. Let us all run in His way and path according to the vocation in which we have been called by the Lord; let no one look back."[68] To Augustine, his role as church

65 For excellent biographies on the life of Augustine and his impact on Christianity see Peter Brown, *Augustine of Hippo* (Berkley, CA: University of California Press, 1967), James J. O'Donnell, *Augustine: A New Biography* (New York, NY: Harper Perennial, 2006), John M. Rist, *Augustine: Ancient Thought Baptized* (Cambridge, UK: The Cambridge University Press, 1994), and R. A. Markus, *Saeculum: History and Society in the Theology of St Augustine* (Cambridge, UK: The Cambridge University Press, 1989).

66 Johnson, *The Rites of Christian Initiation*, 185.

67 Thomas M. Finn, *Early Christian Baptism and the Catechumenate: Italy, North Africa, and Egypt* (Collegeville, MN: Liturgical Press, 1992), 155.

68 Augustine, "Sermon 216: To the Seekers," in *The Fathers Of The Church A New Translation Volume 38*, Translated by Mary Sarah Muldowney, Accessed August 28, 2014 from https://archive.org/stream/fathersofthechur009512mbp/fathersoft-

139

leader was to provide the teaching of the Scriptures. It was the role of the catechumen to practice this teaching. Moral formation was a key component in Augustine's catechumenal process. Augustine, though his practice was similar to other Church Fathers of that time period, provided a vast amount of material that has survived related to the instruction of *catechumens.*

Augustine placed great emphasis on the catechetical process. In Augustine's work, "On the Catechizing of the Uninstructed," a letter written to Deogratias, a teacher in Carthage who was struggling with discouragement in his ministry pertaining to the catechetical process, Augustine functioned as a mentor providing advice to continue carrying out the important function of catechizing new believers.[69] For Augustine, the

---

hechur009512mbp_djvu.txt.

69 Philip Schaff, "On the Catechising of the Uninstructed," *Augustine: On the Holy Trinity, Doctrinal Treatises, Moral Treatises* (Peabody, MA: Hendrickson Publishers, 1994), 616–617.

> You have requested me, brother Deogratias, to send you in writing something which might be of service to you in the matter of catechising the uninstructed. For you have in-formed me that in Carthage, where you hold the position of a deacon, persons, who have to be taught the Christian faith from its very rudiments, are frequently brought to you by reason of your enjoying the reputation of possessing a rich gift in catechising, due at once to an intimate acquaintance with the faith, and to an attractive method of discourse; but that you almost always find yourself in a difficulty as to the manner in which a suitable declaration is to be made of the precise doctrine, the belief of which constitutes us Christians: regarding the point at which our statement of the same ought to commence, and the limit to which it should be allowed to proceed: and with respect to the question whether, when our narration is concluded, we ought to make use of any kind of exhortation, or simply specify those precepts in the observance of which the person to whom we are discoursing may know the Christian life and profession to be maintained. At the same time, you have made the confession and complaint that it has often befallen you that in the course of a lengthened and languid address you have become profitless and distasteful even to yourself, not to speak of the learner whom you have been endeavoring to instruct by your utterance, and the other parties who have been present as hearers; and that you have been constrained by these straits to put upon me the constraint of that love which I owe to you, so that I may not feel it a burdensome thing among all my engagements to write you something on this subject. As for myself then, if, in the exercise of those capacities which through the bounty of our Lord I am enabled to present, the same Lord requires me to offer any manner of aid to those whom He has made brethren to me, I feel constrained not only by that love and service which is due from me

catechumenal process was one of the most important functions of the church.

In summary, the period of the catechumenate from A.D. 313–420 saw an emphasis on communal liturgies involving instructions related to lay teachers (godparents), penitential rites, and catechesis with creed. Exorcisms were a common practice as *competentes* approached the baptismal phase. Specific catechetical procedures were practiced through various regions during this period. These procedures will be examined in the next section.

By the end of the 5th century, the catechumenate was all but extinct. Michel Dujarier provided a picture of the grim remnants of the catechumenate at the end of the 5th century A.D.

> The entry into the catechumenate had lost its character of being a step taken in faith. Since the evangelization had not been thorough enough, the candidates were not ready to "hear the word." They were not truly converted. They saw the Church they entered as a simple institution from which they expected only advantages. ... It is important to understand that the devaluation of the entry into the catechumenate is at the source of the devaluation of the catechumenate, for catechumenal formation cannot be experienced authentically except by subjects who actually believe in Christ. ... The true meaning of baptism became blurred. While access to the sacrament was a matter of "election" for Hippolytus, it seems that from this time on some catechumens looked on it as a right. ... Baptism was even considered by some as a kind of insurance, which one took out at the very last moment to get the maximum advantage for the minimum cost, or as an arduous obligation one had to accept to avoid hell. ... Because of the liberty it [the church] enjoyed from 313 on and the privileges it acquired, it ran the danger of being contaminated by the mentality of the

---

to you on the terms of familiar friendship, but also by that which I owe universally to my mother the Church, by no means to refuse the task, but rather to take it up with a prompt and devoted willingness. For the more extensively I desire to see the treasure of the Lord distributed, the more does it become my duty, if I ascertain that the stewards, who are my fellow-servants, find any difficulty in laying it out, to do all that lies in my power to the end that they may be able to accomplish easily and expeditiously what they sedulously and earnestly aim at.

world and of forgetting that it had to be the "soul of the world" by living evangelically.[70]

The history of the catechumenate saw dramatic advances during the 2nd and 3rd centuries A.D. During the 4th, after the influx of new Christians, the catechumenate struggled to maintain its unique identity as an intense process of initiation for entrance into the church. By the end of the 5th century, the catechumenate was all but extinct as the criteria for initiation dramatically decreased.

Catechumenal Procedures

As indicated in the history of the catechumenate, various traditions from diverse cultures and regions impacted the structure of catechesis.[71] However, in the golden age of the catechumenate (2nd–4th centuries A.D.) a well-defined structure of preparation for baptism was in place.[72] The catechumenal procedures during this period occurred in multiple stages over a multi-year period. The basis for this structure appears to find its origins in the NT writings.

Modern scholarship has postulated that a catechumenal process can be seen in the book of Acts. Michel Dujarier argues that a catechumenal process can be seen as early as Acts 2 at the day of Pentecost. Dujarier highlights the following catechumenal steps:

1. There is a kerygmatic announcement (Acts 2:14–36).
2. There is a conversion of individuals (Acts 2:37).
3. There is a period of catechesis (Acts 2:38–40).
4. This period of instruction ends with a second round of questions regarding whether the convert has applied the message to their lives—"received his word" (Acts 2:41).
5. They are admitted to baptism (Acts 2:41).[73]

---

70 Michel Dujarier, *A History of the Catechumenate: The First Six Centuries* (New York, NY: William H. Sadlier Inc., 1979), 107–109.

71 See Appendix 3 for a summary chart by Maxwell Johnson of the 2nd and 3rd century catechetical structures.

72 See Bradshaw, et. al., *The Apostolic Tradition,* and Pasquato, *Encyclopedia of Ancient Christianity, A–E: Catechumenate-Discipleship.*

73 Michel Dujarier, *A History of the Catechumenate,* 19–21.

Ottorino Pasquato asserts that the salvation to baptism process of the Roman centurion as seen in Acts 10:1–11:18 provides a glimpse into the catechumenal structure that was in place during the 1st century A.D. The catechumenal steps are as follows:

1. Questioning of the new convert by the person in charge—Peter (Acts 10:21).
2. The candidate's response to the questioning (Acts 10:22).
3. The candidate asks to be admitted to catechesis (Acts 10:33).
4. The request rests on assurances from sponsors (Acts 10:4, 22).
5. Catechesis begins (Acts 10:34–43).
6. The focus of instruction is Christ, the one Lord (Acts 10:36–42).
7. The aim of catechesis is to arouse an unconditional faith in Christ and look ahead to confirmation through baptism (Acts 10:43).
8. The authenticity of faith is attested by God, who sends the Holy Spirit (Acts 10:44).
9. Peter baptizes Cornelius (Acts 10:48).[74]

Whether this delineation of procedures from the book of Acts provided the framework for the catechumenate is speculative; however, by the 2nd century A.D. a defined process of catechumenal procedures was in place. The entire catechumenal process took several years to complete, and the new convert proceeded through various stages during these years in preparation for baptism.

1st Stage (preliminaries or entrance)

Entrance to the catechumenate was not granted immediately. There was a period of probation so that the church leaders could determine whether the candidate had experienced conversion. This conversion manifested itself in a changed lifestyle.[75] A question is posed as to whether these individuals who entered the catechumenate were believers or unbelievers.

---

74 Pasquato, *Encyclopedia of Ancient Christianity, A–E: Catechumenate-Discipleship*, 460.

75 Michel Dujarier, *A History of the Catechumenate*, 60.

At the beginning of the *Apostolic Tradition* (an accumulation of material from different sources from a variety of geographical regions dating to the mid-second century A.D.), the following statement appears which provides insight into the question of whether the individuals entering the catechumenal process were believers: "Concerning newcomers, those who will give their assent to the faith."[76] The initial interviewing teacher was further instructed: "Let them be asked the reason why they have given their assent to the faith."[77] One can infer from these statements that the new people coming to the church and entering the catechumenal process have a rudimentary level of faith. They have heard the gospel message and have exercised faith in that message. These individuals, after a profession of faith, now desire to join the community of believers by giving themselves to a period of rigorous study and preparation for baptism.[78]

The first stage of the catechumenal process (*preliminaries*) involved three primary steps. First, the individual was asked a series of questions pertaining to their motives for conversion.[79] Second, the candidate was asked questions regarding status in life.[80] Last, the candidate was asked

---

76 Bradshaw, et. al., *The Apostolic Tradition: A Commentary,* 82.

77 Ibid., 82.

78 Arnold, *JETS,* 42.

79 Bradshaw, et. al., "Apostolic Constitutions 8.32.2–6," *The Apostolic Tradition,* 83. "Let those first coming to the mystery of the godly life be brought by the deacons to the bishop or to the presbyters and let them be examined as to why they came to the Word of the Lord. Let those who brought them give witness to them, after examining the things concerning them." In addition, the "Canons of Hippolytus 10" in *The Apostolic Tradition,* 83 also highlights the initial questioning of the candidate. "Those who come to the church in order to become Christians are to be examined with all rigors for what motive have they abandoned their religion, for fear lest they enter out of mockery." Also, "Testamentum Domini 2.1" in *The Apostolic Tradition,* 83 highlights this initial questioning. "Let those who first come to hear the Word, before they enter among all the people, first come to teachers at home, and let them be examined as to all the cause [of their coming] with all accuracy, so that their teachers may know for what they have come, or with what will. And if they have come with a good will and love, let them be diligently taught."

80 Ibid., 83. *Apostolic Constitutions 8.32.2–6.*

> And let them examine also their manner and life and whether they are slave or free. And if someone is a slave, let him be asked who his master is; and if he is a slave of one of the faithful, let his master be asked if he testifies to him. But if not, let him be rejected until that time he may show himself worthy to the master. But if he does testify to him, let him be accepted. But if he is a house-

questions regarding whether he/she was involved in trades or professions that must be abandoned because they are not compatible with the Christian life.[81] Once the individual provided adequate answers to the above

---

hold slave to a heathen, let him be taught to please his master in order that the Word not be blasphemed. If, then, he has a wife, or the woman a husband, let them be taught to be content in themselves. But if they are not married, let them be taught not to fornicate but to marry in the law. But if his master, being of faith and knowing that he fornicates, does not give him a wife, or a husband to the woman, let him be separated. And if anyone has a demon, let him be taught the godly life, but do not let him enter into the community before he has been purified. But if death is hastening, let him be accepted.

Canons of Hippolytus 10, stated, "If he is a slave and his master idolatrous, and his master forbids him, he is not to be baptized, but it suffices that he is a Christian; even if he dies without having received the gift, he is not to be excluded from the flock." In *Testamentum Domini 2.1*, the following is stated:

But let those who bring them be such as are well on in years, faithful who are known by the church; and let them bear witness about them, if they are able to hear [the Word]. Also let their life and conversation be asked about: if they are not contentious, if quiet, if meek, not speaking vain things or despisers or foul speakers, or buffoons or leaders astray, or ridicule mongers. Also if any of them have a wife or not. ... And also let him who comes be asked if he is a slave or free; and if the slave of one who is faithful, and if also his master permit him, let him hear. But if his master is not faithful and does not permit him, let him be persuaded to permit him. And if [his master] says truly about him that he wishes to become a Christian because he hates his masters, let him be cast out. But if no cause be shown of hatred of servitude, but [if] he [really] wishes to be a Christian, let him hear. But if his master is faithful and does not bear witness to him, let him be cast out. Similarly if [a woman] is the wife of a man, let the woman be taught to please her husband in the fear of God. But if both of them desire to serve purity in piety, they have a reward. Let him who is unmarried not commit fornication, but let him marry in the law. But if he desires to persevere thus, let him abide in the Lord. If anyone is tormented with a devil, let him not hear the Word from a teacher until he is cleansed. For the intelligence, when consumed with a material spirit, does not receive the immaterial and holy Word. But if he is cleansed, let him be instructed in the Word."

81 Ibid., 89–93. *Apostolic Constitutions 8.32.7–13* stated:

If anyone is a brothel keeper, either let him stop his pimping or be rejected. Let a prostitute who comes either stop or be rejected. Let an idol maker who comes either stop or be rejected. If any of them belongs to the theater, whether man, woman, charioteer, gladiator, stadium runner, trainer of athletes, one who participates in the Olympic Games, or one who accompanies the chorus on flute, lute, or lyre, or who puts on a display of dancing or is a fraudulent trader, let them either stop or be rejected. Let a soldier who comes be taught to do no injustice or to extort money, but to be content with his given wages. Let the one who objects be rejected. A doer of unmentionable things, a lustful person, a lascivious person, a magician, a mob leader, a charmer, an astrologer, a diviner, a charmer of wild beasts, a pimp, a maker of charms, one who purifies by applying objects, a fortuneteller, an interpreter of oracles, an interpreter of bodily vibrations, one who, upon encountering them, observes defects of eyes or feet or birds, or cats, or loud noises, or significant chance remarks—let them be examined for a time, for the evil is hard to wash out. Then, let those who stop be received, but let those not persuaded be rejected. Let a concubine who is a slave of some unbeliever, who devotes herself to that one alone, be received. But if she behaves licentiously toward others, let her be rejected. If a person of faith has a concubine, if a slave, let him stop and marry in the law. But if free, let him marry her in the law. But if not, let him be rejected."

Canons of Hippolytus 11–15 stated:

Every craftsman is to be told not to make any image, or any idol, whether he is a sculptor, silversmith, or painter, or of any other art. If they happen after baptism to make any such thing, except what the people need, they are to be excluded until they repent. Whoever becomes director of a theater, or a wrestler, or a runner, or teaches music, or plays before the processions, or teaches the art of the gladiator, or a hunter, or a hairdresser, or a fighter with savage beasts, or a priest of idols, all these, one is not to reveal to them any of the Holy Word, until they are purified first from these impure occupations. Then, during forty days they are to hear the Word, and if they are worthy they are to be baptized. The teacher of the church is the one who judges this matter. A schoolmaster who teaches little children, if he has not a livelihood by which to live except for that, may educate, if he reveals at all times to those he teaches and confesses that what the heathen call gods are demons, and says before them every day there is no divinity except the Father, the Son, and the Holy Spirit. If he can teach his pupils the excellent word of the poet, and better still if he can teach them the faith of the word of truth, for that he shall have a reward. Whoever has received the authority to kill, or else a soldier, they are not to kill in any case, even if they receive the order to kill. They are not to pronounce a bad word. Those who have received an honor are not to wear wreaths on their heads. Whosoever is raised to the authority of prefect or the magistracy and does not put on the righteousness of the gospel is to be excluded from the flock and the bishop is not to pray with him. A Christian must not become a soldier, unless he is compelled by a chief bearing the sword. He is not to burden himself with the sin of blood. But if he has shed blood, he is not to partake of the mysteries, unless he is purified by a punishment, tears, and wailing. He is not to come forward deceitfully but in the fear of God. A fornicator or one who lives on the proceeds of fornication, or an effeminate, and especially one who speaks of shameful [things], or an idler, or a profligate, or a magician or an astrologer, or a diviner, or an interpreter of dreams, or a snake charmer, or an agitator who agitates the people, or one who makes phylacteries, or a usu-

questions or changed his/her manner of life to match with the criteria for acceptance into the catechumenate, he/she could advance to the second stage of the catechumenal process.

---

rer, or an oppressor, or one who loves the world, or one who loves swearing, that is, oaths, or one who makes reproaches against the people, or one who is a hypocrite, or a slanderer of people, or who decides if the hours and the days are favorable, all these and the like, do not catechize them and baptize them, until they have renounced all occupations of this sort, and three witnesses have testified for them that they really have renounced all these vices, because often a man remains in his passions until his old age, unless he is enabled by a great power. If they are found after baptism in vices of this sort, they are to be excluded from the church until they repent with tears, fasting, and alms.

Testamentum Domini 2.2 stated:

If a fornicatress, or a brothel keeper, or a drunkard, or a maker of idols, or a painter, or one engaged in shows, or a charioteer, or a wrestler, or one who goes to the contest, or a combatant [in the games], or one who teaches wrestling, or a public huntsman, or a priest of idols, or a keeper of them, be [among those that come], let him not be received. If any such desires to become faithful, let him cease from these [things]; and being in deed faithful, and being baptized, let him be received and let him partake. And if he does not cease, let him be rejected. If anyone is a teacher of boys in worldly wisdom, it is well if he ceases. But if he has no other craft by which to live, let him be excused. If anyone be a soldier or in authority, let him be taught not to oppress or to kill or to rob, or to be angry or to rage and afflict anyone. But let those rations suffice him that are given to him. But if they wish to be baptized in the Lord, let them cease from military service or from the [post of] authority, and if not let them not be received. Let a catechumen or a believer of the people, if he desires to be a soldier, either cease from his intention, or if not let him be rejected. For he has despised God by his thought, and leaving the things of the Spirit, he has perfected himself in the flesh, and has treated the faith with contempt. If a fornicatress or a dissolute man or a drunkard do not do [these things], and desire, believing, to be catechumens, they may [be admitted]. And if they make progress, let them be baptized; but if not let them be rejected. If a concubine of a man is a servant, and desires to believe, if she educates those who are born [of her] and she separates from her master, or be joined to him alone in marriage, let her hear; and being baptized let her partake in the offering, but if not let her be rejected. He who does things that may not be spoken of, or a diviner or a magician or a necromancer, these are defiled and do not come to judgment. Let a charmer, or an astrologer, or an interpreter of dreams, or a sorcerer, or one who gathers together the people, or a stargazer, or a diviner by idols, either cease, and when he ceases let him be exorcised and baptized; or if not, let him be rejected. If a man has a concubine, let him divorce her and marry in the law and hear the word of instruction.

Origen, in his writings to believers who were facing martyrdom, reminds them of the commitment they made at the beginning of the catechumenate process. If these individuals had not dedicated themselves to complete commitment to Christ, they would not have been accepted by the church leaders to enter catechesis. They were to remember their commitment to Christ.

> At the beginning when you were to be instructed in the Christian faith it would have been reasonable to say to you: "If you do not wish to serve the Lord, choose you this day whom you will serve, whether the gods of your fathers on the far side of the river or the gods of the Amorites, among whom you inhabit the land." And the catechist might have said to you: "As for me and my house, we will serve the Lord, for he is holy." But now it is not possible to say this to you. For at that time you said: "God forbid that we should forsake the Lord and serve other gods. The Lord our God, he is God, who brought us and our fathers up out of Egypt and kept us in all the way in which we journeyed." Moreover, in the agreements concerning religion you long ago made this reply to your instructors: "We will serve the Lord, for he is our God."[82]

This first stage was completed once the church leaders (instructors) had verified that the candidate was a believer who had demonstrated a verifiable conversion and was committed to serving God alone.

2nd Stage (catechesis period)

The catechesis stage of the catechumenal practice typically lasted between 2–3 years in duration.[83] The *Apostolic Tradition* requires that the candidates be taught for no less than three years. However, if one excelled during this catechesis stage the time of his/her baptism could be accelerated to allow an earlier entrance into the community of believers.[84]

---

82 Henry Chadwick and J. E. L. Oulton, *Alexandrian Christianity: Selected Translations of Clement and Origen* (Louisville, KY: Westminster John Knox Press, 2006), 404–405.

83 Pasquato, *Encyclopedia of Ancient Christianity, A–E: Catechumenate-Discipleship*, 461.

84 Bradshaw, et. al., "Apostolic Constitutions 8.32.16," *The Apostolic Tradition*, 97. "Let the one coming to be catechized be instructed for three years. But if anyone is eager and has zeal for the task, let him be received, for it is not the time but the way that is judged."

During the second stage of the catechumenal process, the candidate was identified as a "hearer" and received instruction privately within a class setting. In addition, the hearers were persons admitted to the first part of the Christians' worship service to hear the lectures and oral instruction (*missa catechumenorum*). Origen describes that there was a division of classes within this second stage of the catechumenal process.

> They privately appoint one class consisting of recent beginners who are receiving elementary instruction and have not yet received the sign that they have been purified, and another class of those who, as far as they are able, make it their set purpose to desire nothing other than those things of which Christians approve. Among the latter class some are appointed to inquire into the lives and conduct of those who want to join the community in order that they may prevent those who indulge in trickery from coming to their common gathering; those who do not do this they whole-heartedly receive, and make them better every day.[85]

This second stage involved an increase of scriptural and moral instruction as "hearers" progressed forward toward baptism and entrance into the community. These "hearers" were required to live in a morally acceptable manner approved by the body of believers.

The *Apostolic Tradition* provides a list of several areas of moral obligations that were required of the catechumen during this second inquiry or scrutiny. The catechumens "having been examined (if they lived virtuously while they were catechumens, and if they honored the widows, and if they visited those who are sick, and if they fulfilled every good work), and when those who brought them testify in his behalf that he acted thus, then let them hear the gospel."[86] One can gather that a high priority was placed upon a life of faith and practice of charity and justice.[87]

During this stage of catechesis, the instructor was entrusted with the important task of educating and training catechumens for entrance into the community. They were also the ones who guaranteed the moral

---

85 Henry Chadwick, *Origen: Contra Celsum* (Cambridge, UK: Cambridge University Press, 1953), 163.

86 Bradshaw et. al., *The Apostolic Tradition*, 104.

87 William Harmless, *Augustine and the Catechumenate* (Collegeville, MN: Liturgical Press, 1995), 43.

excellence, conduct, and dignity of the catechumens.[88] Though a specific manual of education that was consistent throughout the church does not exist, lectures from Cyril of Jerusalem, Augustine, and other church fathers reveal the importance that the church leaders placed on the instruction of the Scriptures, theological truths, and moral conduct.

3rd Stage (competentes or election)

The next stage of the catechumenal process involved advanced study of Christian doctrine and tradition. This stage usually took place during the second or third year of training depending upon the Eastern or Western Church's traditions. Before entrance into the 3rd stage, the catechumens were examined again regarding moral living. The sponsors of the catechumens had to testify to the conduct of the catechumens during the 2nd stage (the instructional period).[89] When one had been a hearer for a required length of time, one would undergo a second inquiry to discover if he or she was living a morally satisfactory life by Christian standards. These inquiries were called "scrutinies." The inquiry was a "scrutiny" of life to genuinely attest whether the candidate was living a Christian lifestyle.[90] According to Pasquato, this examination was assessed by the godparents (those believers assigned to the catechumens to mentor the candidates in moral conduct).[91] The *Apostolic Tradition* describes this examination prior to the final stage of the catechumenal process.

> Let them be proved and investigated first, how they have lived while catechumens, if they have honored widows, if they have visited the sick, if they have walked in all meekness and love, if they were earnest in good works. But let them be attested by those who bring them. And when they hear the gospel, let a hand be laid on them daily.[92]

This examination would lead to a period of advanced education before the final stage of baptismal preparation.

---

88 Pasquato, *Encyclopedia of Ancient Christianity, A–E: Catechumenate-Discipleship*, 461.

89 Dujarier, *A History of the Catechumenate*, 52.

90 Sherrill, *The Rise of Christian Education*, 189.

91 Pasquato, *Encyclopedia of Ancient Christianity, A–E: Catechumenate-Discipleship*, 461.

92 Bradshaw et. al., "Testamentum Dominin 2.6," *The Apostolic Tradition*, 105.

During this 3rd stage the catechumens were identified as *competentes*.[93] *Competentes* were approved morally and were now approaching the final instruction that would culminate in their baptism. This final instruction was an intensive educational process that covered aspects of baptism, church membership, and service within the body. When the catechumen became a *competente*, he/she was scrutinized, indoctrinated through an advanced study of scriptural/theological truths, and disciplined. This period was much shorter than the 2nd stage, but the preparation was more intense and specialized.[94]

In the Eastern Church, the bishop examined the *competentes* and required testimony be given by fellow believers as to the quality of lifestyle being lived by the candidates for baptism. If the candidate qualified, he/she had their name registered in the *Diptychs of the Living* along with the name of their sponsor. In *The Pilgrimage of Ethoria*, a 4th-century account of a Galician woman who made a pilgrimage to the Holy Land about 381–384 and wrote an account of her journey in a long letter to a circle of women back at home, the following quotation describes this scrutiny and registration of the *competentes*.

> Then the bishop asks the neighbours of every one who has entered concerning each individual, saying: "Does this person lead a good life, is he obedient to his parents, is he not given to wine, nor deceitful?" making also inquiry about the several vices which are more serious in man. And if he has proved him in the presence of witnesses to be blameless in all these matters concerning which he has made inquiry, he writes down his name with his own hand. But if he is accused in any matter, he orders him to go out, saying: "Let him amend, and when he has amended then let him come to the font (*lavacrum*)." And as he makes inquiry concerning the men, so also does he concerning the women.[95]

---

93 Ibid., 458.

94 Lawrence D. Folkemer, "A Study of the Catechumenate," *Studies in Early Christianity* (New York, NY: Garland Publishing Inc., 1993), 291.

95 M. L. McClure and Charles L. Feltoe. *The Pilgrimage of Ethoria*. Accessed March 14, 2012, from http://www.ccel.org/m/mcclure/etheria/etheria.htm.

Following the registration of the *competentes*, the candidates advance into an advanced training for baptism. This intensive (special) instruction might occupy as many as three hours a day for seven weeks.[96]

4th Stage (baptismal period)

The ensuing step was the process of baptism. The baptismal period appears to coincide with the week prior to Easter Sunday (the Passion Week). On Thursday of the Passion Week the candidates for baptism perform ritual baths. On Friday and Saturday, the candidates fast in preparation for baptism. The *competentes* came to the baptistery on the night prior to Easter Sunday. There they engaged in a prayer vigil throughout the night and a memorization of the Apostles' Creed. Part of this process involved a *suntasso* in which they covenanted themselves to Christ with a preparation of readiness to obey his command.[97]

Ottorino Pasquato lists the order of events that occurred on Saturday night into Easter Sunday.

1. They keep vigil with Bible readings and catechesis.
2. At the cockcrow, there is a renunciation of Satan.
3. Anointing with oil for exorcism.
4. A threefold question of faith.
5. Administration of baptism by immersion.
6. Bishop administers confirmation.
7. The neophytes enter the assembly of the faithful where they participate in the Eucharist with the faithful.[98]

Lewis Sherrill also provides a description of the events that occurred on the Saturday evening into Easter Sunday morning. His description expounds upon certain features throughout the evening in preparation for baptism.

> Their instruction completed, the *competentes* came to the baptistery on the night before Easter. The service began with the renunciation of Satan. Turning to the west, the region of darkness, the candidates stretched out their hands, in some instances striking

---

96 Ibid.

97 Sherrill, *The Rise of Christian Education*, 193.

98 Pasquato, *Encyclopedia of Ancient Christianity, A–E: Catechumenate-Discipleship*, 461.

them together and spitting in defiance, and repeated the formula of renunciation. The second act was a profession of obedience to Christ. Turning to the east, the region of light, the candidate, with hands and eyes lifted to heaven, repeated the words, "I covenant myself to Thee, O Christ." The word *suntasso*, to covenant with, meant to give oneself over to the government of another, in readiness to obey his command. Then came the candidate's profession of faith, uttered in the words of the baptismal creed which might be in use. This creed had been secretly "delivered" to the candidate by the catechist, and now was "given back" as a pledge or symbol of the faith he held. It was deemed a sign or password by which the faithful might be known. Having removed his garments, the candidate entered the baptistery, and was anointed. Replying to the three-fold interrogation he again made his confession of faith in the words of the same creed, and was thrice baptized. Perhaps at this point he prayed the Lord's Prayer; and he partook of his first Communion.[99]

With this final stage completed with the celebration of baptism, the catechumen joined the community of believers.[100]

The catechumenal process was viewed as a critical step in the growth of a new believer by well-known church leaders in the first four centuries of the church. Men such as Origen, Tertullian, Hippolytus, Ambrose, Cyprian, Gregory of Nyssa, John Chrysostom, Theodore of Mopsuestia, Cyril of Jerusalem, Augustine, and others devoted themselves to the task of teaching new believers.[101] As has already been shown, Augustine's interaction with Deogratias shows the importance that was placed upon the catechetical process.[102]

The catechumenate developed as a corporate educational tool to be used to train new believers to understand what they believe, why they believe it, how to defend it, and how to live it in a hostile world. This process was not a quick process (not the customary 4–8 weeks, as is often seen in

99 Lewis J. Sherrill, *The Rise of Christian Education* (New York, NY: The Macmillan Company, 1950), 192–193.

100 A detailed description of the baptismal proceedings are described by Bradshaw et. al., *The Apostolic Tradition*, 105–121. See Appendix 4.

101 Arnold, *JETS*, 45.

102 Philip Schaff, *Augustine: On the Holy Trinity, Doctrinal Treatises, Moral Treatises* (Peabody, MA: Hendrickson Publishers, 1994), 283–314.

churches today) but rather was accomplished through various interviews, lectures, and mentorship over a period of two to three years. The pastors/bishops of the Patristic period saw the value and need for this corporate education for the growth of individuals within their congregations.

Content Taught During the Catechumenate

The Scriptures

Within the entire catechumenal process various theological and biblical topics were taught to the catechumens. One major feature on the catechumenal process was the immersion of new believers in the Word of God. In the *Canons of Hippolytus*, part of the *Apostolic Tradition*, Hippolytus states that catechumens are "to be instructed in the Scriptures."[103] The assumption, because of the oral nature of the culture, is that large portions of Scripture were read to these new believers. However, teachers would also provide explanations of the texts that the catechumens were hearing read to them.[104] Pierre Nautin ("Introduction" in *Homelies sur Jeremie*) argues that, due to the way in which the services were arranged, over the course of three years the whole Bible was read and commented upon by the teacher to the catechumens.[105]

Augustine in "On the Catechizing of the Uninstructed" argues that it is critical for the teacher to provide an overview of "salvation history." The overview that Augustine provides would be equivalent to a modern-day Bible survey course.[106] The early church understood the importance of the study of Scriptures. For them, it was essential that individuals be versed in the whole of Scripture before they could join the church. It is important to note that this biblical understanding/teaching was required of all new believers.

Theological Truths

Not only were catechumens taught Scripture, but they were also instructed in theological topics. Cyril of Jerusalem wrote a series of catechetical

---

103 Bradshaw et. al., *The Apostolic Tradition*, 83.

104 Arnold, *JETS,* 46.

105 Harmless, *Augustine and the Catechumenate*, 42.

106 Schaff, *Augustine: On the Holy Trinity, Doctrinal Treatises, Moral Treatises*, 285–286.

lectures that survive to this day. Within the scope of these lectures, numerous topics are covered. The first of these lectures served as an introduction of the catechumenal process and baptism. In Cyril's fourth catechetical lecture, he provides an overview of the doctrines that were taught to the catechumens during the process of the catechumenate. Those doctrinal categories included: God, Christ, the virgin birth, the cross, His burial, the resurrection, the ascension, the judgment to come, the Holy Ghost, the soul, the body, our bodily resurrection, the Holy Scriptures, among other practical topics.[107]

The doctrinal overview covered the theological topics that are often contained within modern systematic theologies. The remainder of Cyril's theological lectures focused upon detailed treaties of the various phrases of the Apostle's Creed, which was later memorized by the *competentes* before baptism. The following is the list of titles presented by Cyril regarding the Apostle's Creed:

1. Concerning the Unity of God. On the Article, I Believe in One God. Also Concerning Heresies,

2. The Father,

3. Almighty,

4. On the Words, Maker of Heaven, and Earth, and of All Things Visible and Invisible,

5. On the Clause, and in One Lord Jesus Christ, with a Reading from the First Epistle to the Corinthians,

6. On the Words, the Only Begotten Son of God, Begotten of the Father Very God Before All Ages, by Whom All Things Were Made,

7. On the words Incarnate, and Made Man,

8. On the words, Crucified and Buried,

9. On the Words, And Rose Again from the Dead on the Third Day, and Ascended into the Heavens, and Sat on the Right Hand of the Father,

10. On the Clause, And Shall Come in Glory to Judge the Quick and the Dead; Of Whose Kingdom There Shall Be No End,

---

107 Schaff, *Nicene and Post-Nicene Fathers of the Christian Church: Cyril of Jerusalem and Gregory Nazianzen,* 19–28.

11. On the Article, And in One Holy Ghost, the Comforter, Which Spake in the Prophets,

12. Continuation of the Discourse on the Holy Ghost,

13. On the Words, And in One Holy Catholic Church, and in the Resurrection of the Flesh, and the Life Everlasting.[108]

These theological topics were deemed necessary as foundational instructions for the catechumens to be properly prepared for baptism.

The *Constitutions of the Holy Apostles* also provide various theological topics that were critical in the teaching of catechumens. The following topics were required to be taught:

> In the knowledge of the unbegotten God, in the understanding of His only begotten Son, in the assured acknowledgment of the Holy Ghost. Let him learn the order of the several parts of the creation, the series of providence, the different dispensations of Thy laws. Let him be instructed why the world was made, and why man was appointed to be a citizen therein."[109]

This list is representative of the doctrines that instructors were exhorted to teach to the catechumens. Theodore of Mopsuestia went further by teaching the following theological topics prior to baptism during Lent:

1. Reason for creed; One God,

2. Faith; Father; Creator,

3. Son: only begotten,

4. Son: true God, homoousios,

5. Son: incarnation,

6. Son: two natures,

7. Son: death, resurrection, second coming,

8. Son: two natures,

9. Spirit: divinity,

10. Spirit: consubstantial, proceeds; remission of sin; resurrection of flesh,

---

108 Ibid., 33–143.

109 Alexander J. Roberts, *Ante-Nicene Fathers, Vol VII* (Grand Rapids, MI: Eerdmans Pub. Co., 1975), 475.

11. Commentary on prayer,

12. Prebaptismal exorcism,

13. Renunciation; prebaptismal anointing,

14. Immersion, consignation.[110]

One can assert from these examples that a strong emphasis was placed upon an understanding of the Father, the person and work of Christ, and the role of the Spirit, as well as various theological issues deemed important at that time.

In addition to the works of these Church Fathers, there survived for today the sermons which dealt with theological themes by John Chrysostom,[111] Theodore of Mopsuestia,[112] and Ambrose of Milan.[113] Augustine provided for the church a number of sermons and lectures for catechumens in various stages of the catechumenal process.[114] In these works, an abundance of theological and scriptural topics are addressed and clarified as catechumens prepared for baptism and entrance into the church.

Moral Instruction

In addition to the study of Scripture and an examination of theological topics, the catechumenate also placed a high priority on instruction related to moral formation. Cyril of Jerusalem begins his fourth catechetical lecture by stating:

> Vice mimics virtue, and the tares strive to be thought wheat, growing like the wheat in appearance, but being detected by good judges from the taste. ... For the method of godliness consists of these two things, pious doctrines, and virtuous practice: and neither are the doctrines acceptable to God apart from good works, nor does God accept the works which are not perfected with pious doctrines.[115]

---

110 Harmless, *Augustine and the Catechumenate*, 77. See Appendix 7.

111 See Appendix 6.

112 See Appendix 7.

113 See Appendix 8.

114 See Appendices 9–11.

115 Schaff, *Nicene and Post-Nicene Fathers of the Christian Church: Cyril of Jerusalem and Gregory Nazianzen,* 19.

Catechumens were called upon to commit themselves to a biblical standard of living prior to baptism and joining the community. John Chrysostom urged that baptism is not bestowed on individuals who had not turned from sin and lived a virtuous life.

> For this reason I said before, and speak now and will not cease speaking, if any has not rectified the defects in his morals, nor furnished himself with easily acquired virtue, let him not be baptized. For the laver is able to remit former sins, but there is no little fear, and no ordinary danger lest we return to them, and our remedy become a wound.[116]

To Chrysostom, virtuous living was essential before one could join the church.

As stated earlier, a major document used in the catechumenal process was the *Didache*.[117] The first six chapters of this work provide moral or ethical exhortations around the doctrine of the "two ways." The instructor would educate his catechumens to strive to live according to the way of life (virtue) versus living according to the way of death.[118] The *Didache* explains those vices that lead to the way of death:

> But the path of death is this. First of all, it is evil, and full of cursing; there are found murders, adulteries, lusts, fornication, thefts, idolatries, soothsaying, sorceries, robberies, false witnessings, hypocrisies, double-mindedness, craft, pride, malice, self-will, covetousness, filthy talking, jealousy, audacity, pride, arrogance.[119]

One can note that strong teaching and direct admonitions regarding moral transformation were a critical component to the catechumenate.[120]

During this catechumenal process, several characteristics regarding the teaching presented to the catechumens are noteworthy. 1) The teaching focused on ethical living. A candidate was required to understand the

---

116 John Chrysostom, *Instructions to Catechumens: Second Instruction*, Translated by T.P. Brandram, Accessed August 28, 2014, from http://www.newadvent.org /fathers/1908. htm.

117 Sherrill, *The Rise of Christian Education*, 187.

118 Arnold, *JETS*, 50.

119 C.H. Hoole, *Didache*. Accessed March 22, 2012, from http://www.earlychristianwritings.com/text/didache-hoole.html.

120 Arnold, *JETS*, 50.

way of Christian living. 2) The core of the instruction related to the Apostle's Creed, the Lord's Prayer, and ordinances of baptism and the Lord's Supper. 3) The intensive teaching involved instruction in theology and Biblical history/knowledge. The purpose of this teaching was to train the catechumen to live a godly lifestyle in a pagan society. In addition, the catechumen must understand what they believe and how to defend their beliefs in a pagan culture.[121]

Mentorship Practices during the Catechumenate

An important component to the entrance of the candidate for catechesis was the role of the "godparent" to the catechumen. These individuals have also been identified as "sponsors"[122] or "spiritual parents."[123] Often these mentors led the candidate to conversion through faith in Jesus Christ. These mentors accompanied the candidate to the initial examination and bore witness to the faith of the catechumen.[124] *Apostolic Constitutions* stated, "Let those who brought them give witness to them, after examining the things concerning them."[125]

Before admission into the baptismal preparation, the sponsors once again were examined and provided proof that the catechumen has progressed in moral formation. The Canons of Hippolytus described this second examination by the sponsors.

> The catechumen, when he is baptized, and he who presents him attests that he has been zealous for the commandments during the time of his catechumenate, that he has visited the sick or given to the needy, that he has kept himself from every wicked and disgraceful word, that he has hated vainglory, despised pride, and chosen for himself humility, and he confesses to the bishop that he [takes] responsibility for himself, so that the bishop is satisfied about him and considers him [worthy] of the mysteries, and that he has become truly pure, then he reads over him the gospel at that time, and asks him several times, "Are you in two minds, or under

---

121 Sherrill, *The Rise of Christian Education*, 196.

122 Dujarier, *A History of the Catechumenate*, 48.

123 Pasquato, *Encyclopedia of Ancient Christianity, A–E: Catechumenate-Discipleship*, 466.

124 Dujarier, *A History of the Catechumenate*, 48.

125 Bradshaw, et. al. "Apostolic Constitutions 8.32.2–6," *The Apostolic Tradtion*, 83.

pressure from anything, or driven by convention? For nobody mocks the kingdom of heaven, but it is given to those who love it with all their heart."[126]

These documents revealed that the role of the "godparent" was critical during catechesis. These mentors intimately knew their "spiritual children" because they had to attest to the spiritual growth in the candidates. These "godparents" were involved in mentoring the spiritual truths that were taught to the catechumens by the leaders of the church, thus these church members (godparents) played a key role in the spiritual development of the catechumens.

Conclusion

As one examines both the corporate education of the Old Testament and New Testament periods, it is critical to note the important role that corporate teaching had on Israel and the church. In both periods, the emphasis in corporate education was on obedience to God and His Word. The Scriptures demand that corporate education be used as a vital tool in leading people to spiritual maturity. The post-apostolic church utilized the catechumenate as an essential corporate educational tool to train new believers prior to entrance into the church through baptism. A study of the history of the catechumenate, the catechumenal process, the content of the catechumenate, and mentorship in the catechumenate provided an understanding of this important tool to post-apostolic discipleship.

---

126 Ibid., "Canons of Hippolytus," 105.

CHAPTER 5

Summary, Implications, and Recommendations

Synopsis of Research

Chapter 1

This historical study explored the catechumenate and its implications for discipleship in 21st-century churches. Contemporary research related to discipleship revealed several concerns that the church must acknowledge as it seeks to disciple believers. The catechumenate developed as a corporate educational tool to be used to train new believers to understand what they believe, why they believe it, how to defend it, and how to live it in a hostile world. This post-apostolic period from A.D. 150 to A.D. 420 witnessed the rapid growth of Christianity through a deep commitment by believers to Jesus Christ. This growth occurred during a period of persecution by a morally corrupt and heretical culture, government, and society. The catechumenate was the primary discipleship tool utilized by the church during this period of growth.

Are there lessons that we can learn from the early church? Are there practices from the catechumenate that should be incorporated in discipleship programs today? Is essential biblical and theological content omitted today in our discipleship programs that were present in the early church? This research will contribute to current discipleship materials by providing an analysis of a successful discipleship program in church history and provide implications from this program for 21st-century churches.

Chapter 2

As the post-apostolic church prepared to train individuals for membership to their community, it based its foundation for theological teaching and personal commitment upon the instruction of the NT Scriptures. The principles that were gleaned from the NT provided the basis for the catechumenate. An examination of NT instruction regarding discipleship is essential to understanding post-apostolic discipleship as well as discipleship in 21st-century church settings. This section examined select NT passages to provide an understanding of key principles in the development of NT disciples.

Biblical Discipleship Principles from Select NT Passages

This section presented several principles of discipleship that can be gleaned from select NT passages. These NT passages provide a foundation for discipleship in the church age.[1] The principles gleaned from the NT provided the basis for the catechumenate (first educational/discipleship program for the church). Twelve discipleship principles have been garnered from Matthew 28:19–20, Luke 6:40, Luke 14:26–27, John 13:34–35, John 15:7–8, Romans 12:1–2, Ephesians 4:11–16, and 2 Timothy 2:2.

1. Disciples are commanded to make disciples of all peoples.
2. The means by which disciples are made is by baptizing (initiation) and teaching (instruction).
3. Disciples of Christ strive to be like their Master not just cognitively but also in conduct.
4. Disciples are singular in their allegiance to Christ.
5. Disciples must be willing to sacrifice all for Christ.
6. Disciples display genuine love to fellow believers.
7. Disciples are characterized by an intimate relationship with Jesus Christ, a passion for the Bible, a consistent prayer life, and a heart for ministry and service.

---

1 The church age covers the timeframe from Acts 2 until the present.

8. Disciples dedicate their lives as a consistent, blameless sacrifice to God.

9. Disciples consistently allow themselves to be transformed through meditation on the Word of God.

10. Disciples are actively involved in ministry.

11. Disciples are grounded in the truth and are not persuaded to follow false teaching.

12. Disciples replicate themselves into the spiritual lives of others.

Chapter 3

The impetus behind the development of the catechumenate derived from the second part of Jesus' Great Commission to his disciples. Jesus states to His followers that as they make disciples they were to be "teaching them to observe all that I commanded you" (Matt. 28:20). Alan Kreider asserts the following regarding this phrase: "In saying this Jesus, in keeping with the emphases throughout Matthew's gospel, underscored the importance of a lived practical response to his teachings."[2] The desire was to instruct and teach these new followers in the areas of Scripture and theology to produce disciples. As the church moves into the post-apostolic period, there develops widespread testimony of a focused, coherent plan to instruct new believers: the catechumenate.[3] What influences impacted the church which ultimately provided an impetus to begin the catechumenal process? In this chapter, three catalysts were examined that influenced the development of the catechumenate.

Pre-Christian Religious Influences

Historical evidence indicated that the Essene and Jewish traditions influenced the process of baptism and membership into the early Christian church. Baptism no longer immediately followed salvation as was seen at times in Scripture (Acts 2:41; 8:38). Following the influence from the Essene and Jewish traditions, the early church began a process of education

---

2 Alan Kreider, "Baptism, Catechism and the Eclipse of Jesus' Teaching in Early Christianity," *Tyndale Bulletin, 47(2)*, 316.

3 Arnold, *JETS*, 43.

and preparation for both baptism and membership into the Christian community.

Sociological Influences

As the church sought to educate and prepare those interested in joining their community, they created a program (catechumenate) that answered and addressed the sociological influences of society on Christian individuals and the church at large. If a believer intended to join the church, they must be prepared to live according to a different ethical standard than was presented in society. They also needed to be prepared to suffer and possibly die for their commitment to the church and ultimately Jesus Christ. Ottorino Pasquato explains the need for instruction prior to baptism in the 2nd and 3rd centuries A.D. as opposed to baptism described in Acts.

> We note that admission to baptism was more cautious than in the NT period. In fact, in this period, as an antidote to the moral decadence of the Christian communities and to cases of apostasy in the period of persecution, there was the introduction of a twofold examination, the first in the initial phase of orientation toward Christianity, the second at the act of enrollment for baptism. The phase of preparation for baptism was designed to last 2–3 years.[4]

The church established the catechumenate as a means to prepare individuals to address the sociological influences of their day. The two sociological influences that were examined were persecution and immorality.

Persecution was the norm during the post-apostolic church age. Under Nero and the emperors who ruled after him, the believers were regularly persecuted for serving Jesus Christ. The church developed a process (catechumenate) that vetted and prepared individuals to face possible persecution and death.

In addition to the catechumenate preparing a new believer to face persecution, the catechumenate also addressed the purity by which a new believer (and ultimately a member of the early church) needed to live one's life. Secular culture surrounding the early church was a perverse blend of hedonism, sexual immorality, unrestrained appetites, and cruelty to others.

---

4 Ottorino Pasquato, *Encyclopedia of Ancient Christianity, A-E: Catechumenate-Discipleship* (Downers Grove, IL: Intervarsity Press, 2014), 460.

The catechumenate was developed to teach and mentor individuals to cast off vice and replace it with virtue. In addition to the spiritual instruction, the catechumens were discipled/mentored by mature believers. Before baptism, a "scrutiny" was made of the individual's lifestyle to verify that he/she was qualified to join the church. Upon finishing the "scrutiny," the new believers were taken through a multi-level educational process over a lengthy period to teach virtuous living in a degenerate culture.

Doctrinal Influences

As the church dealt with ethical issues and persecution, another issue arose during the expansion of the church. Doctrinal heresies began to surface which challenged the very fabric of Christian teaching. Justo Gonzalez explains the theological climate of the early church.

> The many converts who joined the early church came from a wide variety of backgrounds. This variety enriched the church and gave witness to the universality of its message. But it also resulted in widely differing interpretations of that message, some of which threatened its integrity. The danger was increased by the syncretism of the time, which sought truth, not by adhering to a single system of doctrine, but by taking bits and pieces from various systems. The result was that, while many claimed the name of Christ, some interpreted that name in such a manner that the very core of his message seemed to be obscured or even denied.[5]

The catechumenate sought to educate individuals in theology and apologetics to be able to respond to the doctrinal heresies presented from both within and outside the church. Several heretical influences were examined that impacted the catechumenal process: Gnosticism, Montanism, teaching of Marcion, Arianism, and the teaching of Celsus. Because of the pagan culture in which the early church began, church leaders found it necessary to train believers to forsake vice and seek virtue as well as be prepared to answer the theological disputes of early Christianity. This catechumenal process was a multi-year training period in discipleship.

---

5 Justo L. González, *The Story of Christianity* (Peabody, MA: Prince Press, 1999), 58.

Chapter 4

This chapter sought to examine the characteristics of the catechumenal process. Before examining this process, an overview of the corporate education in the OT and NT was examined. Once the role of corporate education was examined, the chapter examined the catechumenate.

The Catechumenate's Place within the Corporate Education of the Early Church

The first official Christian education program for the church was the catechumenate. The catechumenate, from κατηχεω (in the active meaning "to teach" or "instruct"[6] and in the passive meaning "to listen"[7]) was designed for the education of adult converts prior to joining the church through baptism. Pasquato describes the catechumenate as a critical component in Christian initiation and discipleship.

> By catechumenate, from the neo-Latin *catechumenatus* and its modern derivation from *catechumenus* (*katechoumenos*), is meant the process of formation in the church's *forma vitae*; in the ancient church it pertained to the reception of the three sacraments of Christian initiation [baptism, confirmation, and Eucharist], in view of Christian discipleship.[8]

The catechumenate then involved a period of instruction in which new believers were discipled and initiated to the Christian community.

Pasquato describes this important process of catechumenate as a critical step in preparing individuals for baptism and entrance into the church body.

> Initiation (typical of every religion) in primitive Christianity was aimed at introducing persons coming from paganism or Judaism to Christian discipleship. ... The catechumenate was a basic part of Christian initiation. The early church's effort in selecting and preparing candidates for baptism was substantial: a process of

---

6 Walter Bauer, William F. Arndt, Wilbur Gingrich, and Fredrick W. Danker, *A Greek-English Lexicon of the New Testament and Other Early Christian Literature,* 2nd. Ed. (Chicago, IL: University of Chicago Press, 1979), 423.

7 Ottorino Pasquato, *Encyclopedia of Ancient Christianity, A–E: Catechumenate-Discipleship* (Downers Grove, IL: Intervarsity Press, 2014), 458.

8 Ibid., 458.

initiation, growth and apprenticeship through which the whole person was transformed, orienting his life in a radically new way toward the God of Jesus Christ and the church community.[9]

The goal then of the catechumenate was to take a new convert to Christianity through a process of initiation into the church family.

Three intended purposes are noticeable as the church created this Christian educational program. The first purpose was to help develop a disciplined lifestyle among new believers. A second purpose was to acquaint the catechumen with the Christian tradition. The final purpose was to create a profound devotion to the Christian faith and way of life.[10] Individuals passed through stages of increasingly intimate fellowship and participation within the Christian community. As they progressed through these stages, the catechumens would be introduced to deeper instruction until they were admitted to baptism and then participation in the Lord's Supper. Cyril of Jerusalem provides insight as to why a process of systematic education was important.

> Suppose, pray, that the Catechising is a kind of building: if we do not bind the house together by regular bonds in the building, lest some gap be found, and the building become unsound, even our former labour is of no use. But stone must follow stone by course, and corner match with corner, and by our smoothing off inequalities the building must thus rise evenly. In like manner we are bringing to thee stones, as it were, of knowledge.[11]

The desire of the catechumenal process was to equip and "build" new believers through an understanding of God's Word, moral teachings from Scripture, and theological truths derived from the Bible.

The church in the first through sixth centuries lived in a pagan, immoral, and hostile world. This community of Christians had sworn loyalty to Christ and pledged themselves to obey and follow His will. Christians considered themselves soldiers of Christ and fellow soldiers with other

---

9 Ibid., 459.

10 Lewis J. Sherrill, *The Rise of Christian Education* (New York, NY: The Macmillan Company, 1950), 186.

11 Philip Schaff, *Nicene, and Post-Nicene Fathers of the Christian Church: Cyril of Jerusalem and Gregory Nazianzen*, Vol. VII (Grand Rapids, MI: WM. B. Eerdmans Publishing Company, 1978), 3.

believers. At their baptism they were "enlisted" in Christ's army. Their baptism served as a *sacramentum*, or pledge, which would be the equivalent of a military oath. They were members of the camp of Christ, and His Word served as their orders.[12] The catechumenal process prepared them to enter this militant Christian lifestyle.

This chapter examined several aspects of the catechumenate. An analysis of the history of the catechumenate was provided by examining the period from A.D. 150–313. The study then examined the period of the catechumenate following the "Constantinian turn" in A.D. 313. This period marked a dramatic change in the catechumenal process. Initially, the catechumenate resembled the catechumenal process of the 2nd and 3rd century. However, as a flood of new converts entered the church due to the "Constantinian turn" the catechumenate began to lose its defining features and ultimately became a remnant of its former self by the end of the 5th century A.D.

Next the study examined the catechumenal procedures (those procedures that were evident in the golden age of the catechumenate). The catechumenate developed as a corporate educational tool to be used to train new believers to understand what they believe, why they believe it, how to defend it, and how to live it in a hostile world. This process was not a quick process (not the customary 4–8 weeks, as is often seen in churches today) but rather was accomplished through various interviews, lectures, and mentorship over a period of two to three years. The pastors/ bishops of the Patristic period saw the value and need for this corporate education for the growth of individuals within their congregations.

The next section of this chapter examined the content that was taught during the catechumenate. The main content features that are evident from catechetical lectures are an emphasis on the Scriptures, theological truths, and moral formation. The following section examined the mentorship practices during the catechumenate.

An important component to the entrance of the candidate for catechesis was the role of the "godparent" to the catechumen. These individuals have also been identified as "sponsors"[13] or "spiritual parents."[14] Often they were those individuals who through evangelism had led the

---

12 Sherrill, *The Rise of Christian Education*, 187.

13 Dujarier, *A History of the Catechumenate*, 48.

14 Pasquato, *Encyclopedia of Ancient Christianity, A–E: Catechumenate-Discipleship*, 466.

candidate to conversion through faith in Jesus Christ. These mentors accompanied the candidate to the initial examination and bore witness to the faith of the catechumen.[15] *Apostolic Constitutions* stated, "Let those who brought them give witness to them, after examining the things concerning them."[16]

Before admission into the baptismal preparation, the sponsors once again were examined and provided proof that the catechumen has progressed in moral formation. The Canons of Hippolytus described this second examination by the sponsors.

> The catechumen, when he is baptized, and he who presents him attests that he has been zealous for the commandments during the time of his catechumenate, that he has visited the sick or given to the needy, that he has kept himself from every wicked and disgraceful word, that he has hated vain-glory, despised pride, and chosen for himself humility, and he confesses to the bishop that he [takes] responsibility for himself, so that the bishop is satisfied about him and considers him [worthy] of the mysteries, and that he has become truly pure, then he reads over him the gospel at that time, and asks him several times, "Are you in two minds, or under pressure from anything, or driven by convention? For nobody mocks the kingdom of heaven, but it is given to those who love it with all their heart."[17]

These documents revealed that the role of the "godparent" was critical during catechesis. These mentors intimately knew their "spiritual children" because they had to attest to the spiritual growth in the candidates. These "godparents" were involved in mentoring the spiritual truths that were taught to the catechumens by the leaders of the church. These church members (godparents) played a key role in the spiritual development of the catechumens.

Chapter 4 concluded with principles that can be gleaned from the catechumenate that affect modern discipleship. The post-apostolic church placed a high priority on training and educating new believers before they joined the church community. In a world of persecution, vice, and doctrinal heresies, it was critical to train new converts in the teachings

---

15 Dujarier, *A History of the Catechumenate*, 48.

16 Bradshaw, et. al., "Apostolic Constitutions 8.32.2–6," *The Apostolic Tradition*, 83.

17 Ibid., "Canons of Hippolytus," 105.

of Scripture, doctrinal orthodoxy, and moral purity. The early church developed the catechumenate to accomplish this important corporate education of new believers. The success of the catechumenate can be seen though a historical lens. History reveals that the church flourished and expanded during the first six centuries A.D. One reason, among many, for this expansion was due to the training of believers to know what they believed, why they believed it, and how to defend it in a hostile environment. Clinton Arnold accurately states: "By contrast, many evangelical churches today place a minimal emphasis on the training of new believers, especially when compared to the prominence and importance of the catechumenate in the ancient church."[18]

Implications for 21st-Century Churches

After examining the cultural difficulties that the early church faced, one is impressed that current society reflects many of the same immoral influences. One needs to merely turn on the computer or television or read a popular magazine to discover issues such as pornography, homosexuality, divorce, promiscuity, violence, etc. are immediately apparent. Churches are battling doctrinal heresies from both within the church (annihilationism, open theism, non-virgin birth, challenges to inerrancy, etc.) and from outside (evolution, cults, challenges to the deity of Christ, etc.). Churches today would be wise to heed the example of the early church and create a program in which new believers are trained both to know their faith and to defend it in the face of opposition. Immorality is prevalent in our society, and churches would also be wise to instruct and create mentoring programs in which the Christian ethic is taught and exemplified to new believers within the church. The catechumenate was a powerful training method in its day. Churches today might benefit by critically evaluating the catechumenal model as they seek to educate the next generation of believers.

An important factor to examine is whether contemporary "new believers' classes" are adequately equipping new Christians to impact our current culture (Matt 5). Clinton Arnold challenged the church to ask several important questions:

- Is a four-week (six-week, or eight-week) new Christians' class enough?

---

18 Arnold, *JETS*, 44.

- Are we getting new believers adequately immersed into the Scriptures?
- Have we downplayed the importance of creed?
- Are we helping new believers repent completely of sinful lifestyles and practices?
- Are we taking the spiritual warfare dynamic seriously enough in helping new believers grow?[19]

Similarly, Michel Dujarier challenges churches to understand the importance of systematically and intentionally training new believers:

> Whether we are concerned with a young Church, or a Church already matured by the centuries, it is always necessary to safeguard the traditional spirit of a serious and progressive catechumenal formation. The modes may change, and indeed they must be adapted to the concrete historical situation. But the journey of the individual to his or her Lord must be respected, just as the Lord has respected it to approach us.[20]

The post-apostolic church placed a high priority upon training and equipping new believers to live for Christ in a hostile world.

Many practices and procedures of the catechumenate were directly related to the issues the post-apostolic church faced on a regular basis. Several of those practices would not be relevant or necessary for discipleship in 21st-century churches. For instance, this writer would perform the ordinance of baptism far closer to salvation than after a two- to three-year period of instruction. However, though today's church may never return to the catechumenal procedures (nor in some cases should they), several lessons should be learned from the catechumenal process and implemented in current discipleship programs.

The Value of the Catechumenate for Discipleship

Corporate Christian education is more than just a suggestion; it is a mandate. Perry Downs accurately asserts, "*How* the church teaches is open to a variety of cultural expressions, but *that* the church teaches is nonnegotiable. The Scriptures demand that the church educate its people for

---

19 Ibid., 40.

20 Dujarier, *A History of the Catechumenate*, 114.

spiritual maturity."[21] Corporate education by the church is critical to the formation of the believer in progressive sanctification. It is the church's responsibility to teach the believer the Scriptures, doctrinal truth, and moral purity. Each of these factors is a critical component in the process of discipleship.

The post-apostolic church placed a high priority upon training and equipping new believers to live for Christ in a hostile world. Several lessons should be learned from the catechumenal process.

1. Catechumens were serious about their commitment to Christ.

2. Catechumens believed they were engaging in spiritual warfare and by joining the church they must obey the Commander, Jesus Christ.

3. Church leaders developed a systematic Christian educational program to instruct new believers in the Scriptures, theology, and moral conduct.

4. Catechumens did not join the church immediately, but rather were tested to see if they were truly committed to Christ.

5. Catechumens were assigned, or brought with them from the beginning, spiritual mentors who became actively involved in the education (specifically moral education) of the new believers.

6. These spiritual mentors (godparents) knew the catechumens' spiritual lifestyle because the mentors would ultimately give attestation to the spiritual growth of their assigned catechumen.

7. At the culmination of the catechumenal process, these new members of the church were fully committed to Christ and to their fellow brothers/sisters in the Lord.

Lessons from the Catechumenate

Though the catechumenate had a varied history and there were dissimilarities in catechumenal practices in different locations, several key lessons can be drawn from this discipleship program of the early church.

---

21 Downs, *Teaching for Spiritual Growth*, 29.

Lesson 1: Catechumens were serious about their commitment to Christ.

The catechumenal process occurred over a 2–3-year period. In addition, the process was filled with extensive instruction but also evaluation of moral conduct and application of the lessons that were taught by the church. The catechumens were called upon to serve extensively within the church. The commitment that the catechumenal process demanded was a serious commitment to Christ and the church. The questions arise today, are our churches filled with believers that are fully committed to Christ? Do we as a church demand commitment to Christ? Or have we reduced Christianity to "easy believism"? The catechumenal process challenges today's church to evaluate our commitment to Christ.

Lesson 2: Catechumens believed they were engaging in spiritual warfare and by joining the church they must obey the Commander, Jesus Christ.

In a culture of opposition and persecution, the catechumens viewed the Christian walk as spiritual warfare. By joining the church, they were obeying their "Commander." Whatever Christ asked of them, they needed to obey. Does the 21st-century church view the Christian life as a spiritual battle (Eph 6:12—"For our struggle is not against flesh and blood, but against the rulers, against the powers, against the world forces of this darkness, against the spiritual *forces* of wickedness in the heavenly *places*")? Often in Western cultures, where persecution is not the norm in the 21st-century context, the Christian life is not an intense struggle. Are we acutely aware of the conflict we are in? Do we view Christ as our "Commander in Chief"? Do we have a commitment to go to war for Him?

Lesson 3: Early church leaders developed a systematic Christian educational program to instruct new believers in the Scriptures, theology, and moral conduct.

The catechumenate was an intense educational program that taught in areas of moral conduct, theological issues, and scriptural guidelines and principles. The goal of the catechumenal process was comprehensive spiritual change. Do churches today have an intentional program to educate new believers? Are our discipleship programs comprehensive in their scope? Do we have a prescribed sequence of instruction to prepare modern believers to answer the difficult questions they are facing in today's world?

Lesson 4: Catechumens did not join the church immediately, but rather were tested to see if they were truly committed to Christ.

Part of the reason for the 2–3-year catechumenal process was to prove and approve of the new believers before entrance into the church community. During a time of persecution, it was important for the early church to vet individuals who wished to join the church. In addition, these new believers needed to be approved before joining the church to make sure that they were living a morally acceptable life that followed the principles expressed in the Bible. Though 21st-century western churches do not face the same persecution as the early church or as other churches face in various locations around the globe today, it is important that believers are committed to Christ and the church body before joining the church. This writer agrees with the questions posed by Clinton Arnold. "Is a four-week (six-week, or eight-week) new Christians' class enough? Are we getting new believers adequately immersed into the Scripture? Are we helping new believers repent completely of sinful lifestyles and practices?"[22] In addition to these questions it may be important for our churches to ask, do our candidates for membership understand what is involved when they join our church? Do they fully understand and accept our church's bylaws and constitution? Can a full understanding of our church's procedures be achieved in a few days or in a couple of weeks?

Lesson 5: Catechumens were assigned, or brought with them from the beginning, spiritual mentors who became actively involved in the education (specifically moral education) of the new believers.

The catechumens were not only instructed through corporate education by church leaders but also through mentorship by church members. Do our churches today have an active mentorship program where new believers are practically trained by mature believers? Are we intentional in our mentorship endeavors? Or has discipleship been reduced to simply lectures from the pulpit or in the classroom?

---

22 Arnold, *JETS*, 40.

Lesson 6: These spiritual mentors (godparents) knew the catechumens' spiritual lifestyle because the mentors would ultimately give attestation to the spiritual growth of their assigned catechumen.

Not only were the "godparents" involved in the moral education of the catechumens, but they also had intimate knowledge of the spiritual growth of their assigned catechumen. The "godparents" were involved in the "scrutinies" before entrance to baptism. They had to answer questions as to the growth within the life of their assigned catechumen. Do we have intimate knowledge of our fellow believers in our churches? Do we understand the struggles and sins that the people in our congregations are facing? Do we even ask about the spiritual growth of one another much less hold each other accountable?

Lesson 7: At the culmination of the catechumenal process, these new members of the church were fully committed to Christ and to their fellow brothers/sisters in the Lord.

By joining the church, the catechumens were allowed intimate spiritual fellowship with their brothers/sisters in Christ. This fellowship was earned as they endured the catechumenal process. Are we committed to one another as believers in Christ? Do we defend one another in the face of opposition? Are we intentional about expressing our love through service within the church?

Though 21st-century churches may never fully integrate a 2–3-year training program before baptism and membership into the body of Christ, it is critical that we understand the implications that can be drawn from the catechumenal process. Many good features and examples are found within the catechumenate. Twenty-first-century churches would do well to learn these important lessons as we minister in our contexts.

Biblical Discipleship Principles from the NT

In chapter 2, twelve discipleship principles were gleaned from Matthew 28:19–20, Luke 6:40, Luke 14:26–27, John 13:34–35, John 15:7–8, Romans 12:1–2, Ephesians 4:11–16, and 2 Timothy 2:2. Are our churches today practicing these NT principles? The church would be wise to re-examine the NT principles regarding discipleship and seek to develop programs and procedures that implement these principles. One of the reasons that the church is facing dire issues as expressed in chapter one is that we have neglected to follow NT discipleship principles. It is time for the 21st-century church to practice the principles provided in the NT regarding spiritual growth and discipleship.

Biblical Discipleship Principle 1: Disciples are commanded to make disciples of all peoples.

- Are we reproducing ourselves in the lives of others?
- Are we actively involved in both evangelism and discipleship?
- Have we neglected Jesus' primary command to the church, to disciple the nations?

Biblical Discipleship Principle 2: The means by which disciples are made is by baptizing (initiation) and teaching (instruction).

- Are we actively teaching new believers that baptism is a critical component to spiritual obedience?
- Are we intentional in developing curriculum for comprehensive spiritual change?

Biblical Discipleship Principle 3: Disciples of Christ strive to be like their Master not just cognitively but also in conduct.

- Are we seeking to replicate the example of the Master?
- Are we living our lives focused on being spiritually, morally, ethically different from the world around us?

Biblical Discipleship Principle 4: Disciples are singular in their allegiance to Christ.

- Are we allowing the world to pull our allegiance away from Christ?
- Are we consumed by selfish desires, or is Christ our single devotion?

Biblical Discipleship Principle 5: Disciples must be willing to sacrifice all for Christ.

- Is our comfort our utmost priority?

- Are we willing to sacrifice our comforts to follow Christ?
- Are there things or individuals that we place before Christ?
- Are we willing to lay aside our desires to follow our Savior?

Biblical Discipleship Principle 6: Disciples display genuine love to fellow believers.

- Do we actively display love for others?
- Are our churches characterized by love or division?
- Do we set aside our desires or comforts to minister to one another?

Biblical Discipleship Principle 7: Disciples are characterized by an intimate relationship with Jesus Christ, a passion for the Bible, a consistent prayer life, and a heart for ministry and service.

- Are our churches today reflecting these characteristics?
- Would the world look at believers and identify them as "unique" or "different" because we display these characteristics?

Biblical Discipleship Principle 8: Disciples dedicate their lives as a consistent, blameless sacrifice to God.

- Are our churches filled with believers who remain distinct from the world?
- Do believers today view their lives as a sacrifice, or are we determined to make our lives easy?
- Would others view us as living blamelessly in this present world?

Biblical Discipleship Principle 9: Disciples consistently allow themselves to be transformed through meditation on the Word of God.

- Do we regularly read and study God's Word?
- Do believers understand what meditation is?
- Are we seeking to be biblically literate—understanding God's truths for our lives?

Biblical Discipleship Principle 10: Disciples are actively involved in ministry.

- Are our churches characterized by service?
- Do our church members actively participate in ministry, or expect the "paid staff" to carry out the work of the ministry?

Biblical Discipleship Principle 11: Disciples are grounded in the truth and are not persuaded to follow false teaching.

- Do believers understand doctrinal truth?
- Can the members of our churches distinguish what is truth and what is heresy?

Biblical Discipleship Principle 12: Disciples replicate themselves into the spiritual lives of others.

- Are our churches involved in mentorship?
- Do we as believers share our faith with a lost and dying world?
- Do we actively seek to impact the next generation for Christ?

Recommendations for Church Leaders of Disciple-Making Ministries

With the current state of discipleship (as noted in chapter 1), it is critical that leaders of disciple-making ministries address problems facing today's evangelical church. After a study of the catechumenate, several recommendations are provided for church leaders.

Recommendation 1: Church leaders must recognize the current state of discipleship today.

The church today is seeing a rise of biblical illiteracy, a lack of involvement, an exodus of believers, and a de-emphasis in discipleship in our churches. The early church was intentional about educating believers and grounding them in the truths of Scripture. The serious level of commitment of early believers is evident as one examines the catechumenate.

Recommendation 2: Church leaders must develop systematic and intentional discipleship curriculum and programs for their churches.

Too often churches teach random biblical topics without examining scope and sequence. The church must be intentional about teaching core biblical content and theological truths to new believers.

Recommendation 3: Church leaders must develop discipleship procedures that produce comprehensive change in the lives of new believers.

Have we reduced our discipleship programs to either classroom instruction or to only mentorship? If our churches today only focus on one component of discipleship, we will not produce comprehensive spiritual change in the lives of believers. Corporate instruction is a critical component of discipleship. Without teaching how will the new believer know what is necessary for godliness? In addition, without practical instruction (mentorship), how can the new believer know what the truths of Scripture "look like" in practical situations?

Recommendation 4: Church leaders must emphasize mentorship in our churches today.

Discipleship has often been reduced to simply teaching from the pulpit or in the Sunday School (Adult Bible Fellowship) classroom. The early church was intentional about assigning new believers to an older, biblically established believer who helped implement the lectures that were taught in the church. These "godparents" knew their assigned catechumen. They had to attest to the growth that the new believer experienced during catechesis. Do established believers in our church know the intimate spiritual lives of the new believers in our congregation? The church must become intentional in mentoring new Christians. Titus 2:1–8 states:

> But *as for* you, speak the things which are fitting for sound doctrine. Older men are to be temperate, dignified, sensible, sound in faith, in love, in perseverance. Older women likewise *are to be* reverent in their behavior, not malicious gossips nor enslaved to much wine, teaching what is good, so that they may encourage the young women to love their husbands, to love their children, *to be* sensible, pure, workers at home, kind, being subject to their own husbands,

so that the word of God will not be dishonored. Likewise urge the young men to be sensible; in all things show yourself *to be* an example of good deeds, *with* purity in doctrine, dignified, sound *in* speech which is beyond reproach, so that the opponent will be put to shame, having nothing bad to say about us.

The church is not called simply to educate individuals in a lecture classroom, but the church is also called to educate individuals through mentoring relationships.

Conclusion

The primary goal of this research study was to examine the catechumenate and its implications for discipleship in 21st-century churches. To achieve this goal, current issues facing discipleship were examined, an exegesis of several NT passages and the principles that derive from these passages regarding discipleship were provided, an analysis of post-apostolic culture and religious setting that influenced the start of the catechumenate was discussed, and an analysis of the catechumenal process was conducted to provide a basis for implications for modern disciple-making ministries. This chapter provided an overall survey of the research as well as a synthesis of the principles from this study that impacts modern discipleship.

Twenty-first-century churches would do well to examine how the post-apostolic church viewed and practiced discipleship. Though today's church may never return to the catechumenal procedures (nor in some cases should they), several lessons should be learned from the catechumenal process and implemented in current disciple-making ministries. The catechumenate is an important ministry tool to understand as the church seeks to disciple believers in today's context.

APPENDIX 1

CRUCIFIXION—THE ARCHAEOLOGICAL EVIDENCE

Quote from Vassilios Tzaferis's article "Crucifixion—The Archaeological Evidence" regarding the horrors of the crucifixion process.

Once a defendant was found guilty and was condemned to be crucified, the execution was supervised by an official known as the *Carnifix Serarum*. From the tribunal hall, the victim was taken outside, stripped, bound to a column and scourged. The scourging was done with either a stick or a *flagellum*, a Roman instrument with a short handle to which several long, thick thongs had been attached. On the ends of the leather thongs were lead or bone tips. Although the number of strokes imposed was not fixed, care was taken not to kill the victim. Following the beating, the horizontal beam was placed upon the condemned man's shoulders, and he began the long, grueling march to the execution site, usually outside the city walls. A soldier at the head of the procession carried the *titulus*, an inscription written on wood, which stated the defendant's name and the crime for which he had been condemned. Later, this *titulus* was fastened to the victim's cross. When the procession arrived at the execution site, a vertical stake was fixed into the ground. Sometimes the victim was attached to the cross only with ropes. In such a case, the *patibulum* or crossbeam, to which the victim's arms were already bound, was simply affixed to the vertical beam; the victim's feet were then bound to the stake with a few turns of the rope.

If the victim was attached by nails, he was laid on the ground, with his shoulders on the crossbeam. His arms were held out and nailed to the two ends of the crossbeam, which was then raised and fixed on top of the vertical beam. The victim's feet were then nailed down against this vertical stake.

Without any supplementary body support, the victim would die from muscular spasms and asphyxia in a very short time, certainly within two or three hours. Shortly after being raised on the cross, breathing would become difficult; to get his breath, the victim would attempt to draw himself up on his arms. Initially he would be able to hold himself up for 30 to 60 seconds, but this movement would quickly become increasingly difficult. As he became weaker, the victim would be unable to pull himself up and death would ensue within a few hours.

In order to prolong the agony, Roman executioners devised two instruments that would keep the victim alive on the cross for extended periods of time. One, known as a *sedile*, was a small seat attached to the front of the cross, about halfway down. This device provided some support for the victim's body and may explain the phrase used by the Romans, 'to sit on the cross.' Both Erenaeus and Justin Martyr describe the cross of Jesus as having five extremities rather than four; the fifth was probably the *sedile*. To increase the victim's suffering, the *sedile* was pointed, thus inflicting horrible pain. The second device added to the cross was the *suppedaneum*, or foot support. It was less painful than the *sedile*, but it also prolonged the victim's agony. Ancient historians record many cases in which the victim stayed alive on the cross for two or three or more days with the use of a *suppedaneum*. The church father Origen writes of having seen a crucified man who survived the whole night and the following day. Josephus refers to a case in which three crucified Jews survived on the cross for three days. During the mass crucifixions following the repression of the revolt of Spartacus in Rome, some of the crucified rebels talked to the soldiers for three days.[23]

---

23 Vassilios Tzaferis, "Crucifixion—The Archaeological Evidence," *BAR* Jan/Feb (1985), 49–50.

APPENDIX 2

PHILO ON THE ESSENES

Quote from Philo, The Works of Philo, trans. C. D. Yonge (Peabody, MA: Hendrickson, 1993), 689–690.

Moreover Palestine and Syria too are not barren of exemplary wisdom and virtue, which countries no slight portion of that most populous nation of the Jews inhabits. There is a portion of those people called Essenes, in number something more than four thousand in my opinion, who derive their name from their piety, though not according to any accurate form of the Grecian dialect, because they are above all men devoted to the service of God, not sacrificing living animals, but studying rather to preserve their own minds in a state of holiness and purity. (76) These men, in the first place, live in villages, avoiding all cities on account of the habitual lawlessness of those who inhabit them, well knowing that such a moral disease is contracted from associations with wicked men, just as a real disease might be from an impure atmosphere, and that this would stamp an incurable evil on their souls. Of these men, some cultivating the earth, and others devoting themselves to those arts which are the result of peace, benefit both themselves and all those who come in contact with them, not storing up treasures of silver and of gold, nor acquiring vast sections of the earth out of a desire for ample revenues, but providing all things which are requisite for the natural purposes of life; (77) for they alone of almost all men having been originally poor and destitute, and that too rather from their own habits and ways of life than from any real deficiency of good fortune, are nevertheless accounted very rich, judging contentment and frugality to be great abundance, as in truth they are. (78) Among those men you will find no makers of arrows, or javelins, or swords, or helmets, or breastplates, or shields; no makers of arms or of military engines; no one, in short, attending to any employment whatever connected with war, or even to any of those occupations even in peace which are easily perverted to wicked purposes; for they are utterly ignorant of all traffic, and of all commercial dealings, and of all navigation, but they repudiate and keep aloof from everything which can possibly afford any inducement to covetousness; (79) and there is not a single slave among them, but they are all free, aiding one another with a reciprocal interchange of good offices; and they condemn masters, not only as unjust, inasmuch as they corrupt the very principle of equality, but likewise as impious, because they destroy the ordinances of nature, which generated them all equally, and brought them up like a mother, as if they were all legitimate brethren, not in name only, but in reality and truth. But in their view this natural relationship of all men to one another has been thrown into disorder by designing covetousness, continually wishing to surpass others in good fortune, and which has therefore engendered alienation instead of affection, and hatred instead of friendship; (80) and leaving the logical part of philosophy, as in no respect necessary for the acquisition of virtue, to the word-catchers, and the natural part, as being too sublime for human nature to master, to those who love to converse about high objects (except indeed so far as such a study takes in the contemplation of the existence of God and of the creation of the universe), they devote all their attention to the moral part of philosophy, using as instructors the laws of their country which it would have been impossible for the human mind to devise without divine inspiration. (81) Now these laws they are taught at other times, indeed, but most especially on the seventh day, for the seventh day is accounted sacred, on which they abstain from all other employments, and frequent the sacred places which are called synagogues, and there they sit according to their age in classes, the younger sitting under the elder, and listening with eager attention in becoming order. (82) Then one, indeed, takes up the holy volume and reads it, and another of the men of the greatest experience comes forward and explains what is not very intelligible, for a great many precepts are delivered in enigmatical modes of expression, and allegorically, as the old fashion was; (83) and thus the people are taught piety, and holiness, and justice, and economy, and the science of regulating the state, and the knowledge of such things as are naturally good, or bad, or indifferent, and to choose what is right and to avoid what is wrong, using a threefold variety of definitions, and rules, and criteria, namely, the love of God, and the love of virtue, and the love of mankind. (84) Accordingly, the sacred volumes present an infinite number of instances of the disposition devoted to the love of God, and of a continued and uninterrupted purity throughout the whole of life, of a careful avoidance of oaths and of falsehood, and of a strict adherence to the principle of looking on the Deity as the cause of everything which is good and of nothing which is evil. They also furnish us with many proofs of a love of virtue, such as abstinence from all covetousness of money, from ambition, from indulgence in pleasures, temperance, endurance, and also moderation, simplicity, good temper, the absence of pride, obedience to the laws, steadiness, and everything of that kind; and, lastly, they bring forward as proofs of the love of mankind, goodwill, equality beyond all power of description, and fellowship, about which it is not unreasonable to say a few words. (85) In the first place, then, there is no one who has a house so absolutely his own private property, that it does not in some sense also belong to every one: for besides that they all dwell together in companies, the house is open to all those of the same notions, who come to them from other quarters; (86) then there is one magazine among them all; their expenses are all in common; their garments belong to them all in common; their food is common, since they all eat in messes; for there is no other people among which you can find a common use of the same house, a common adoption of one mode of living, and a common use of the same table more thoroughly established in fact than among this tribe: and is not this very natural? For whatever they, after having been working during the day, receive for their wages, that they do not retain as their own, but bring it into the common stock, and give any advantage that is to be derived from it to all who desire to avail themselves of it; (87) and those who are sick are not neglected because they are unable to contribute to the common stock, inasmuch as the tribe have in their public stock a means of supplying their necessities and aiding their weakness, so that from their ample means they support them liberally and abundantly; and they cherish respect for their elders, and honour them and care for them, just as parents are honoured and cared for by their lawful children: being supported by them in all abundance both by their personal exertions, and by innumerable contrivances.

APPENDIX 3

CHART OF CATECHESIS IN THE 2ND AND 3RD CENTURIES A.D.

Summary Chart of Catechesis and Baptism in the 2nd–3rd Centuries A.D.[1]

Figure 3.1

Rites	Didache	Justin Martyr	Syrian Documents	Egypt	North Africa (Tertullian/Cyprian)	Rome (?) (Apostolic Tradition)
Preparation	Instruction in the "Two Ways" Two days of fasting in immediate preparation	Instruction in the "truth" Preparatory fasting and prayer	Catechesis (possibly three weeks in length)	Possibly "40 days" of catechesis after "Epiphany"; associated with Jesus' temptation	Catechesis of unspecified length; included vigils, fasting, prayer	Three-year catechumenate Election to baptism Immediate preparation; included fasting, prayer, daily exorcism
Prebaptismal			Anointing(s) as the high point of the rite associated with the gift of the Holy Spirit	Anointing associated with the Holy Spirit	Sanctification of the waters Renunciation	Blessing of water and oils Renunciation of Satan Anointing/exorcism
Baptism Proper	Baptism in "running water" with trinitarian formula	"Regenerated" and "enlightened" with possible interrogations	Baptism with trinitarian "formula"; "new birth," "adoption"; possible use of Ps 2:7	"Regeneration" and "new birth"; associated with crossing the Jordan; formula or interrogation	Baptism connected to three-fold interrogation and profession of faith	Baptism connected to three-fold interrogation and profession of faith
Postbaptismal		Led to the assembly for common prayers and kiss			Anointing Handlaying related to Holy Spirit Consignation (Cyprian)	Anointing by presbyter Handlaying prayer for "grace" by bishop Anointing by bishop with consignation
Eucharist	Only for the baptized	Eucharist as culmination	Eucharist as culmination	Unclear if Eucharist was immediate culmination	Included "milk and honey"	Included "milk and honey"

---

1 Maxwell E. Johnson, *The Rites of Christian Initiation: Their Evolution and Interpretation* (Collegeville, MN: The Liturgical Press, 2007), 111.

188

APPENDIX 4

BAPTISMAL PROCESS AS DESCRIBED IN THE APOSTOLIC TRADITION

A detailed description of the baptismal proceedings are described by Bradshaw et. al., The Apostolic Tradition, 105–121.

The catechumen, when he is baptized, and he who presents him attests that he has been zealous for the commandments during the time of his catechumenate, that he has visited the sick or given to the needy, that he has kept himself from every wicked and disgraceful word, that he has hated vainglory, despised pride, and chosen for himself humility, and he confesses to the bishop that he [takes] responsibility for himself, so that the bishop is satisfied about him and considers him [worthy] of the mysteries, and that he has become truly pure, then he reads over him the gospel at that time, and asks him several times, "Are you in two minds, or under pressure from anything, or driven by convention? For nobody mocks the kingdom of heaven, but tis given to those who love it with all their heart." Those who are to be baptized are to bathe in water on the fifth day of the week and eat. They are to fast on Friday. If there is a woman and she has her menstrual period, she is not to be baptized on that occasion, but she is to wait until she is purified. On Saturday the bishop assembles those who are to be baptized. He makes them bow the head toward the east, extends his hand over them, and prays and expels every evil spirit from them by his exorcism, and these never return to them from that time on through their deeds. When he has finished exorcising them, he breathes on their face and signs their breast, their forehead, their ears, and their nose. They are to spend all their night in the sacred Word and prayers. One is to position them at cockcrow near the water, water from a river, running and pure, prepared, and sanctified. Those who reply for the little children are to strip them of their clothes first; then those who are capable of answering for themselves; then the women are to be last of all to divest themselves of their clothes; they are to remove their jewels, whether they are of gold or others, and loosen the hair of their head, for fear that something of the alien spirits should go down with them into the water of the second birth. The bishop blesses the oil of exorcism and gives it to a presbyter; then he blesses the oil of anointing, that is the oil of thanksgiving, and gives it to another presbyter. He who holds the oil of exorcism stands on the left of the bishop, and he who holds the oil of anointing stands on the right of the bishop. He who is to be baptized turns his face toward the west and says, "I renounce you, Satan, and all your service." When he has said that, the presbyter anoints him with the oil of exorcism that has been blessed, so that every evil spirit may depart from him. He is handed over by a deacon to the presbyter who stands near the water. A presbyter holds his right hand and makes him turn his face toward the east, near the water. Before going down into the water, his face toward the east and standing near the water, he says this after having received the oil of exorcism: "I believe, and submit myself to you and to all your service, O Father, Son, and Holy Spirit." Thus he descends into the waters; the presbyter places his hand on his head and questions him, saying, "Do you believe in God the Father Almighty?" He who is baptized replies, "I believe." Then he immerses him in the water once, his hand on his head. He questions him a second time, saying, "Do you believe in Jesus Christ, Son of God, whom the virgin Mary bore by the Holy Spirit, who came for the salvation of the human race, who was crucified in the time of Pontius Pilate, who died and was raised from the dead the third day, ascended into heaven, is seated at the right hand of the Father, and will come to judge the living and the dead?" He replies, "I believe." Then he immerses him in the water a second time. He questions him a third time, saying, "Do you believe in the Holy Spirit, the Paraclete flowing from the Father and the Son?" When he replies, "I believe," he immerses him a third time in the water. And he says each time, "I baptize you in the name of the Father, of the Son, and of the Holy Spirit, equal Trinity." Then he comes up from the water. The presbyter takes the oil of thanksgiving and signs his forehead, his mouth, and his breast, and anoints all his body, his head, and his face, saying, "I anoint you in the name of the Father, of the Son, and of the Holy Spirit." And he wipes him with a cloth, which he keeps for him. He dresses him in his clothes, and takes him into the church. The bishop lays his hand on all the baptized and prays thus: "We bless you, Lord God Almighty, for the fact that you have made these worthy to be born again, that you pour your Holy Spirit on them, and to be one in the body of your church, not being excluded by alien works; but, just as you have granted them forgiveness of their sins, grant them also the pledge of your kingdom; through our Lord

Jesus Christ, through whom be glory to you, with him and the Holy Spirit, to ages of ages. Amen." Next he signs their forehead with the oil of anointing and gives them the kiss, saying, "The Lord be with you." And those who have been baptized also say, "And with your spirit." He does this to each of the baptized. After that they pray with all the people of the faithful and they give them the kiss and rejoice with them with cries of gladness. Then the deacon begins the liturgy and the bishop completes the Eucharist of the body and blood of the Lord.

APPENDIX 5

CATECHESIS OF CYRIL OF JERUSALEM

Summary Chart of Catechesis of Cyril of Jerusalem[2]

The Catecheses of Cyril of Jerusalem

Number	Text	Trans	Topic	Subjects Covered
I. LENTEN CATECHESIS				
Pro-catechesis	Cross	FC 61	Opening of Lent	Greeting, suspect motives catechesis, daily exorcism, secrecy
1	PG 33	FC 61	[Creed]	One baptism for the forgiveness of sins
2	PG 33	FC 61	[Creed]	Repentance
3	PG 33	FC 61	[Creed]	Meaning of baptism
4	PG 33	FC 61	Ten Doctrines	God, Christ, virgin birth, cross, resurrection, ascension, judgment, Spirit, soul/body, Scriptures
5	PG 33	FC 61	Faith	Abraham, in Gospels, assent, receive Creed
6	PG 33	FC 61	Creed	Unity of God
7	PG 33	FC 61	Creed	God the Father
8	PG 33	FC 61	Creed	Omnipotent
9	PG 33	FC 61	Creed	Creator
10	PG 33	FC 61	Creed	One Lord Jesus Christ
11	PG 33	FC 61	Creed	Only-begotten Son of God
12	PG 33	FC 61	Creed	Made Flesh
13	PG 33	FC 64	Creed	Crucified and buried
14	PG 33	FC 64	Creed	Rose from dead, ascended
15	PG 33	FC 64	Creed	Judge of living/dead; kingdom without end
16	PG 33	FC 64	Creed	Spirit
17	PG 33	FC 64	Creed	Spirit
18	PG 33	FC 64	Creed	Church, resurrection of flesh, eternal life, hand back Creed
II. MYSTAGOGICAL CATECHESES (DURING EASTER WEEK)				
1	Cross	FC 64, MF 5 Yarnold	Baptism	Renunciation, profession
2	Cross	FC 64, MF 5 Yarnold	Baptism	Immersion
3	Cross	FC 64, MF 5 Yarnold	Baptism	Chrism
4	Cross	FC 64, MF 7 Yarnold	Eucharist	Body and Blood of Christ
5	Cross	FC 64, MF 7 Yarnold	Eucharist	Liturgy: Kiss, dialogue, sanctus, epiclesis, Our Father, Communion

---

2 William Harmless, *Augustine and the Catechumenate* (Collegeville, MN: Liturgical Press, 1995), 78.

APPENDIX 6

CATECHESIS OF JOHN CHRYSOSTOM

Summary Chart of Catechesis of John Chrysostom[3]

The Catecheses of John Chrysostom

I. THE CATECHUMENATE: PASSING REFERENCES

Sermon	Text	Trans	Topic
In s. Johannis, Sermon 18	PG 59	FC 41	Denounces delays
In s. Johannis, Sermon 25	PG 59	FC 41	Denounces delays
In ep. 2 Cor, Sermon 2	PG 61	NPNF 12	Commentary on prayer for dismissal of catechumens
In s. Matthaei, Sermon 4	PG 57	NPNF 10	Baptized vs. catechumens

II. LENTEN INSTRUCTIONS

Harkins's Numbering	Manuscript Numbering	Text	Trans	Delivered
1	Stavronikita 1	SC 50	ACW 31	10 days, 390
2	Stavronikita 2	SC 50	ACW 31, MF 5	Just before Easter, 390
9	Papadopoulous-Kerameus 1 = Montfaucon 1	PG 49	ACW 31	10 days into Lent, 388
10	Papadopoulous-Kerameus 2	P-K2	ACW 31	20 days into Lent, 388
11	Papadopoulous-Kerameus 3	P-K3	ACW 31	Holy Thursday, 388
12	Montfaucon 2	PG 49	ACW 31	20 days into Lent, 390(?)

	Topics
1	Spiritual marriage: mystery, contract, gifts; belief in Trinity; yoke of Christ; portrait of meek and humble heart; adornment of women; against omens, oaths, spectacles; "Christian"
2	Baptism: Adam; eyes of faith; exorcisms; sponsors; renunciation; adherence to Christ; anointing; immersion; baptismal formula
9	Deathbed baptisms; bath of regeneration; baptism and Jewish baths; training of *photizomenoi*; sins of speech; avoid swearing
10	Swearing; Easter; baptism as death/resurrection; three days in tomb; exorcism; oaths; Herod
11	Spiritual marriage; wedding garb; "faithful"; renunciation; covenant with Christ; anointing; baptism; pray for Church; sacred kiss
12	"Faithful"; "Newly-illumined"; excellent conduct; evil habits; recruits; contest with Satan; adornment of women; renunciation; omens, charms, incantations

III. EASTER WEEK INSTRUCTIONS

Harkins's Numbering	Manuscript Numbering	Text	Trans	Delivered
3	Stavronikita 3 = Sermo ad neophytos	SC 50	ACW 31	Just after baptism, 388–390

---

3 William Harmless, *Augustine and the Catechumenate* (Collegeville, MN: Liturgical Press, 1995), 75.

APPENDIX 6 Continued[4]

The Catecheses of John Chrysostom

Harkins's Numbering	Manuscript Numbering	Text	Trans	Delivered
	= Papadopoulous-Kerameus 4			
4	Stavronikita 4	SC 50	ACW 31	Easter Sun or Mon 390
5	Stavronikita 5	SC 50	ACW 31	Easter Tues 390
6	Stavronikita 6	SC 50	ACW 31	Easter Wed 390
7	Stavronikita 7	SC 50	ACW 31	Easter Fri 390
8	Stavronikita 8	SC 50	ACW 31	Easter Sat 390

	Topics
3	Neophytes greeted; graces of baptism; Blood of Christ; baptism and exodus
4	Neophytes as joy of Church; Paul as model of neophyte; new creation; conduct
5	No laxity; drunkenness; danger of relaxing; Paul vs. Simon Magus; conversion to regain innocence
6	Christians at spectacles; do all for God's glory; fraternal correction; a neophyte for life
7	Tombs of martyrs; martyrs as physicians; martyrs as models; be dead to world; almsgiving; Cornelius
8	Welcome to countryfolk; Abraham as model; vanity of world; neophyte's daily program

---

4 Ibid., 76.

APPENDIX 7

CATECHESIS OF THEODORE OF MOPSUESTIA

Summary Chart of the Catechesis of Theodore of Mopsuestia[5]

The Catecheses of Theodore of Mopsuestia

I. CATECHESES GIVEN DURING LENT

Tonneau's Number/Text	Trans	Topic	Subjects Covered
1	Mingana	Creed	Reason for creed; One God
2	Mingana	Creed	Faith; Father; Creator
3	Mingana	Creed	Son: only-begotten
4	Mingana	Creed	Son: true God, *homoousios*
5	Mingana	Creed	Son: incarnation
6	Mingana	Creed	Son: two natures
7	Mingana	Creed	Son: death, resurrection, second coming
8	Mingana	Creed	Son: two natures
9	Mingana	Creed	Spirit: divinity
10	Mingana	Creed	Spirit: consubstantial, proceeds; remission of sin; resurrection of flesh
11	Mingana	Our Father	Commentary on prayer
12	Mingana	Baptism	Prebaptismal exorcism
13	Mingana, Yarnold	Baptism	Renunciation; prebaptismal anointing
14	Mingana, MF 5 Yarnold	Baptism	Immersion, consignation

II. CATECHESES GIVEN AFTER THE VIGIL

Tonneau's Number/Text	Trans	Topic	Subjects Covered
15	Mingana, Yarnold	Eucharist	Preparation of altar; dialogue of anaphora
16	Mingana, Yarnold	Eucharist	Anaphora; communion

Syriac Text: *Les homélies catéchétiques de Théodore de Mopsueste*, Studi e Testi 145. Eds. R. Tonneau and R. Dovreesse.

Translation: A. Mingana, *Woodbrooke Studies* 5–6 (Cambridge).

Translation: Edward Yarnold, *The Awe-Inspiring Rites of Initiation: Baptismal Homilies of the Fourth Century*.

---

5 William Harmless, *Augustine and the Catechumenate* (Collegeville, MN: Liturgical Press, 1995), 77.

APPENDIX 8

CATECHESIS OF AMBROSE OF MILAN

Summary Chart of the Catechesis of Ambrose of Milan[6]

The Catecheses of Ambrose of Milan

Work	Text	Trans	Topics Covered
I. THE CATECHUMENATE: PASSING REFERENCES			
De Cain et Abel	CSEL 32.1	FC 42	*Disciplina arcani*
Exp. ps 148, Sermon 2	CSEL 32	---	*Disciplina arcani*
Exp. ps 148, Sermon 20	CSEL 32	---	Suspect motives
Exp. ev. Luc, Sermon 4	SC 45	---	Call to put in names
Epistola 20	PL 16	FC 26	Timing of *traditio*
II. LENTEN SERMONS (TO THE WHOLE ASSEMBLY)			
De Helia et ieiunio	PS 19	PS 19	Begin Lenten discipline
De Abraham 1	CSEL 32.1	---	Abraham: faith, marriage
Exp. ps 136–140	CSEL 44	---	Senses of Scripture; exhorts *competentes*
[Paulinus, *Vita* 38	PS 16	FC 15	Ambrose as catechist]
III. *TRADITIO SYMBOLI* (TO THE *COMPETENTES*)			
Expositio symboli	Connolly	Connolly	Hands over, explains Creed phrase by phrase
IV. MYSTAGOGICAL WORKS **(TO NEOPHYTES DURING EASTER WEEK)**			
De Sacramentis			
1 (Tues)	SC 25	FC 44, MF 6	Ephephtha; first anointing; renunciation
2 (Wed)	SC 25	FC 44, MF 6	Baptism: OT figures; font as "crucifixion"
3 (Thurs)	SC 25	FC 44, MF 6	Washing of feet; Chrism
4 (Fri)	SC 25	FC 44, MF 7	Eucharist: Roman canon; consecration; Amen
5 (Sat)	SC 25	FC 44, MF 7	Eucharist: sober intoxication, Lord's Prayer
6 (Sun)	SC 25	FC 44	Prayer: where, how, order
De Mysteriis	SC 25	FC 44	

Topics: Rationale of Lenten pedagogy; *disciplina arcani; ephephtha; apotaxis;* water: OT figures, invisible powers, anointing; washing of feet; new robes; seal; "ancient" sacraments; consecration; Amen; Eucharist.

---

6 William Harmless, *Augustine and the Catechumenate* (Collegeville, MN: Liturgical Press, 1995), 106.

APPENDIX 9

CATECHESIS OF AUGUSTINE

Summary of Augustine's Catechesis[7]

Sermons and Works Addressed to Catechumens

Sermon	Verbraken #	Text	Trans	Scripture/Feast
1. Cross on the Forehead				
*32	32	BAC 7	---	Ps 143
*107	107	BAC 10	NPNF 6	Lk 13:13-21
*302	302	BAC 25	---	St. Lawrence
Bibliotheca Cas 2, 114	97A	BAC 10	---	Luke 5:31-32
Denis 17	301A	BAC 25	---	Luke 14:28-33
*En in Ps 68,1	---	CCSL 39	LF 30	Ps 68
*En in Ps 141	---	CCSL 40	LF 39	Ps 141
*Tract Jn 3	---	CCSL 36	FC 78	John 1:15-18
Tract Jn 11	---	CCSL 36	FC 79	John 2:22-3:5
*Tract Jn 50	---	CCSL 36	NPNF 7	John 11:55-12:11
*Tract Jn 53	---	CCSL 36	NPNF 7	John 12:37-43
2. Catechumens Ignorance of "Secrets"				
131	131	BAC 23	NPNF 6	John 6:54-56
132	132	BAC 23	NPNF 6	John 6:56-57
235	235	BAC 24	FC 38	Luke 24:13-35
307	307	BAC 25	---	St. John the Baptist
En in Ps 80	---	CCSL 39	LF 32	Ps 80
En in Ps 109	---	CCSL 40	LF 37	Ps 109
Epistola 140	---	CSEL 44	FC 20	---
Tract Jn 11	---	CCSL 36	FC 79	John 2:22-3:5
3. Catechumens as Examples to Illustrate a Point				
46	46	BAC 7	---	Ezek 34:1-16
232	232	BAC 24	FC 38	Luke 24:13-35
Denis 20	16A	BAC 7	---	Ps 38:13
Tract Jn 4	---	CCSL 36	FC 78	John 1:19-23
Tract Jn 5	---	CCSL 36	FC 78	John 1:33
Tract Jn 13	---	CCSL 36	FC 79	John 3:22-29
Tract Jn 44	---	CCSL 36	NPNF 7	John 9:1-41
4. Admonition to Seek Baptism				
132	132	BAC 23	NPNF 6	John 6:56
135	135	BAC 23	NPNF 6	John 9:1-41
392	392	BAC 26	---	---
Bibliotheca Cas 2, 114	97 A	BAC 10	---	Luke 5:31
En in Ps 80	---	CCSL 39	LF 32	Ps 80
En in Ps 109	---	CCSL 40	LF 37	Ps 109
Epistola 151	---	CSEL 44	FC 20	---
Epistola 258	---	CSEL 57	FC 32	---
Epistola 2* (Divjak)	---	CSEL 88	FC 81	---
Lambot 10	136 B	BAC 23	---	John 9:1-41

7 William Harmless, *Augustine and the Catechumenate* (Collegeville, MN: Liturgical Press, 1995), 191.

APPENDIX 10

AUGUSTINE'S SERMONS TO THE COMPETENTES

A Summary Chart of Augustine's Sermons to the Competentes[8]

Sermons to the *Competentes*

Sermon	Verbraken #	Text	Trans
1. *Lenten Discipline: to whole assembly, beginning of Lent*			
205	205	BAC 24	FC 38
206	206	BAC 24	FC 38
207	207	BAC 24	FC 38
208	208	BAC 24	FC 38
209	209	BAC 24	FC 38
210	210	BAC 24	FC 38
De utilitate ieiunii (?)	---	CCSL 46	PS 85, FC 16
2. *Scrutiny: to the* competentes, *probably early in Lent*			
216	216	BAC 24	FC 38
3. Traditio symboli: *to the* competentes, *two weeks before vigil*			
212	212	BAC 24	FC 38, Weller
213 = Guelf 1	213	BAC 24	FC 38
214	214	BAC 24	FC 38
De symbolo ad catechumenos	---	CCSL 46	FC 27
4. Redditio symboli: *to the* competentes, *one week before vigil*			
215	215	BAC 24	FC 38
5. Traditio orationis: *to the* competentes, *one week before vigil*			
56	56	BAC 10	FC 11, Weller
57	57	BAC 10	NPNF 6
58	58	BAC 10	NPNF 6
59	59	BAC 10	NPNF 6
6. *Other sermons in which* competentes *are addressed*			
5	5	BAC 7	---
352	352	BAC 26	---
392	392	BAC 26	---

Weller = Philip T. Weller, *Selected Easter Sermons of Saint Augustine* (St. Louis: Herder Book Co., 1959)

---

8 William Harmless, *Augustine and the Catechumenate* (Collegeville, MN: Liturgical Press, 1995), 297.

APPENDIX 11

AUGUSTINE'S SERMONS DURING EASTER

Summary Chart of Augustine's Sermons to the Catechumens during Easter Week[9]

Special Easter Week Catecheses

Sermon	Verbraken #	Text	Trans
1. Seven Days of Creation (fragments)	229R–229V	BAC 24	---
2. *Tractatus epistolam Ioannis, 1–6 (7–8?)*	---	SC 75	LCC 8, NPNF 7
3. *De resurrectione corporum, contra Gentiles*	240–242	BAC 24	FC 38
4. Special question-and-answer sessions:			
De divinatione daemonum	---	CSEL 41	FC 27
[cf. *Sermon 259, 7*]	259	BAC 24	FC 38

---

9 William Harmless, *Augustine and the Catechumenate* (Collegeville, MN: Liturgical Press, 1995), 345.

BIBLIOGRAPHY

Aland, Kurt et al. *Novum Testamentum Graece.* 28th Edition. Stuttgart: Deutsche Bibelgesellschaft, 2012.

Alcin, Linda. "Causes for the Fall of the Roman Empire." Accessed July 28, 2014, from http://www.tribunesandtriumphs.org/roman-empire/causes-for-the-fall-of-the-roman-empire.htm.

Allen, Willoughby C. *A Critical and Exegetical Commentary on the Gospel according to St. Matthew.* 3rd ed. Edinburgh: T. & T. Clark, 2000.

Arius. *Confession of Faith of Arius and his Followers to Bishop Alexander of Alexandria.* Accessed August 11, 2014, from http://www.fourthcentury.com/index.php/urkunde-6.

_____. *Letter of Arius to Eusebius of Nicomedia.* Accessed August 11, 2014, from http://www.fourthcentury.com/index.php/urkunde-1.

Arn, Win and Charles Arn. *The Master's Plan for Making Disciples.* Grand Rapids, MI: Baker Books, 1998.

Arnold, Clinton E. "Early Church Catechesis and New Christians' Classes in Contemporary Evangelicalism." *JETS, 47* (2004): 39–54.

_____. *Ephesians: Zondervan Exegetical Commentary on the New Testament.* Grand Rapids, MI: Zondervan, 2010.

Auguet, Roland. *Cruelty and Civilization: The Roman Games.* New York: Routledge, 1994.

Augustine. "Sermon 216: To the Seekers," in *The Fathers of The Church a New Translation, Volume 38.* Translated by Mary Sarah Muldowney. Accessed August 28, 2014, from https://archive.org/stream/fathersofthechur009512mbp/fathersofthechur009512mbp_djvu.txt.

_____. *The First Catechetical Instruction.* Mahwah, NJ: Paulist Press, 1946.

Baker, Alan. *The Gladiator: The Secret History of Rome's Warrior Slaves.* Cambridge, MA: Da Capo Press, 2000.

Barclay, William. *The Gospel of Matthew. Vol. 2.* Philadelphia, PA: Westminster Press, 1958.

_____. *The Letters to Timothy, Titus and Philemon.* Philadelphia, PA.: Westminster, 1957.

Barna, George. *Growing True Disciples: New Strategies for Producing Genuine Followers of Christ.* Colorado Springs, CO: WaterBrook Press, 2001.

Bauer, Walter, William F. Arndt, Wilbur Gingrich, and Fredrick W. Danker. *A Greek-English Lexicon of the New Testament and Other Early Christian Literature.* 2nd ed. Chicago, IL: University of Chicago Press, 1979.

Baumgarten, Albert L. *The Flourishing of Jewish Sects in the Maccabean Era: An Interpretation.* Leiden, the Netherlands: Brill, 1997.

Beall, Todd S. *Josephus' Description of the Essenes Illustrated by the Dead Sea Scrolls.* Cambridge, UK: Cambridge University Press, 1988.

Berg, Jim. *Changed into His Image.* Greenville, SC.: BJU Press, 1999.

Bernard, John H. *The Pastoral Epistles.* Grand Rapids, MI: Baker Book House, 1980.

Best, Ernest. *ICC: Ephesians.* London, England: T & T Clark, 2004.

Blomberg, Craig L. *NAC: Matthew.* Nashville, TN: B&H Publishing Group, 1992.

Bock, Darrell L. *Luke.* Grand Rapids, MI: Baker Books, 1994.

Boice, James M. *Christ's Call to Discipleship.* Chicago, IL Moody Press, 1986.

_____. *Romans.* Grand Rapids, MI: Baker, 1995.

Borchert, Gerald L. *NAC: John 1–11.* Nashville, TN: Broadman & Holman, 1996.

_____. *NAC: John 12–21.* Nashville, TN: Broadman & Holman, 2002.

Bounds, E. M. *The Weapon of Prayer.* New Kensington, PA.: Whitaker House, 1996.

Bovon, Francois. *Luke a Commentary on the Gospel of Luke 1:1–9:50*. Minneapolis, MN: Fortress Press, 2002.

_____. *Luke a Commentary on the Gospel of Luke 9:51–19:27*. Minneapolis, MN: Fortress Press, 2013.

Bradshaw, Paul F. "The Profession of Faith in Early Christian Baptism." *Evangelical Quarterly*, *78*(2), 101–115.

_____. "The Gospel and the Catechumenate in the Third Century." *Journal of Theological Studies 50:1* (April 1999), 143–152.

Bradshaw, Paul F., Maxwell E. Johnson, L. Edward Phillips, and Harold W. Attridge. *The Apostolic Tradition: A Commentary*. Minneapolis, MN: Fortress Press, 2002.

Bray, Gerald L. *Ancient Christian Commentary on Scripture: Romans*. Downers Grove: IL: InterVarsity Press, 1998.

Breneman, Mervin. *New American Commentary: Ezra, Nehemiah, Esther*. Nashville, TN: Broadman & Holman Publishers, 1993.

Brown, Peter. *Augustine of Hippo*. Berkley, CA: University of California Press, 1967.

Bruce, A. B. *The Training of the Twelve*. Lexington, KY.: ReadaClassic.com, 2010.

Bruce, F. F. *The Book of the Acts* (Rev. ed.). Grand Rapids, MI: William B. Eerdmans Publishing Co, 1988.

_____. *The Gospel of John*. Grand Rapids, MI: Eerdmans Pub. Co., 1983.

_____. *NICNT: The Epistle to the Colossians, to Philemon, and to the Ephesians*. Grand Rapids, MI: Eerdmans, 1984.

_____. *Tyndale New Testament Commentary: Romans*. Grand Rapids, MI: William B. Eerdmans Publishing Co. 1993.

Brown, Francis, S. R. Driver, and Charles A. Briggs. *The New Brown, Driver, Briggs, Gesenius Hebrew and English Lexicon: With an Appendix Containing the Biblical Aramaic*. Peabody, MA: Hendrickson, 1979.

Brown, Raymond E. *The Gospel According to John (xii-xxi).2nd ed*. Garden City, NY: Doubleday, 1966.

Buchanan, Edward A. "The Catechumenate of the Early Church with Implication for the Church of the 21st Century." Valley Forge, PA: ETS Annual Conference, 2005.

Burggraff, Andrew. "Developing Discipleship Curriculum: Applying the Systems Approach Model for Designing Instruction by Dick, Carey, and Carey to the Construction of Church Discipleship Courses." *Christian Education Journal* 12 (2015): 397–414.

Cansdale, Lena. *Qumran and the Essenes: A Re-Evaluation of the Evidence.* Tubingen: J. C. B. Mohr and Paul Siebeck, 1997.

Carson, Donald A. *EBC: Matthew (vol. 8).* Grand Rapids, MI: Zondervan Pub. House, 1984.

_____. *The Gospel According to John.* Grand Rapids, MI: Wm. B. Eerdmans Publishing Co., 1990.

_____. *New Bible Commentary, 21st Century Edition.* Leicester, England: Inter-Varsity Press, 1994.

Carson, Donald A., Douglas J. Moo, and Leon Morris. *An Introduction to the New Testament (2nd ed.).* Grand Rapids, MI: Zondervan, 2005.

Chadwick, Henry. *Origen: Contra Celsum.* Cambridge, UK: Cambridge University Press, 1953.

_____. and J. E. L. Oulton. *Alexandrian Christianity: Selected Translations of Clement and Origen.* Louisville, KY: Westminster John Knox Press, 2006.

Charlesworth, James H. *The Dead Sea Scrolls. Vol. 1. Rule of the Community and Related Documents.* Louisville, KY: Westminster John Knox Press, 1994.

Chateaubriand, François-René de. *The Martyrs.* New York, NY: Derbyand Jackson, 1859.

Christensen, Duane L. *Word Biblical Commentary: Deuteronomy.* Nashville, TN: Thomas Nelson, 2002.

Chrysostom, John. *Against the Circuses and Theatre: Homily of St. John Chrysostom, Archbishop of Constantinople, our Sainted Father: Against Those who have Abandoned the Church and Deserted it for Hippodromes and Theatres.* Translated by Mark Vermes. Accessed July 29, 2014, from http://www.tertullian.org/fathers/chrysostom_against_theatres_and_circuses.htm.

_____. *Baptismal Instructions*. Mahwah, NJ: Paulist Press, 1963.

_____. *Instructions to Catechumens: Second Instruction*. Translated by T.P. Brandram. Accessed August 28, 2014, from http://www.newadvent.org / fathers/1908.htm.

Clement of Alexandria. *Instructor*. Accessed August 27, 2014, from http://www.ccel.org/ccel/schaff/anf02.vi.iii.i.vi.html.

_____. *Paedagogos*. Translated by William Wilson. Accessed July 30, 2014, from http://www.newadvent.org/fathers/02093.htm.

_____. *The Stromata*. Accessed August 27, 2014, from http://www.ccel.org/ccel/schaff/anf02.vi.iv.ii.xviii.html.

Cohick, Lynn. *Women in the World of the Earliest Christians: Illuminating Ancient Ways of Life*. Grand Rapids, MI: Baker Academic, 2009.

Collins, Raymond F. *1 & 2 Timothy and Titus: A Commentary*. Louisville, KY: Westminster John Knox Press, 2002.

Connolly, R. Hugh. *Didascalia Apostolorum*. Oxford, England: Clarendon Press, 1929. Accessed from July 30, 2014, from http://www.earlychristianwritings.com/text/didascalia.html

Cranfield, Charles. E. B. *ICC: A Critical and Exegetical Commentary on the Epistle to the Romans: Volume 2*. Edinburgh, Scotland: T. & T. Clark, 2000.

Cross, F. L. and E. A. Livingstone. "Ebionites." *Dictionary of the Christian Church*. Peabody, MA: Hendrickson Publishers, 1997.

Davids, Peter. H. *The Letters of 2 Peter and Jude*. Grand Rapids, MI: William B. Eerdmans Pub. Co., 2006.

Davies, Philip R. *Behind the Essenes: History and Ideology in the Dead Sea Scrolls*. Atlanta, GA: Scholars Press, 1987.

Davies, Philip R., George J. Brooke, and Phillip R. Callaway. *The Complete World of the Dead Sea Scrolls*. New York, NY: Thames & Hudson, 2002.

Davies, W. D. and Dale C. Allison. *ICC: A Critical and Exegetical Commentary on the Gospel According to Saint Matthew*. London, England: T & T Clark, 2004.

Davis, Michael T., and Brent A. Strawn. *Qumran Studies: New Approaches, New Questions*. Grand Rapids, MI: William B. Eerdmans Pub. Co., 2007.

Dibelius, Martin and Hans Conzelmann. *The Pastoral Epistles: A Commentary on the Pastoral Epistles*. Philadelphia, PA: Fortress Press, 1972.

Dickerson, John S. *The Great Evangelical Recession: 6 Factors That Will Crash the American Church...and How to Prepare*. Grand Rapids, MI: Baker Books, 2013.

Dohrmann, Natalie B. and Annette Y. Reed. *Jews, Christians, and the Roman Empire*. Philadelphia, PA: University of Pennsylvania Press, 2013.

Downs, Perry G. *Teaching for Spiritual Growth*. Grand Rapids, MI: Zondervan Pub. House, 1994.

Duerlinger, James. *Ultimate Reality and Spiritual Discipline*. New York, NY: Paragon House Publishers, 1984.

Duggan, Robert D. *Conversion and the Catechumenate*. Mahwah, NJ : Paulist Pr., 1984.

Dujarier, Michel. *A History of the Catechumenate: The First Six Centuries*. New York, NY: William H. Sadlier Inc., 1979.

Dunn, James D. *WBC: Romans*. Dallas, TX: Word Books, 1988.

Dunn, Rita and Kenneth Dunn. *Teaching Secondary Students Through Their Individual Learning Styles*. Boston MA: Allyn and Bacon, 1993.

Dupont-Sommer, Andre. *The Essene Writings from Qumran*. Cleveland, OH: Meridian Books, 1962.

_____. *The Jewish Sect of Qumran and the Essenes: New Studies on the Dead Sea Scrolls*. London, England: Vallentine, Mitchell & Co., 1954.

Edersheim, Alfred. *The Life and Times of Jesus the Messiah. Vol. 1*. Grand Rapids, MI: WM. B. Eerdmans Publishing Co., 1883.

Edwards, James R. *NIBC: Romans*. Peabody, MA: Hendrickson, 1992.

Eims, Leroy. *The Lost Art of Disciple Making*. Grand Rapids, MI: Zondervan, 1978.

Eldridge, Daryl. *The Teaching Ministry of the Church: Integrating Biblical Truth with Contemporary Application*. Nashville, TN: Broadman & Holman, 1995.

Elowsky, Joel C. *Ancient Christian Commentary on Scripture: John 11–21*. Downers Grove, IL: InterVarsity Press, 2007.

Epstein, I. "Yebamoth: Folio 47 a-b." *Soncino Babylonian Talmud*. London, England: Soncino Press, 1948.

_____. "Yebamoth: Folio 47 b." *Soncino Babylonian Talmud*. London, England: Soncino Press, 1948.

Erickson, Millard J. *Christian Theology*. Grand Rapids, MI: Baker Books, 1998.

Evans, Craig A. *NIBC: Luke*. Peabody, MA: Hendrickson Publishers, 1990.

Fagan, Garrett G. *Bathing in Public in the Roman World*. Ann Arbor, MI: The University of Michigan Press, 2002.

Fee, Gordon D. *NIBC: 1 and 2 Timothy, Titus*. Peabody, MA: Hendrickson, Publishers, 1988.

_____. *NICNT: Paul's Letter to the Philippians*. Grand Rapids, MI: W.B. Eerdmans Pub. Co., 1995.

_____. *The First Epistle to the Corinthians*. Grand Rapids, MI: W.B. Eerdmans Publishing Co., 1987.

Fensham, F. Charles. *The New International Commentary on the Old Testament: Ezra and Nehemiah*. Grand Rapids, MI: W. B. Eerdmans, 1982.

Ferguson, Everett. *Backgrounds of Early Christianity*. Grand Rapids, MI: W. B. Eerdmans Pub. Co., 2003.

_____. *Baptism in the Early Church: History, Theology, and Liturgy in the First Five Centuries*. Grand Rapids, MI: William B. Eerdmans Publishing Company, 2009.

Finn, Thomas. M. *Early Christian Baptism and the Catechumenate: Italy, North Africa, and Egypt*. Collegeville, MN: Liturgical Press, 1992.

_____. *Early Christian Baptism and the Catechumenate: West and East Syria*. Collegeville, MN: Liturgical Press, 1992.

Finney, Paul C., David Scholer, and Everett Ferguson. *Conversion, Catechumenate, and Baptism in the Early Church*. New York, NY.: Garland, 1993.

Fitzmyer, Joseph A. *Romans: A New Translation with Introduction and Commentary*. New Haven, CT: Yale University Press, 2008.

_____. *The Dead Sea Scrolls and Christian Origins*. Grand Rapids, MI: William B. Eerdmans Publishing Company, 2000.

Flusser, David. *Judaism of the Second Temple period*. Vol. 1. Grand Rapids, MI: William B. Eerdmans Pub., 2007.

Folkemer, Lawrence D. "A Study of the Catechumenate." *Studies in Early Christianity*. New York, England: Garland Publishing Inc., 1993.

Foster, Richard J. *Celebration of Discipline, The Path to Spiritual Growth*. San Francisco, CA: HarperOne, 1989.

France, R. T. *NICNT: The Gospel of Matthew*. Grand Rapids, MI: William B. Eerdmans Pub., 2007.

Frank, Tenney. *A History of Rome*. New York, NY: Henry Hold and Company, 1923.

Frend, W. H. C. *The Rise of Christianity*. Philadelphia, PA: Fortress Press, 1984.

Gaebelein, Frank. E. *EBC: Matthew, Mark, Luke*. Grand Rapids, MI: Zondervan Pub. House, 1984.

Gangel, Kenneth O. and Benson, Warren S. *Christian Education: Its History and Philosophy*. Chicago, IL: Moody Press, 1983.

Gantt, Susan D. *Catechetical Instruction as an Educational Process for the Teaching of Doctrine to Children in Southern Baptist Churches*. Ph. D. diss. The Southern Baptist Theological Seminary. 2004.

Gardner, Howard. *Multiple Intelligences: New Horizons in Theory and Practice*. Rev. and updated ed. New York, NY: BasicBooks, 2006.

Garland, David E. *1 Corinthians*. Grand Rapids, MI: Baker Academic, 2003.

_____. *Luke*. Grand Rapids, MI: Zondervan, 2011.

Gavin, Frank S. B. *The Jewish Antecedents of the Christian Sacraments*. New York, NY: Cosimo Inc., 2005.

Geiger, Eric, Michael Kelley, and Philip Nation. *Transformational Discipleship: How People Really Grow*. Nashville, TN: B & H Publishing Group, 2012.

Geldenhuys, Norval. *NICNT: The Gospel of Luke*. Grand Rapids, MI: Eerdmans, 1983.

Gibbon, Edward. *Decline and Fall of the Roman Empire*. Accessed July 28, 2014 from http://sacred-texts.com/cla/gibbon/02/daf02043.htm.

Gibbon, Edward. *Gibbon's Decline and Fall of the Roman Empire: Abridged and Illustrated.* London, England: Bison Books, 1985.

Ginsburg, Christian D. *The Essenes: Their History and Doctrines.* London, England: Routledge & Kegan Paul LTD, 1956.

Golb, Norman. *Who Wrote the Dead Sea Scrolls? The Search of the Secret of Qumran.* New York, England: Scribner, 1995.

González, Justo L. *The Story of Christianity.* Peabody, MA: Prince Press, 1999.

Gourlay, Kenneth H. *An Assessment of Bible Knowledge Among Adult Southern Baptist Sunday School Participants.* Ed.D. diss. Southeastern Baptist Theological Seminary, 2010.

Green, Joel B. *The Gospel of Luke.* Grand Rapids, MI: W.B. Eerdmans Pub. Co., 1997.

Green, Joel B., Jeannine K. Brown, and Nicholas Perrin. *Dictionary of Jesus and the Gospels.* Second ed. Downers Grove, IL: InterVarsity Press, 2013.

Grudem, Wayne. *Systematic Theology.* Leicester, England: InterVarsity Press, 1994.

Gundry, Robert H. *Matthew: A Commentary on His Literary and Theological Art.* Grand Rapids, MI: W.B. Eerdmans Pub. Co., 1982.

Guthrie, George H. *Will We Rise to Biblical Literacy?* Accessed March 12, 2013, from http://www.bpnews.net/bpnews.asp?id=34558.

Haenchen, Ernst. *John.* Philadelphia, PA: Fortress Press, 1984.

Hagner, Donald A. *WBC: Matthew 14–28.* (Vol. 33b). Nashville, TN: Word Incorporated, 1995.

Harmless, William. *Augustine and the Catechumenate.* Collegeville, MN: Liturgical Press, 1995.

Harrington, Bobby and Alex Absalom. *Discipleship that Fits: The Five Kinds of Relationships God Uses to Help Us Grow.* Grand Rapids, MI: Zondervan, 2016.

Hauerwas, Stanley. *Matthew.* Grand Rapids, MI: Brazos Press, 2006.

Harvey, Susan A. and David G. Hunter. *The Oxford Handbook of Early Christian Studies.* Oxford, UK: Oxford University Press, 2008.

Hengel, Martin. *Crucifixion in the Ancient World and the Folly of the Message of the Cross.* Philadelphia, PA: Fortress Press, 1977.

Heron, James. *The Church of the Sub-Apostolic Age: Its Life, Worship, and Organization, in the Light of "The Teaching of the Twelve Apostles."* London, England: Hodder and Stoughton, 1888.

Hodge, Charles. *Ephesians.* Grand Rapids, MI: W.B. Eerdmans Pub., 1994.

Hoehner, Harold W. *Ephesians: An Exegetical Commentary.* Grand Rapids, MI: Baker Academic, 2002.

Hoffman, R. Joseph. "Translation of Celsus," in *On the True Doctrine, A Discourse Against the Christians.* USA: Oxford University Press, 1987.

Hoole, C.H. *Didache.* Accessed March 22, 2012, from http://www.earlychristianwritings.com/text/didache-hoole.html.

Howlett, Duncan. *The Essenes and Christianity.* New York, NY: Harper and Brothers Publishers, 1957.

Hudgins, Thomas W. *Luke 6:40 and the Theme of Likeness Education in the New Testament.* Ed.D. Diss., Southeastern Baptist Theological Seminary, 2013.

Hughes, Kent R. *Disciplines of a Godly Man.* Wheaton, IL: Crossway Books, 1991.

Hull, Bill. *The Complete Book of Discipleship.* Colorado Springs, CO: NavPress, 2006.

_____. *The disciple-making church.* Old Tappan, NJ: F.H. Revell Co., 1990.

Irenaeus. *Against Heresies.* Translated by Alexander Roberts and William Rambaut. Accessed July 31, 2014, from http://www.newadvent.org/fathers/0103123.htm.

Jackson, Pamela. "Cyril of Jerusalem's Use of Scripture in Catechesis." *Theological Studies 52.* (1991), 431–450.

Jeffers, James S. *The Greco-Roman World of the New Testament Era, Exploring the Background of Early Christianity.* Downers Grove, IL: Intervarsity Pr., 1999.

Jeffrey, David L. *Luke.* Grand Rapids, MI: Brazos Press, 2012.

Jewett, Robert. *Romans: A Commentary*. Minneapolis, MN: Fortress Press, 2007.

Johnson, Maxwell E. "Christian Initiation," in *The Oxford Handbook of Early Christian Studies*. New York, NY: Oxford University Press, 2008.

_____. "From Three Weeks to Forty Days: Baptismal Preparation and the Origins of Lent," in *Living Water, Sealing Spirit*. Collegeville, MN: The Liturgical Press, 1995.

_____. *The Rites of Christian Initiation: Their Evolution and Interpretation*. Collegeville, MN: The Liturgical Press, 2007.

Jones, Arnold H. M. *The Later Roman Empire, 284–602: A Social, Economic, and Administrative Survey*. Baltimore, MD: Johns Hopkins Press, 1986.

Josephus, Flavius. *The Works of Josephus: Complete and Unabridged*. New updated ed. Peabody, MA: Hendrickson Publishers, 1987.

Justin Martyr. *First Apology*. Translated by Marcus Dods and George Reith. Accessed July 31, 2014, from http://www.newadvent.org/fathers/0126.htm.

Keener, Craig S. *The Gospel of John: A Commentary*. Peabody, MA: Hendrickson Publishers, 2003.

_____. "Matthew's Missiology: Making Disciples of the Nations." (Matthew 28:19–20), *Asian Journal of Pentecostal Studies, 12 (1)*. (2009), 3–20.

_____. *The Gospel of Matthew: A Socio-Rhetorical Commentary*. Grand Rapids, MI: William B. Eerdmans Pub., 2009.

Keil, Carl F. and Delitzsch, Franz. *Commentary on the Old Testament: The Pentateuch*. Grand Rapids, MI: Eerdmans, 1975.

Kinnaman, David. *You Lost Me: Why Young Christians are Leaving Church...and Rethinking Faith*. Grand Rapids, MI: Baker Books, 2011.

Kittel, Gerhard. *Theological Dictionary of the New Testament: Vol.4*. Edited by G. Kittel; edited and translated by G.W. Bromiley. Grand Rapids, MI: Wm. B. Eerdmans Pub. Co., 1967.

Klein, Gottlieb. *Der älteste christliche Katechismus und die jüdische Propaganda-Literatur*. Berlin: G. Reimer, 1909.

Knight, George W. *The Pastoral Epistles: A Commentary on the Greek Text*. Grand Rapids, MI: W.B. Eerdmans, 1992.

Knowles, David. *Christian Monasticism*. New York, NY: McGraw-Hill, 1969.

Köstenberger, Andreas. J. *John*. Grand Rapids, MI: Baker Academic, 2004.

Kreider, Alan. "Baptism, Catechism, and the Eclipse of Jesus' Teaching in Early Christianity." *Tyndale Bulletin, 47(2)*. (Nov. 1996), 315–348.

_____. *The Change of Conversion and the Origin of Christendom*. Eugene, OR: Wipf & Stock Pub., 2007.

Kruse, Colin G. *Paul's Letter to the Romans*. Grand Rapids, MI.: William B. Eerdmans Pub. Co., 2012.

Latourette, Kenneth S. *A History of Christianity*. Peabody, MA: Prince Press, 1997.

Lea, Thomas D. and Hayne P. Griffin. *NAC: 1, 2 Timothy, Titus*. Nashville, TN: Broadman Press, 1992.

Leedy, Paul D. and Ellis J. Ormrod. *Practical Research: Planning and Design* (9th ed.). Upper Saddle River, NJ: Merrill, 2010.

Liddell, Henry G. and Robert Scott. *A Greek-English Lexicon*. 8th ed. New York, NY: American Book Company, 1882.

Liefeld, Walter L. *1 & 2 Timothy/Titus: the NIV Application Commentary from Biblical Text--To Contemporary Life*. Grand Rapids, MI: Zondervan, 1999.

Lightfoot, J. B. *The Shepherd of Hermas*. Accessed August 27, 2014, from http://www.earlychristianwritings.com/text/shepherd-lightfoot.html.

Limburg, James. *Psalms*. Louisville, KY: Westminster John Knox, 2000.

Lincoln, Andrew T. *WBC: Ephesians*. Waco, TX: Word Books, 1990.

Loftness, John and C. J. Mahaney. *Disciplined for Life: Steps to Spiritual Strength*. Gaithersburg, MD: People of Destiny International, 1992.

Longenecker, Richard N. *EBC: John–Acts*. Grand Rapids, MI: Zondervan Pub. House, 1981.

_____. *Patterns of Discipleship in the New Testament*. Grand Rapids, MI: William B. Eerdmans Pub, 1996.

Longman III, Tremper and Peter Enns. *Dictionary of the Old Testament: Wisdom, Poetry & Writings*. Downers Grove, IL: InterVarsity Press, 2008.

Longus. *Daphnis and Chloe*. Translated by William B. Tyrrell. Accessed April 20, 2014, from https://www.msu.edu/~tyrrell/daphchlo.htm.

Luz, Ulrich. *Matthew 21–28: Hermeneia*. Philadelphia, PA: Fortress Press, 2005.

Lynch, Joseph H. *Godparents and Kinship in Early Medieval Europe*. Princeton, NJ: Princeton University Press, 1986.

MacArthur, John. *Ephesians*. Chicago, IL: Moody Press, 1986.

_____. *Romans 9–16*. Chicago, IL: Moody Press, 1994.

_____. *2 Timothy*. Chicago, IL: Moody Press, 1995.

Markus, R. A. *Saeculum: History and Society in the Theology of St Augustine*. Cambridge, UK: The Cambridge University Press, 1989.

Marlin, Steve. *Barna Research Group: Megatheme: Biblical Illiteracy!* Accessed March 14, 2012, from http://hopeforbrazil.com/wordpress/barna-research-group-megatheme-biblical-illiteracy/.

Marshall, I. Howard. *The Gospel of Luke: A Commentary on the Greek Text*. Grand Rapids, MI: Eerdmans, 1978.

_____. *ICC: A Critical and Exegetical Commentary on the Pastoral Epistles*. London, England: T & T Clark, 2004.

Martínez, Florentino, Julio C. Barrera, and Wilfred G. E. Watson. *The People of the Dead Sea Scrolls*. Leiden, The Netherlands: E.J. Brill, 1995.

Marzano, Robert J., Debra Pickering, and Jane E. Pollock. *Classroom Instruction That Works: Research-Based Strategies for Increasing Student Achievement*. Alexandria, VA: Association for Supervision and Curriculum Development, 2001.

Mason, Steve. *Josephus, Judea, and Christian Origins: Methods and Categories*. Peabody, MA: Hendrickson Publishers, 2009.

McClure, M. L. and Charles L. Feltoe. *The Pilgrimage of Ethoria*. Accessed March 14, 2012, from http://www.ccel.org/m/mcclure/etheria/etheria.htm

McDonnell, Kilian and George T. Montague. *Christian Initiation and Baptism in the Holy Spirit: Evidence from the First Eight Centuries*. Collegeville, MN: Liturgical Press, 1991.

McGrath, Alister E. *Historical Theology: An Introduction to the History of Christian Thought*. Malden, MA: Blackwell Publishing, 1998.

McMillan, James H. *Educational Research: Fundamentals for the Consumer* (6th ed.). Boston, MA: Pearson, 2012.

Merdinger, J. E. *Rome and the African Church in the Time of Augustine*. New Haven, CT: Yale University Press, 1997.

Michaels, J. Ramsey. *NIBC: John*. Peabody, MA: Hendrickson Publishers, 1989.

_____. *NICNT: The Gospel of John*. Grand Rapids, MI: William B. Eerdmans Pub., 2010.

Mintz, Sidney W. and Eric R. Wolf. "An Analysis of Ritual Co-Parenthood (Compadrazgo)." *Southwestern Journal of Anthropology. Vol. 6, No. 4* (Winter, 1950), 341–368.

Mohler, Albert. *The Scandal of Biblical Illiteracy: It's Our Problem*. Accessed March 22, 2013, from http://www.albertmohler.com/2005/10/14/the-scandal-of-biblical-illiteracy-its-our-problem/.

Monroe, Paul. *A Cyclopedia of Education*. New York, NY: The Macmillan Company, 1919.

Moo, Douglas J. *NICNT: The Epistle to the Romans*. Grand Rapids, MI: W.B. Eerdmans Pub. Co., 1996.

Moreland, J. P. *Love Your God with all Your Mind*. Colorado Springs, CO: NavPress, 1997.

Morris, Leon. *The Epistle to the Romans*. Grand Rapids, MI: W.B. Eerdmans, 1988.

_____. *The Gospel According to John* (Rev. ed.). Grand Rapids, MI: William B. Eerdmans Publishing Co., 1995.

Mounce, Robert H. *NAC: Romans*. (Vol. 28). Nashville, TN: Broadman & Holman Pub., 1995.

_____. *NIBC: Matthew: Based on the New International Version*. Peabody, MA: Hendrickson, 1998.

Mounce, William D. *WBC: Pastoral Epistles*. Waco, TX: Word Books, 2000.

Murphy Center for Liturgical Research. (1976). *Made, Not Born: New Perspectives on Christian Initiation and the Catechumenate*. University of Notre Dame Press, 1976.

Murray, John. *NICNT: The Epistle to the Romans*. Grand Rapids, MI: Wm. B. Eerdmans Pub. Co., 1965.

Nicarchus, "Anthologia Graeca, 11.243," *Greek Anthropology, Vo. 4*. Edited by W.R. Paton, Accessed July 30, 2014, from http://www.perseus.tufts.edu/hopper/text?doc=Perseus%3Atext%3A2008.01.0475%3Abook%3D11%3Achapter%3D243.

Nolland, John. *WBC: Luke*. Dallas, TX: Word Books, 1989.

_____. *NIGTC: The Gospel of Matthew: A Commentary on the Greek Text*. Grand Rapids, MI: W.B. Eerdmans Pub. Co., 2005.

O'Brien, Peter T. *The Letter to the Ephesians*. Grand Rapids, MI: W.B. Eerdmans Publishing Co., 1999.

O'Donnell, James J. *Augustine: A New Biography*. New York, NY: Harper Perennial, 2006.

Olson, Roger E. *The Story of Christian Theology, Twenty Centuries of Tradition & Reform*. Downers Grove, IL: Intervarsity Pr., 1999.

Origen. *Against Celsus*. Translated by Frederick Crombie. Accessed August 27, 2014, from http://www.newadvent.org/fathers/04163.htm.

Orr, James. *The International Standard Bible Encyclopedia*. Hendrickson Publishers, Inc. Peabody, MA: Hendrickson Publishers, 1984.

Osborne, Grant R. *Matthew*. Grand Rapids, MI: Zondervan, 2010.

Ovid. *Metamorphoses*. Translated by A. S. Kline. Accessed April 20, 2014, from http://ovid.lib.virginia.edu/trans/Metamorph2.htm#476707488.

Parrett, Gary A. and S. Steve Kang. *Teaching the Faith, Forming the Faithful: A Biblical Vision for Education in the Church*. Downers Grove, IL: IVP Academic, 2009.

Pasquato, Ottorino. *Encyclopedia of Ancient Christianity, A-E: Catechumenate-Discipleship*. Downers Grove, IL: Intervarsity Press, 2014.

Pate, C. Marvin. *The Writings of John: A Survey of the Gospel, Epistles, and Apocalypse.* Grand Rapids, MI: Zondervan, 2011.

Pfann, Stephen J. "The Essene Yearly Renewal Ceremony and the Baptism of Repentance." *The Provo International Conference on the Dead Sea Scrolls: Technological Innovations, New Texts, and Reformulated Issues.* Eds. D. Parry and E. Ulrich, Leiden, The Netherlands: Brill, 1999, 336–352.

Phillips, John. *Exploring Romans.* Grand Rapids, MI: Kregel Publications, 1969.

_____. *Exploring the Gospel of John: An Expository Commentary.* Grand Rapids, MI.: Kregel Publications, 2001.

Philo. *The Works of Philo.* Translated by C. D. Yonge. Peabody, MA: Hendrickson, 1993.

_____. *Apology* in Eusebius. *Praeparatio Evangelica.* Translated by E.H. Gifford. 1903. Accessed June 9, 2014, http://www.tertullian.org/fathers/eusebius_pe_08_book8.htm#13.

Pliny. *Natural History.* Accessed July 30, 2014, from http://penelope.uchicago.edu/Thayer/L/Roman/Texts/Pliny_the_Elder/29*.html.

Plummer, Alfred. *ICC: St. Luke.* Edinburgh, Scotland: T & T Clark, 1953.

_____. *The Gospel According to St. John.* Cambridge, England: Cambridge University Press, 1906.

Prothero, Stephen R. *Religious Literacy: What Every American Needs to Know--and Doesn't.* New York, NY: HarperOne, 2008.

Pusey, Karen. *Jewish Proselyte Baptism.* Swansea, Great Britain: The Phoenix Press, 1993.

Rankin, Russ. "Baptist Press—Lack of Bible literacy is Spotlighted—News with a Christian Perspective." *Baptist Press—Baptist Press News with a Christian Perspective.* Accessed March 22, 2012, from http://www.bpnews.net/bpnews.asp?id=35125.

Reese, Michael P. *An Assessment of Bible Knowledge of Churches of Christ in West Virginia and Related Variables* Ed.D. diss. Southeastern Baptist Theological Seminary, 2010.

Reu, Johann Michael. *Catechetics: Or, Theory and Practice of Religious Instruction.* Chicago, IL: Wartburg Publishing House, 1918.

Rist, John M. *Augustine: Ancient Thought Baptized.* Cambridge, UK: The Cambridge University Press, 1994.

Roach, David. "Bible Reading Drops During Social Distancing." Accessed May 4, 2022, from https://www.christianitytoday.com/news/2020/july/state-of-bible-reading-coronavirus-barna-abs.html.

Roberts, Alexander J. *Ante-Nicene Fathers. (Vol VII).* Grand Rapids, MI: Eerdmans Pub. Co., 1975.

Ryan, Thomas P. *Disciplines for Christian Living: Interfaith Perspectives.* New York, NY: Paulist Press, 1993.

Ryrie, Charles C. *Basic Theology: A Popular Systemic Guide to Understanding Biblical Truth.* Chicago, IL: Moody Press, 1999.

Saarinen, Risto. *The Pastoral Epistles with Philemon & Jude.* Grand Rapids, MI: Brazos Press, 2008.

Sanders, E. P. *Judaism Practice and Belief: 63 BCE–66 CE.* Philadelphia, PA.: Trinity Press International, 1992.

Schaff, Philip. *Augustine: On the Holy Trinity, Doctrinal Treatises, Moral Treatises.* Peabody, MA: Hendrickson Publishers, 1994.

_____. *Creeds and Cristendom.* Accessed August 11, 2014, from http://www.ccel.org/ccel/schaff/creeds1.iv.iii.html.

_____. *Nicene and Post-Nicene Fathers of the Christian Church: Cyril of Jerusalem and Gregory Nazianzen*, Vol. VII. Grand Rapids, MI: WM. B. Eerdmans Publishing Company, 1978.

_____. *Origen: Against Celsus.* Accessed August 25, 2014, from http://www.ccel.org/ccel/schaff/anf04.pdf.

_____. *The New Schaff-Herzog Encyclopedia of Religious Knowledge: Embracing Biblical, Historical, Doctrinal, and Practical Theology and Biblical, Theological, and Ecclesiastical Biography from the Earliest Times to the Present Day.* New York, NY: Funk and Wagnalls Company, 1908.

Schmidt, Alvin J. *Under the Influence: How Christianity Transformed Civilization.* Grand Rapids, MI: Zondervan, 2001.

Schreiner, Thomas R. *Romans.* Grand Rapids, MI: Baker Books, 1998.

Schuré, Edouard. *Jesus, the Last Great Initiate*. Chicago, IL: Yogi Publication Society, 1908.

Schürer, Emil. *A History of the Jewish People in the Time of Jesus Christ*. 5th printing. Peabody, MA: Hendrickson Pub., 2008.

Seeberg, Alfred. *Die Didache des Judentums und der Urchristenheit*. Leipzig, Germany: Georg Bohme, 1908.

Shephard, John W. *The Christ of the Gospels*. Grand Rapids, MI: WM. B. Eerdmans Publishing Companry, 1947.

Sherrill, Lewis J. *The Rise of Christian Education*. New York, NY: The Macmillan Company, 1950.

Simon, Marcel. *Jewish Sects at the Time of Jesus*. Philadelphia, PA: Fortress Press, 1967.

Smither, Edward L. *Augustine as Mentor: A Model for Preparing Spiritual Leaders*. Nashville, TN: B & H Publishing Group, 2008.

Spicq, Ceslas. *Theological Lexicon of the New Testament*. *Vol. 2*. Peabody, MA: Hendrickson, 1994.

Spinks, Bryan D. (2006). *Early And Medieval Rituals And Theologies of Baptism: From the New Testament to the Council of Trent (Liturgy, Worship and Society Series)* (New edition.). Burlington, VT: Ashgate Pub Co., 2006.

Sproul, R. C. "Burning Hearts are Not Nourished by Empty Heads." *Christianity Today, September* (3). (1982), 100.

Stark, Rodney. *The Rise of Christianity, A Sociologist Reconsiders History*. (7th ed.). Princeton, NJ: Princeton Univ. Pr., 1996.

Stegemann, Hartmut. "The Qumran Essenes—Local Members of the Main Jewish Union in Late Second Temple Times." *The Madrid Qumran Congress: Proceedings of the International Congress on the Dead Sea Scrolls, Madrid, 18–21 March 1991*. Edited by Julio C. Barrera and Luis Montaner. Leiden, The Netherlands: E. J. Brill, 1992.

Stemberger, Günter. *Jewish contemporaries of Jesus: Pharisees, Sadducees, Essenes*. Minneapolis, MN: Fortress Press, 1995.

Tacitus. *Loeb Classical Library edition of Tacitus, vol. 5, Book 15*. Cambridge, MA: Harvard University Press, 1937.

Tertullian. *Tertullian: Adversus Marcionem*. Translated by Ernest Evans. Oxford, England: Oxford University Press, 1972.

The Barna Group. "Barna Studies the Research, Offers a Year-in-Review Perspective." *The Barna Group—Barna Update*. Accessed March 22, 2012, from http://www.barna.org/barna-update/article/12-faithspirituality/325-barna-studies-the-research-offers-a-year-in-review-perspective.

_____. *Report Examines the State of Mainline Protestant Churches*. Accessed March 22, 2012, from https://www.barna.org/barna-update/article/17-leadership/323-report-examines-the-state-of-mainline-protestant-churches.

_____. *Six Megathemes Emerge from Barna Group Research in 2010*. Accessed March 22, 2012, from https://www.barna.org/barna-update/culture/462-six-megathemes-emerge-from-2010.

_____. *Are Christians More Like Jesus or More Like the Pharisees?* Accessed March 12, 2013, from https://www.barna.org/barna-update/faith-spirituality/611-christians-more-like-jesus-or-pharisees.

Theodore of Mopseustia. *Commentary on the Lord's Prayer, Baptism and the Eucharist*. Translated by Alphonse Mingana, 1933. Accessed August 28, 2014, from http://www.ccel.org/ccel/pearse/morefathers/files/theodore_of_mopsuestia_lordsprayer_02_text.htm#3.

Thiering, B. E. *The Qumran Origins of the Christian Church*. Sydney, Australia: Theological Explorations, 1983.

Thiselton, Anthony C. *The First Epistle to the Corinthians: A Commentary on the Greek Text*. Grand Rapids, MI: W.B. Eerdmans, 2000.

Thomas, David. *The Gospel of St. Matthew: An Expository and Homiletic Commentary*. Grand Rapids, MI: Baker Book House, 1956.

Thomas, George E. *Personal Power through the Spiritual Disciplines*. New York, NY: Abingdon Press, 1960.

Thompson, J. A. *New American Commentary: 1, 2 Chronicles*. Nashville, TN: Broadman & Holman, 1994.

Thompson, Norma H. *Religious Education and Theology*. Birmingham, AL: Religious Education Press, 1982.

Towner, Philip H. *NICNT: The Letters to Timothy and Titus*. Grand Rapids, MI: William B. Eerdmans Pub. Co., 2006.

Tribunes and Triumphs. *Causes for the Fall of the Roman Empire*. Accessed March 12, 2012, from http://www.roman-colosseum.info/roman-empire/causes-for-the-fall-of-the-roman-empire.htm.

Turner, David L. *Matthew*. Grand Rapids, MI: Baker Academic, 2008.

Turner, Paul. *Hallelujah Highway: A History of the Catechumenate*. Chicago: IL: Liturgy Training Publications, 2000.

Tzaferis, Vassilios. "Crucifixion—The Archaeological Evidence," *BAR* Jan/Feb (1985), 44–53.

Vaux, Roland D. *Ancient Israel: Its Life and Institutions*. London, England: McGraw Hill Book Company, 1961.

Vincent, Marvin R. *Word studies in the New Testament: Volume III*. Peabody, MA: Hendrickson, 1991.

Waggoner, Brad J. *The Shape of Faith to Come: Spiritual Formation and the Future of Discipleship*. Nashville, TN: B & H Pub. Group, 2008.

Walker, Williston. *A History of the Christian Church*. New York, NY: Charles Scribner's Sons, 1970.

Wallace, Daniel B. *Greek Grammar Beyond the Basics: An Exegetical Syntax of the New Testament with Scripture, Subject, and Greek Word Indexes*. Grand Rapids, MI: Zondervan, 1996.

Walvoord, John F. and Roy B. Zuck, *The Bible Knowledge Commentary: New Testament Ed.* (New Testament Edition ed.). Wheaton, IL: Victor Books, 1983.

Ward, Roy B. "Women in Roman Baths," *Harvard Theological Review*. Vol. 85, No. 2 (April 1992): 125–147.

Weber, Stu K. *HNTC: Matthew*. Nashville, TN: Broadman & Holman, 2000.

Whitney, Donald S. *Spiritual Disciplines for the Christian Life*. Colorado Springs, CO: NavPress, 1991.

Wilkins, Michael J. "Disciples," in *Dictionary of Jesus and the Gospels: A Compendium of Contemporary Biblical Scholarship*, ed. Joel B. Green, Scot McKnight, and I. Howard Marshall. Downers Grove, IL: InterVarsity, 1992.

_____. *Discipleship in the Ancient World and Matthew's Gospel (2nd ed.)*. Grand Rapids, MI: Baker Books, 1995.

_____. *Following the Master*. Grand Rapids, MI: Zondervan, 1992.

Willard, Dallas. *The Spirit of the Disciplines*. New York, NY: HarperCollins Pub., 1988.

Winkler, Gabriele. "The Original Meaning of the Prebaptismal Anointing and Its Implication," in *Living Water, Sealing Spirit*. Collegeville, MN: The Liturgical Press, 1995.

Wright, N. T. *The New Interpreter's Bible, Vol. X: Letter to the Romans*. Nashville, TN: Abingdon Press, 2002.

Wright, S. Paul, Sandra P. Horn, and William L. Sanders. "Teacher and Classroom Context Effects on Student Achievement: Implications for Teacher Evaluation." *Journal of Personal Evaluation in Education 11* (1997), 57–67.

Author

Andy Burggraff is Assistant Professor of Christian Education and the Director of Student Services at Shepherds Theological Seminary in Cary, NC. He earned a BA in Biblical Studies from Maranatha University, an MDiv from Calvary Baptist Theological Seminary, and an EdD from Southeastern Theological Seminary.

Andy served as Senior Pastor at Bible Baptist Church in Spring Hill, FL, and at Grace Baptist Church in Owatanna, MN. Before taking his current role, Andy was Discipleship Pastor at The Shepherd's Church (previously Colonial Baptist Church) in Cary, NC. He also has extensive missionary experience, including as the former Director of Discipleship for Communities of Grace International, and served as a hospital chaplain.

Andy and his wife, Delecia, have a blended family of five children.

Made in the USA
Middletown, DE
13 September 2023

38159421R00139